ORDINARY HEROES
Untold Stories of World War Two

With Best Wishes
Sharon Wells Wagner
Stew Wagner

Lester Groff's stories:
p. 36
102
111
116
147
250
295
Picture 334

STEVE WAGNER &
SHARON WELLS WAGNER

ORDINARY HEROES
Untold Stories of World War Two

2008

ORDINARY HEROES
Untold Stories of World War Two

TABLE OF CONTENTS

A Note of Thanks

Steve Wagner for helping to bring this book to life
Robert "Red" Wells for starting the ball rolling
Rick Wagner for research, editing and proofreading
Stephanie Wagner for running the household
when I couldn't be there
Kathleen Wagner for support beyond measure
And all my dear friends who have waited patiently
in the wings

I love you all!
Sharon Wells Wagner

"'Were you in the Service?' he asked.
'Yes', I replied.
'I want to thank you for serving our country,' he said,
firmly shaking my hand.
No one had ever said that to me before."

John C. Hoffman
U.S. Navy 1951-1955

This book is dedicated to my cousin
John C. Hoffman
with love and gratitude

And to every man and woman
who served our nation,
particularly those extraordinary individuals herein,
whose stories, told to me with grace and courage,
shall never be forgotten

And especially to
Stewart E. Lerch, George Vath and Richard B. Becker
who made the ultimate sacrifice

Sharon Wells Wagner

This is for the men and women who served,
so that those who could not
might learn from those who did.

Steve Wagner

This book is about enlisted men – ordinary men whose families struggled to survive the Great Depression. Ordinary men who grew up in cities, in small towns, and on farms. Men of little privilege and seemingly little consequence. When they were called upon to serve, and asked to make a sacrifice for the greater good, they rose to the challenge. They did not turn their backs to the face of war, but met it head on.

They brought peace to a world at war.

1

THE AWAKENING
PEARL HARBOR

"I didn't know there was a war going on... the Utah was upside down. I knew it was the bottom of a ship, but why would a ship be upside down? Then I heard machine gun fire from the planes... Jap planes with the red ball..."

Lyle Koenig, Pearl Harbor, 1941

Dawn broke upon the island in its usual way. At half past six a glimmer of light shone on the horizon, glinting in the Pacific waves and creeping skyward. As minutes ticked by, the golden morning climbed higher and higher, tracing the hilly green contours of sleeping volcanoes and greeting the wide blue sky. And in the valleys below, slumbering in the shadows of cloud-tipped peaks, citizens and soldiers dreamed quietly. It was the start of a beautiful day, and by all accounts a perfectly ordinary Sunday in Honolulu.

Lew Carter rolled over in his bunk and glanced sleepily at the clock. *Time to get up.* He stretched and gave a great yawn, tossing his blanket aside and swinging his feet down to the floor. As he sat rubbing sleep from his eyes, the familiar sense of alertness began to return. Being company bugler had its perks, but the privilege of rising before everyone else certainly wasn't one of them. Just as he'd done every day for months, Lew threw on his army uniform, grabbed his bugle, and stepped outside into the morning light. The day had only begun but already the Hawaiian air was fresh and clear. Even in December it was comfortable here.

Punctual as always, Lew arrived near the center of Schofield Barracks and checked his watch. Half past seven, on the dot. Wetting his lips, he raised the bugle and blew reveille. The notes were crisp in the quiet air. It was always a bit startling, but he felt a certain satisfaction in hearing the brassy tune pierce the morning calm. It was his wakeup call to the base, but the music was also his own mark – his little imprint upon the lives of his fellow soldiers. It made him feel proud.

Lew inhaled deeply and started back for the barracks, savoring the quiet as he walked. The gentle breeze, the singing birds; it almost reminded him of home. But Hawaii was far from Pennsylvania, and Pearl Harbor was nothing like Birdsboro, really. There were no military bases, no palm trees, and certainly no battleships where he lived. The people were just as friendly, though, so maybe it wasn't that different after all. Almost five thousand miles away and it still felt familiar. With this in his mind, he put on a smile and thought about his family. He wondered how the Army was treating his brother.

At six minutes to eight, Lew returned to the reveille spot with bugle in hand. Most of the base was awake by now, and a general bustle of movement and voices could be heard in every direction. With an eye on his watch, he counted down to seven fifty five. *Three, two, one...* Chow call, unlike reveille, was a much welcome sound. Hungry soldiers emerged from the barracks around him as a testament to this fact. A rumbling from his belly urged him to join the herd at breakfast, so he took a step in the direction of the mess hall. But something stopped him cold.

Gunfire. He could hear it on the horizon, erupting from somewhere up the valley. Staccato cracks pierced the air, drawing closer and closer until he saw what was happening. There were planes in the sky, screaming towards him in a fearsome swarm. Bugle dangling at his side, Lew turned and looked helplessly as they overtook the base in a flash. They came in low over the barracks, weapons flickering madly as tracers sliced through the air above his head. He was stunned. Frozen in place, he watched as a pair of fighters skimmed the two story building he called home. They were so low he could see the pilots' eyes and teeth. And he could see the fearsome emblem they bore – the fiery red rising sun. Bombs fell and guns crackled. Soldiers sprinted across the base in a frenzy of motion. But Lew remained still. His world had been shattered - thrown into chaos in the span of an instant. Time seemed to crawl as the fighting escalated around him. Only when a bomb landed nearby was he jarred back to attention. He turned, shaken, and saw the motor pool burning, belching dark smoke skyward. It was incredible. It was insane. Yet it was happening. The Japanese were attacking Pearl Harbor.

Not far offshore, the destroyer USS Tucker sat sleeping at anchor in the East Loch. In its belly, George Hatza was relaxing in his bunk with a newspaper. But a sound from the corridor outside grabbed his attention. Craning his neck, he saw a flicker of movement as a boatswain's mate sprinted past the door to his quarters in the aft section of the ship.

"Japanese air attack! Japanese air attack! This is not a drill!" The man sounded frantic.

George bolted upright. He could feel the hairs on the back of his neck stand up.

"What the hell are they doing," he muttered, "Don't tell me they're having maneuvers on Sunday."

Most of the Tucker's crew was still asleep, enjoying their well-earned day of rest. Right now they were scattered about the ship, lounging in their bunks or relaxing somewhere. How could there be a drill? It didn't make sense, but it was his job to respond. So he dropped his wrinkled newspaper and looked at the ceiling with a furrowed brow. *Is that gunfire?* It couldn't be. *There, again!* It was unmistakable. Someone was firing up on deck; the crack of a fifty caliber machine gun rattled its way through the ship and met his ears. *The alert and the guns*, he thought, *it just doesn't add up.* He couldn't rationalize what was happening – it was just too unusual.

He had to obey orders, though. If this was a drill, it was something he hadn't seen before.

Hopping to the floor, George pulled trousers over his hips. His mind was racing; he tried to make sense of the situation but he couldn't. *The only guy who'd be manning that fifty is Walter,* he realized. And while his buddy was gung-ho enough to sleep in a hammock by his gun, he was certainly no fool. If Walter was firing at something up there, he had a damn good reason for it. Somehow this only made George feel worse, and as he left his quarters and tackled the topside ladder, unease was growing in his mind.

A stiff breeze whipped George's face as he emerged onto the Tucker's deck. He shielded his eyes with a hand and listened. Puzzling sounds drifted in from everywhere at once. *Are those explosions?* They seemed to be, but he was still skeptical. Then he noticed the dark smoky haze gathering in the sky, fed by small plumes rising across the island. This erased any doubt in his mind: something bad was happening. *But what exactly?* A sudden burst from the fifty caliber drew his attention and he spun around just in time to see Walter firing wildly at a plane coming in low over the water. Looking down and to the side, George watched as a tiny aircraft zoomed barely thirty feet above the harbor, jerking through the air as it struggled to shrug off the machine gun rounds flying its way. Dodging the fire, it pulled up and banked hard, revealing its allegiance painted on the fuselage.

For an instant, George thought he was mistaken. Had the navy repainted its planes for training? The rising sun was just for show – it had to be. *It's all an elaborate drill.* He hoped desperately that he was right, that this wasn't real. But then the plane passed above him and he saw its pilot - and he knew the truth. In a moment of horrifying clarity, time seemed to slow as he stared into the cockpit of that tiny plane and the enemy returned his gaze. The two men, eyes locked, shared that instant. Then the plane screamed skyward and was gone.

George felt his pulse quicken, and he took a step backwards, mind reeling. Looking down, he suddenly realized he'd forgotten his shoes. But it didn't even matter. There were bigger things to worry about now. "Uh oh," he said to himself, "This is the real McCoy."

A mile and a half to the south, Ralph Mason was getting ready for a quiet Sunday. He ran a towel across the mirror, wiping steam from the glass and clearing his reflection. Setting his razor down, he checked for nicks on his skin. None today. The water was calm where the light cruiser USS Honolulu sat moored in the Navy Yard; at the moment everything was still.

Ralph gathered his things and stepped into the corridor outside the head, moving in the direction of his quarters. The ship was as quiet as it was still, and he took the opportunity to sort out his schedule for the day. As he walked, his thoughts drifted to the plans he'd made with his brother. *Head to the YMCA club to meet Stuart, hang out there for a while, then take a bus somewhere for a bite to eat later on.* They'd probably go to that nice restaurant he'd heard about, the one where you could get a T-bone steak dinner for seventy five cents. Afterwards, they could go to the beach and relax for a while. *Heck, maybe I'll even go swimming.* He'd have to remember to suggest that to Stuart.

Ralph's brother served on the aircraft carrier USS Enterprise, which was due into Honolulu very soon. On occasions when the two ships met, the brothers had a tradition of spending time with one another. Sometimes just a meal, other times a whole day, they took every opportunity to visit when they could. Since Ralph was on watch today, he had early liberty. *More than enough time to get ready,* he thought. So he'd gone down to shower and shave immediately after breakfast.

He was almost lost in thought when a voice came over the ship's speaker system. *General quarters,* it squawked, *battle stations.* Ralph hesitated for a moment, fingers wrapped around the sleeve of his liberty uniform in its locker. *They can't be serious.* The base had been having more and more air attack drills lately. He wasn't in the mood for another one – especially not now - but it looked like he'd have to postpone the day with his brother. Sighing, he shoved the liberty uniform back in and pulled out his duty whites instead. *If they're calling us up on a Sunday morning, there's probably a good reason for it,* he realized. With this thought in the back of his mind, he dressed quickly and started for his station on the signal bridge.

Back in the East Loch, Lyle Koenig was already rushing to duty aboard the destroyer USS Aylwin. Pulse racing, he jogged through the ship's corridors on his way to general quarters. Squeezing past other sailors racing about, he navigated the maze of passages through sheer instinct, for his mind was elsewhere at the moment. He'd never been in combat before, and this was a hell of a way to start. Everything was confusing. *They said the Japanese were attacking,* he recalled, *but why?* Did it even matter? Not to him, at least not now. He just had to make it topside and join the fight. And he knew something big was happening from the noises that were echoing in from outside. The thundering booms and crackling gunfire made his skin crawl, and as he emerged onto the deck he was thrust into a nightmare.

The first thing Lyle noticed, apart from the rush of activity, was an enormous capsized hull floundering astern of the Aylwin about a mile away. It was the Utah. *Why would a ship be upside down?* He was dumbstruck. *This makes no sense,* he thought as he watched the keel protruding from the harbor. Men were in the water around it, kicking up tiny splashes as they swam towards land and the nearby motor launches. They appeared tiny from this distance, but he could see them struggling to escape the mess. Then he noticed the planes – little yellow ones with red wing tips – and he realized exactly what was happening. The Japanese aircraft were strafing the swimmers with gunfire, swooping low and firing as they passed overhead. Until now, he had been prepared to believe it was all a drill. But seeing the Utah dead in the water, its crew shot to pieces amidst the smoking chaos, all doubt in his mind quickly vanished. *This is war,* he realized, alarmed but unafraid. *I have to get moving.* And with this Lyle turned and bolted towards his battle station.

The number two gun was dry when he arrived, its crew scuttling about in an effort to pass ammunition from number three. Squeezing between two sailors, Lyle joined the ammo train and began passing five inch shells by hand. As he worked, the battle raged on. The crack of gunfire, the thundering echo of bomb and torpedo strikes; it was a hellish cacophony that grew worse by the minute. Planes were screaming through the air in waves, dropping explosives into the water and across the decks of anything they could hit. Antiaircraft fire from ships and land guns flickered skyward in a frantic attempt to fend off the attackers. And high up, gliding in the open blue, enemy bombers loomed silent and menacing. Some had already dropped their payloads, and others were about to. Lyle could already see the horrifying result of their work as men tried desperately to extinguish fires across the harbor.

Yet he wasn't afraid. Something held back the fear. Was it faith in men around him, confidence in the soldiers and sailors he'd trained with for so long? Or was it simply the timing? Perhaps he'd had too little warning, and the horror of his position hadn't sunk in yet. He wondered about this as he passed shells along the line.

"Hey, look at that!" A sailor nearby gestured skyward.

Lyle squinted through the gun smoke haze and saw what the man was pointing at. A handful of navy planes were coming in for a landing at Ford Island, or at least they were trying to. Japanese fighters were firing at them as the American pilots zigzagged back and forth wildly. They couldn't fight back from their position; it seemed they were just trying to live long enough to get on the ground. But the enemy planes weren't the only problem: friendly antiaircraft fire was targeting them too. Some of the gun crews couldn't tell friend from foe in the confusion, even though the planes they were shooting at had their landing gear and flaps down. Lyle watched as the Americans wagged their wings and made recognition maneuvers, but it didn't seem to help. They only managed to shake off their Japanese pursuers and fly over the airfield in a wide arc before passing out of sight.

Lyle could only imagine how those pilots must have felt, accidentally thrust into an air attack and fired upon by their own forces. It must have been terribly confusing. But he couldn't wonder for long, for another shell came down the line and he passed it ahead. There was work to be done, fighting to be endured. And this was only the beginning.

"All engineers line up and pass ammunition by hand!" The battleship USS Pennsylvania's intercom system blared loudly, barking order after order as its crew scrambled to fend off aerial attacks. Heart pounding, Joe Yaklowich took hold of a five inch shell with sweaty palms and swung it into the waiting grasp of the sailor next to him. He tried to block out the sounds of fighting, to concentrate on his task, but he couldn't. From just outside the corridor, from the open air of the battleship's main deck, a thundering symphony of gunfire and explosions was rolling in. Something terrible was happening out there.

A blast rattled the metal beneath his feet and Joe thought for a moment about his usual battle station several decks down. Any other day, he would be down there, manning a headset and relaying orders in the number one engine room. But the ship was in dry dock and had no use for its engines. Even if they wanted to, the crew couldn't use them, for they were in pieces – dismantled for overhaul. So here he was, on the upper deck passing ammunition with all the other engineers. Joe wondered if this twist of fate would preserve him or place him in more danger. But there was no way to tell, at least not yet. He'd just have to wait and see.

Ralph Mason raced onto the Honolulu's signal bridge just in time to witness something terrible. As he stepped into the room, he caught a flash of fire in the corner of his vision. Something huge was burning less than a mile to the north. It was a battleship, the USS Arizona, smoldering fiercely out on the water. It was engulfed in thick smoke from bow to stern and listing badly. Then it happened. As Ralph looked on, a tremendous explosion rocked the crippled ship and it erupted in a rippling chain of fireballs. Gigantic chunks of debris went screaming into the air in all directions, trailing smoldering contrails and tongues of flame. And the smoke – it poured from the ruined hull in great sheets, smothering the blue sky and choking out the sun. It was one of the most terrible things he'd ever seen. The Arizona was gone.

With a look of disgust and a pit in his stomach, Ralph turned his gaze toward the submarine base. There, upon the water tank, a message flew boldly. It was telling them to sortie, to leave the harbor. He relayed the order but wondered if it was too late. From the look of things around him, few ships had managed to comply. And the Honolulu hadn't moved an inch.

Deep in the Tucker's emergency radio room, George Hatza expertly manned the dials on the equipment in the tiny compartment. It was eerily quiet down here, and as he worked a strange sense of calm began creeping its way into his head. But it was only momentary. He knew that, only a short distance above, there were men fighting and dying. This was his battle station, though he couldn't stay long. The radio room upstairs was being manned by a pair of rookie sailors he'd put in charge temporarily. It wasn't ideal, but it was the best he could do at the moment. Everyone was making do with what they had, given the circumstances. Sailors were scrambling to bring the big guns online even now, and the antiaircraft batteries had been firing from the start. And in the belly of the ship, it was George's job to maintain communications with the submarine base. That's why he hurried.

As he stepped back into the radio room, the chaos of battle greeted him once more. Vibrations rattled the ship and voices bounced around the room, competing with the radio chatter and mechanical noises coming from the equipment. He kept an ear on the speaker system as he worked, trying to pick details out of the confusion. Reports came in of a mini-sub in the harbor. Were the Japanese infiltrating? He felt the shudder of depth charges detonating nearby, strengthening his fears. Then rumors passed of paratroopers landing on the island. He couldn't believe it. *What the hell*, he thought, *paratroopers?* Was this the beginning of the end? Or was it even worse? For all he knew, Japanese soldiers were ransacking parts of Honolulu already. His imagination ran wild, but there was no point speculating.   With a deep breath, he refocused his attention at the task at hand.

But then a familiar voice called his name.   "Hey George!" It was the gunner's mate, coming over the radio. "Come on out, the Arizona just blew up!" Maybe things were as bad as he thought.

George raced topside and hit the railing looking south. From across the harbor he looked on and realized with horror that the whole island, even the water itself, was burning.   And there, in the center of his vision, sat the Arizona.   Even from a mile away, he knew the ship wouldn't make it.   Still reeling from a tremendous explosion, the battleship belched great plumes of fire and smoke skyward as burning debris rained down like meteors. At this distance it almost looked like fireworks. But it wasn't. Men were dying over there and there was nothing he could do. A sudden sense of smallness – of unimportance – washed over him. It seemed he was just a pawn in some terrible game with no rules. It took all his strength to peel his hands from the railing and return below deck, but duty tugged at his conscience. As he started back down the ladder he wondered, quite seriously, if any of them would emerge from this unscathed. Perhaps none of them would.

A tremendous shudder rocked the Pennsylvania, sending Joe Yaklowich and his buddies reeling. He braced himself against a bulkhead with one arm, a shell cradled tightly in the other. The lights flickered overhead, and for a moment everything was calm. The only sound was an unearthly groan coming from the walls as metal stressed and buckled. It seemed that the ship was screaming. Then the vibrations ceased and the noises from the harbor came drifting back in. The shock began to wear off as Joe regained his footing and passed the ammunition forward. Ears ringing, he craned his neck to catch a glimpse of the action outside. But smoke billowed past, obscuring the view. *We must have taken a direct hit,* he thought. The ship was in dry dock, so it couldn't have been a torpedo. And judging from the noise, it probably hit close to where he was standing. Was it the engine room? Maybe he'd gotten lucky after all.

A tap on the shoulder and a loud voice from behind got his attention. "Come on, we're going for ammo." It was a sailor from somewhere below. "Let's move!"

The man pushed his way past and Joe followed him outside. Stepping out into the breeze, he was struck by a powerful odor drifting across the open harbor. The stench of burning oil nearly choked him. He braced his senses and hurried to the gangplank where a group of sailors was gathering.

Jogging along the edge of the dry dock, Joe noticed something odd. This morning the dock had been empty, but now it was full of water. Had it been damaged? Maybe that blast on the Pennsylvania had been a torpedo after all. It was all so frantic and confusing. Nobody seemed to know exactly what was happening. But as he neared the battleship's bow, his question was answered. Ahead of the Pennsylvania, in the same dry dock, sat a pair of destroyers side by side. One was listing badly, resting against the other, and both were burning. One was barely recognizable. Men dashed about frantically trying to extinguish the flames, and Joe realized they must have flooded the dock in order to contain the fire. But it was barely helping. One of the destroyers was little more than a shell engulfed by dense jets of smoke. As he passed by, he gave silent thanks that his own ship had not shared its fate. At least not yet.

All along the harbor small boats were darting quickly in every direction, shuttling sailors from ship to ship and fishing others out of the water. Barely an hour into the battle, Pearl Harbor was in shambles. It seemed they were already losing the war, and it had only just begun. But he had little time to reflect on his dismay, for the men around him were quickening their pace. There was work do be done and they would have to move fast. On the horizon, another swarm of enemy planes was approaching.

Smoke. It was everywhere. From his vantage point at Schofield Barracks, Lew Carter could look to the southeast and see Pearl Harbor burning. It was nine miles away, but the dark plumes were clearly visible, rising into the sky from ruined ships and bomb-riddled buildings. They were like tornadoes, frozen in silence and perching above the battle, waiting for something to set them in motion. They lifted into the air and dissipated in an inky haze that threatened to engulf the whole island. It was incredibly eerie, even without the constant symphony of gunfire and explosions that drifted in from everywhere at once. He wanted to hide, to curl up into himself and forget what was happening. But he had to man the guard house. *And besides*, he *realized, I'm lucky.* Men were fighting and dying all over the island. Enemy planes and bullets were screaming through the skies. Yet he hadn't even fired his weapon. At least not yet. Lew's unit had been sent to Hickam Field but he'd been left behind as a guard. For all he knew, his friends were being killed at this very moment. From what he was seeing, that seemed likely. Then it hit him. *I'm the luckiest guy in the world,* he thought, *I wouldn't trade this for a million dollars.*

And as the battle raged in front of him - as he stood there in awed silence - Lew wondered what would become of them all.

Lew wasn't alone in his concern. For the men and women on Oahu, December 7 was a long day of uncertainties. From the initial surprise to the invasion rumors to the final hours of dark apprehension, an overwhelming sense of confusion reigned. No one expected the attack and few were prepared for the shock and devastation that ensued, but everyone rose to the challenge. Soldiers, sailors, and even civilians accepted the reality of what was happening. They gritted their teeth and fought, and some of them paid the ultimate price.

Long after the Japanese planes retreated over the horizon, Pearl Harbor was a bustling hive of activity. Salvage and repair operations were underway, ships sortied from the harbor, and search parties scoured the water for survivors. But even as they struggled to recover, some of the men wondered if the enemy was just waiting to strike again.

Squinting ahead into the night, Ralph Mason watched intently as the barge's light swept back and forth across the water. The harbor's surface gleamed slick and bright beneath the moon, its sheen broken only by the shifting silhouettes of debris floating in the tide. Bits of wood and metal, lengths of rope, and countless other scraps bumped against the boat as it slid through the darkness. His eyes flicked from one to the next, nerves tense as he searched for anything that might resemble a periscope. Were the reports wrong? Had the Japanese retreated entirely? He certainly hoped so, but hope meant little at the moment. The only thing he knew for sure was that they hadn't found any submarines. At least not yet. If something was lurking out there in the dark, it was hiding from them, waiting patiently. This thought unnerved him a little, and as he flashed his signal lamp toward the dock he wondered if they were letting their guard down again. It wasn't up to him, thought. An order came in over the radio: the search was called off.

The admiral had sent them to investigate rumors of a Japanese submarine and it was Ralph's job to man the flashing signal light on the tiny craft. But, finding nothing, they were recalled. So with a wide sweeping turn, the barge began heading back. For now, it was enough of a challenge for the sailors to navigate the ever-shifting maze of debris and bodies drifting quietly on the tide. They passed dead men bobbing in the water, smothered under a thick film of bunker fuel leaking from damaged ships. But it was impossible to retrieve them. Such work was best left to the motor launches. Ralph certainly didn't envy them.

2

TOTAL WAR
THE HOMEFRONT

"A constant humming in the east... but could not see a plane anywhere. The humming sounded very much like a plane; perhaps one had landed, or maybe a plane was taking off. Turns out a farmer was filling his silo!"

DeLight Breidegam, Pennsylvania, 1942

Red Wells had just lost his mother, a sad victim of difficult post-depression years. Although he was thirteen years old, she had only been with him for little more than a year. Lovingly mothered during those short months, it was a happy time for him. Circumstances had kept them apart; his tuberculosis took him from her at a very early age. And when they were finally reunited, she slipped away too soon. She was gone for good now, this time forever.

The funeral was sparsely attended by a few friends from the neighborhood and members of her family, many of whom were strangers to Red. In his brief year and a half under her wing, he'd spent most of his time outdoors, exploring the world and all that he had missed when he was in the hospital. Because he'd been on his own for so long, getting close to other people was uncomfortable. So standing by her grave, he kept his distance from everyone else. He'd never felt so alone in his life.

Robert was Red's given name but his mother called him Bobby. She had loved him dearly, though he wouldn't realize it for many years to come. Love had little meaning in his life, as it had eluded him for most of his thirteen years.

Although he'd received good care from the staff of the numerous hospitals and tuberculosis sanitariums where he'd spent his early life, Red never felt he belonged to anyone. Especially now that his mother was gone, he wondered what would become of him. Even though Red had no feelings for his mother, she had been kind to him and had given him a home - a place to begin each day's adventure and a bed in which to rest and dream.

As fate would have it, he was sent to live with Aunt Laura, his father's sister, who owned a boarding house in Reading, Pennsylvania. She was a thorn in Red's side from the moment they met, as she took it upon herself to control his every waking moment. But living with her had its perks; she was an excellent cook, and Red would come to know and admire his paternal grandfather whom Aunt Laura doted over like a child.

Red's grandfather, John Wells, was living in the front room on the second floor of the boardinghouse. Although he was ninety-three years old, John spoke proudly and clearly of his years as soldier during the Civil War. He regaled Red, whom he affectionately called Bobby, with stories about Rebels and slaves. His favorite story, which he told often, was about the time he met and shook the hand of President Abraham Lincoln. Grandpop, as Red called him, was missing an eye, though Red never mentioned it for fear that the old man might show him what lurked beneath the eye patch. Red only knew he had lost it in the war.

In the months that Red lived with Aunt Laura, he and his Grandpop became great friends. The feeling Red had for the proud old man might have been love, but he wasn't sure. He did know that he greatly admired his Grandpop, and hung onto every word he spoke. The time they spent together gave meaning to Red's life, and it thrilled Red to think that Grandpop's blood flowed in his own veins - that they were one and the same. This fortuitous meeting and its ensuing friendship set into motion the boy's desire to become just like his grandfather – the desire to become a soldier. And for the first time in his life, Red was deeply happy.

By summer's end Red was sent to live with his mother's sister, Aunt Margaret. He rarely saw his grandfather after that, but Red would never forget him. Three years later, in August of 1939, his beloved Grandpop died at the age of ninety-six. Two years after that, Red walked into the post office in Reading, Pennsylvania on his eighteenth birthday and enlisted in the United States Army. It was the second of August, 1941 – the start of a new life for Red.

He was a soldier now, just like his grandfather. And though he had little idea of what lay ahead, he couldn't have been more excited. Adventure waited over the horizon; he felt that no matter what happened, it would be a worthy experience. But what Red didn't know – what he couldn't have known - was that in four short months, the Japanese would attack Pearl Harbor and his life would be changed forever.

DeLight Breidegam was an ambitious boy from the time he was a youngster. He was the youngest of three children and his parents' only son. His father had two girls first, and then DeLight came along. He thought the sun rose and set on the boy.

By age thirteen, DeLight was hard at work on a neighbor's farm earning fifty cents a day. A half dollar bought a lot in 1939, but he was frugal with his money, putting some of each day's earnings aside for a rainy day. He also had a job picking potatoes part time for twenty-five cents an hour, earning a whopping total of $4.50 a week. That was quite a windfall for a hard-working youngster, and a few weeks of picking potatoes netted him a brand new bicycle.

DeLight's work ethic wasn't born entirely out of necessity. Rather, it was largely due to the guidance of the honest, hard-working man whom he most admired: his father. The tough depression years spared few, and Delight's family was no exception. Theirs was just one of millions of families who could not meet their mortgage payments and experienced the heartbreak of losing their home. The day his father went into town and surrendered the deed to their Fleetwood home to the bank was a difficult one for the proud man. It was sad for them all.

Undaunted, the Breidegam family relocated to the small community of Lyons, moving into the house behind the store that his father rented. The store was filled with groceries, dry goods and fresh produce and before long the close-knit family was comfortably settled in.

DeLight learned the value of a dollar at a very young age. Instead of paying ten cents to ride the bus, he rode his new bicycle to and from school and saved himself an extra twenty cents each day. By the time he was fourteen years old, he was earning enough money to buy all his own clothing and he still had a little spending money left over.

DeLight's family kept abreast of what was going on in the world, particularly Hitler's activities in Europe. But on Sunday morning, December 7, 1941, they were completely unaware of the events that were taking place in Hawaii as they climbed into their 1937 Ford and drove to church. After the service, they dined at home before visiting relatives in Reading. They returned home at 8 o'clock that evening and retired to bed. Because no member of the Breidegam family turned on a radio that entire day, none of them knew that the Japanese had bombed Pearl Harbor.

The following day, Delight jumped on his bicycle and raced to school in his usual manner. That is when he first heard the devastating news. But it didn't have a tremendous impact on him. Pearl Harbor was so far away it almost didn't seem real. DeLight knew he should be concerned, though, for his country was headed for war. Only fifteen years old, DeLight was still too young to enlist, but he made a decision to help out. In fact, the attack on Pearl Harbor encouraged the whole Breidegam family to get involved in the war effort.

The family became spotters, volunteers who watched the sky for enemy planes. They were given a few gallons of gasoline to cover the drive to their station. Too young to drive himself, DeLight shared his shift with an older guy from Lyons who had a car.

DeLight's station stood on a hill in the middle of an orchard in New Jerusalem, Pennsylvania. It was a small shack with spotter cards and a telephone. He spent hours at a time just watching the sky and jotting down details whenever he saw a plane. Aircraft type, number of engines, altitude, and direction – that's what they looked for. Though he was never sure of the altitude, he confidently estimated a number and stuck with his educated guess. Then he would pick up the phone and make his report. It looked like an ordinary enough telephone, but it rang straight through to a secret location in New York. He liked to imagine it was a direct line to some top government agency, and he felt tremendously important each time he called.

"Single engine plane, 3,000 feet, heading west," he would say, speaking clearly into the receiver as he read from the notation he'd just written in the log book.

"Thanks, good job."

That was the usual response from the unseen authority on the end of the line. DeLight heard it often enough; in the course of an average shift he saw a plane about once every twenty minutes. He and his friend certainly kept busy. It felt good to be part of the war effort, and he was proud to do it.

Spotters took their responsibility very seriously, and to DeLight's amusement, one particular incident was quite memorable. His sister and her husband were on duty in New Jerusalem one afternoon with some people from Reading. The group could hear a constant humming in the east, but couldn't see a plane anywhere. The humming sounded very much like an airplane; perhaps one had landed or was trying to take off. The group was obviously concerned enough to report the incident, and after one of the women noted it in the log, she picked up the telephone. *A constant humming in the east,* she called it.

The assembly never knew whether or not the humming was investigated, but they later learned that a farmer filling his silo was the culprit. The strange sound had come from a tractor that he'd been running for most of the day.

DeLight had a great home life. By the time he was sixteen in 1943, he'd saved enough money to buy his first car, a beautiful eight-year-old 1935 Chevy that cost him a hundred and fifty dollars. In the meantime, his father, who had given up the grocery business and was working for a battery maker, set up shop in a one-room shack and began building his own hand-made batteries. DeLight would eventually help his father transform this new venture into one of the largest battery-making operations in the world. But not yet. By 1944 the war was well underway, the Allies had invaded Normandy, and to his father's chagrin, DeLight made the decision to enlist.

On December 3, 1944, two months after DeLight's seventeenth birthday, he said goodbye to his family and the life he loved, and joined the Army Air Force.

David Voigt was in the dining hall at the Hershey Industrial School. It was Sunday evening – cold cuts night. He could smell the freshly baked bread stacked high with his favorite meats and cheeses. It was delicious.

David was a half-orphan, having lost his father, an English professor, at an early age to heart disease and pneumonia. The second of six children, David was just thirteen years old when he became a ward of the Hershey Industrial School. His mother, a college home economics professor, had made a wise decision in sending him there. He would always be grateful to her for that.

The students and house parents were sitting in the dining hall, listening to the radio and eating when the news came on. The Japanese had attacked Pearl Harbor. It hit them like a shock. The news announcer tried to put a positive spin on the news, as though the American forces were rallying. Everybody started cheering because it seemed they were making a comeback. But at the same time they were angry – very angry. David and his buddies knew all the swear words in those days, but they weren't allowed to say them at school. And they didn't, at least not loud enough for anyone to hear.

When Gabe Fieni and his younger brother, Andy, were teenagers, their dad owned a corner store in downtown Pottstown, Pennsylvania. The quaint little shop, with a soda fountain and a jukebox, was the perfect place for the Fieni brothers and all of their buddies to hang out. The corner was a great spot to socialize and watch the local girls go by before going inside for a bite to eat. The Fieni gang numbered about eight and they were good boys for the most part, but boys none the less – baseball-playing, girl-watching boys who took their studies seriously and helped out at home.

On a chilly December afternoon the boys were in their usual spot when a fellow named Henry Pyott came running up the street.

"Pearl Harbor was hit," he shouted over and over, skidding to a stop in front of the store.

The stunned group stood quietly for a long moment, gaping at Henry in shock. Then the anger kicked in and Gabe felt a swell of patriotism. Running into the store, he faced his father and boldly announced, "Dad, tomorrow I'm going to go and sign up in the army."

Gabe was adamant about his decision.

"Son, please don't," his father said, "They'll take you soon enough anyway. You can wait until then."

But there was no changing the boy's mind. Over the next few days he spent hours trying to convince his parents to let him enlist, but to no avail. Gabe's father was firm, and because he was a good son, Gabe obeyed.

Gabe didn't sign up, but he was angry. He wanted to go right then and there and his buddies wanted to go, too; at least the four who hadn't signed up already. Half of them enlisted in the service the day after the attack. They felt it was their duty to help out. Gabe wondered how their families felt about losing their sons.

In January of 1943, the opportunity for Gabe to serve his country finally presented itself when he was drafted into the army. Even though more than a year had passed since the attack at Pearl Harbor, Gabe never lost his desire to serve. He had high hopes of joining the paratroopers or the infantry, or maybe becoming a rear gunner in a bomber, but the army had other plans for Gabe; he would become a medic.

Gabe was devastated. *Being a medic is for sissies,* he thought, *it's like being a nurse. It's a woman's job!* He was going to war all right, but not with the paratroopers or the infantry or on a bomber, and he wouldn't even be permitted to carry a weapon!

The day was Sunday, the seventh of December. George Moore, a fifteen year old high school junior, was pretty much unaware of what was going on in the world. Following his usual Sunday morning routine, George went to Sunday school with his Grandmother. The day was uneventful right up to the moment the news came over the radio – the Japanese had bombed Pearl Harbor. The gravity of the event didn't hit right away; it took awhile. But when it occurred to him that he was a young kid who might be going to war, the reality sank in.

Some weeks later George went to the movies with friends. It was there that he saw newsreels of the devastation that had taken place at Pearl Harbor; ships were burning, some lay on their sides, and bodies were floating in the oil-slicked bay. He was horrified by the casualties, and he suddenly hoped he would never have to go to war.

But to his great dismay, George was drafted. In April of 1944, along with thousands of other young men, he was inducted into the army. George would go through the training and do whatever he had to do. But he knew it would be no picnic.

Eighteen-year-old Ed Taggert was riding in a car with a bunch of kids on a cold Sunday afternoon in his hometown of Philadelphia. An urgent message interrupted the professional football game the boys were enjoying on the car radio. The anxious announcer was talking about a place called Pearl Harbor. Because none of them had any idea where Pearl Harbor was, they'd never heard of it, they didn't really understand the significance of the events that had taken place there just a few hours earlier. The boys were too young to realize that the deadly attack by the Japanese on Pearl Harbor would change their lives forever.

Ed, who'd graduated from Northeast Public High School in January, should have been a bit more knowledgeable about world events, particularly since his father was in the 28th National Guard Division and they, along with other units, had been called up about a year before the war started. Because Ed's father was involved with the war effort, and the Guard was gearing up for war, he was not against Ed enlisting in the service right away. The decision was Ed's alone.

He would have gone down the next day and joined just for the adventure of it, because it seemed the right thing to do. But he needed money, so he opted to go to work instead. So, having prior experience as a tool factory messenger boy, he landed a job as the mail boy in a defense factory.

When Ed was ten years old, his father surprised him by taking him along to Guard camp for two weeks of training. The camp at that time was in Mt. Gretna, Pennsylvania. Ed never knew how his father got away with bringing a young child to camp, but Ed's experience there was a good one. He'd even befriended some of the soldiers.

The military aspect of that visit influenced Ed greatly. Like his father, he would join the ranks of young men who would proudly serve their country; but first, he would take some time to grow up.

Finally, on February 9, 1942, just two short months after the attack on Pearl Harbor, Ed enlisted in the United States Army. In a bittersweet moment, Ed's proud father accompanied him to the recruiting office in downtown Philadelphia. From the time Ed was a boy he was very easy going, not prone to being nervous about anything. But that particular day his legs shook uncontrollably as he and his father walked down Chestnut Street to the recruiting office. Certain he would be accepted, Ed hoped to get into the marines or the navy, but was turned down because he wore glasses. So, with his father's blessing, Ed enlisted in the army.

Going into the service seemed natural to Ed; he figured it would be a big adventure. Little did he know what lay ahead.

Willard Bickel was visiting the Pagoda on top of Mt. Penn in Reading, Pennsylvania, with Margaret, the lovely young lady he would eventually marry. Margaret's sister and brother-in-law were in the back seat of the car enjoying the view from the top of the mountain. The day was clear and from the best vantage spot in the city, the young folks could see for miles. They were chatting cheerfully and enjoying each other's company when

Willard reached for the radio on the dashboard. It was Monday, about mid day when the group first heard Roosevelt's steady voice in his address to Congress.

Shocked, Willard and his friends sat in silence and listened to the devastating news. The President was announcing that Pearl Harbor had been deliberately attacked by naval and air forces of the Empire of Japan.

A calm but stunned Willard looked at the others and said, "Well, here we go...we're on our way."

His future brother-in-law, too stunned to reply, nodded his response.

Greatly concerned, he knew now that war was inevitable. This saddened him. *Are we ready for this*, he wondered, *are we prepared?* Eighteen-year-old Willard knew what he had to do.

When Willard returned home later that day, he looked at his father squarely and announced his decision to enlist.

His father's reply was firm: "You get your education first!"

Willard obeyed his father's wishes and postponed enlisting, attending the University of Pennsylvania on a part-time basis working towards a degree in accounting. For extra money he worked in a music store on Fridays and as a bank teller on Saturdays. Upon completing only one and a half semesters of his college studies, Willard was drafted into the Army in 1943 along with one hundred ninety-five others; the largest contingent of men to leave Pottstown for world war two.

Geraldine Houp was in the bathtub when the news came over the radio. A nurse at George Washington

University Hospital in Washington, D.C., she had just finished her shift. President Roosevelt was reporting the grim news that the Japanese had struck Pearl Harbor. Geraldine was shocked by the news as she thought about all of those people who were killed and the families whose lives would be changed forever.

So many things had happened already; Geraldine was well aware of what was going on with Hitler in Europe. But the event at Pearl Harbor was the main reason Geraldine decided to go into the military.

As a nursing student, Geraldine could see the war coming. In nursing school she was encouraged to sign up for Red Cross nursing, but she signed up for the Army Reserves instead. Then she went to Washington to take a three-month course in psychiatric nursing, and found it was not her cup of tea. So, she went to work at George Washington University Hospital.

Geraldine had a strong sense of duty, having first learned about responsibility and the meaning of hard work at a very young age. She was one of seven children born and raised on a farm in the beautiful Oley Valley in Berks County, Pennsylvania. The children were all given chores from a very early age and Geraldine couldn't wait until she was old enough to milk the family's very docile cow. She was just five or six when she was given this chore, and she loved it. The children did whatever they had to do in order to help the family survive those tough years.

Everyone was poor in those days, and her close-knit family was no exception. But neighbors helped each other, sharing workloads and even food. In 1927 when a cyclone took the second floor off her family's house and destroyed the barn, Geraldine's father, with the help of neighboring farmers, built it all back in no time.

When Geraldine was fifteen years old, tragedy struck her family. Her father was killed in a fall from a cherry tree, and her mother was left alone to run the farm and care for seven children.

From childhood, especially after the death of her father, Geraldine had a strong sense of responsibility, first to her family, then to her patients at George Washington University Hospital, and to the corpsmen she had trained there who would ultimately go to war. It just seemed natural for her to help out wherever she was needed. And Geraldine knew the time had come for her to move on. There was a greater calling; the navy needed her now.

Because his father had served in World War I, Paul Fett followed the war on the radio. He enjoyed listening to the commentators and dispatchers, though he often suspected that the news didn't really emphasize the enormity of what was taking place in the world. It was December 8, 1941, and he was upstairs in his bedroom writing a paper for Miss Dick's eleventh grade English class. Suddenly he heard President Roosevelt's voice on the radio. He got a sinking feeling, thinking something might be wrong. Pausing to listen, he let the pencil slip from his fingers when he heard the news about Pearl Harbor. It was stunning. The conflict had seemed so far away, so unreal. He had no feel for the number of casualties. But it suddenly hit home in a very personal way.

Paul knew this act of Japanese aggression would have an effect on his life. Inevitably, the United States would be drawn into war and he would be called to serve.

Upon graduating from high school in June of 1943, Paul was drafted and told to report for duty in July. He failed the physical, though, and was sent home where he went to work for Wilson Safety Products in Reading, Pennsylvania. But the army wouldn't forget him. On December of that same year, he was ordered to New Cumberland. This time Paul passed the physical; he belonged to the army now.

Margaret Schatz Wolf graduated from Mohnton High School in 1939, but with little prospect of attending college.

"I can't afford to send you to college," her father said, "but if I can borrow the money, do you want to become a nurse?"

Her answer was clear: "Anything to get out of this community!"

The tiny village of Mohnton, in Berks County, Pennsylvania, had little to offer this ambitious young woman. Its only industry was a stocking factory, and she didn't want to end up there. Her dream was to become an airline stewardess, which in 1939 required a nursing degree. So, in spite of her paternal grandmother's insistence that she'd never make it through nursing school, she set out to prove herself.

Margaret's experience at the Reading Hospital School of Nursing was scary at times. Her head nurse was a holy terror and as stiff as the uniform; *everything* had to be done by the book. Nursing school was tough but Margaret prevailed and proudly graduated in September of 1942.

Seeking a change of scenery, Margaret and her friend Helen went to work at Allentown Hospital after graduation. The girls were very aware of a world at war, and Helen began thinking that she might enlist, that her nursing skills might be better used in the war effort. Margaret agreed, and decided to enlist also.

Margaret's brother John was already in the army with Coastal Artillery stationed in Hawaii. For two frightening weeks after the attack at Pearl Harbor, Margaret and her family had no contact from John, and they feared the worse. Margaret's family was greatly relieved to learn that John, who'd been stationed thirty miles from Pearl Harbor, was safe. There were distressed, however, when Margaret spoke of going into the service.

A short time later, the girls went to the navy recruiting center in Allentown and signed up. But only Helen made it in. Margaret was taken into a large room and asked to remove her glasses, then walk up to a chart on the opposite wall until she could see the large letter E. But when Margaret politely asked where the chart was, she immediately failed the eye test and was turned away.

Unfazed that the navy wouldn't take her, Margaret went directly to the army recruiting station and was accepted on the spot. It was February of 1943 and she was into her army uniform before Helen even got her navy uniform.

Within a year after Margaret's enlistment, her younger sister, Anna May, enlisted in the marines in 1944. The war years were difficult for the Schatz family. Margaret's mother often lamented, "I only have one boy, but I have three children in the service."

Lester Groff's father gave his son a Bible before Lester left for the army. He walked his son down the street from their home in Pottstown to the place where Lester was to be inducted. There were seventy-five young men waiting that day; it was the only time he ever saw his father cry.

"I don't know what this is going to do for you," Walter Groff said to his son, placing the small book into Lester's hands, "but I want you to take it along and put it in your pocket."

Walter wept while he held Lester's hand and told his son the story of a World War I soldier whose life was saved when a bullet lodged in the Bible in the man's breast pocket. Lester agreed to carry the Bible.

When Lester took the Bible from his father, he didn't know that many of the men he would meet never knew God. But they would know that Lester knew God, that he was religious, and that he prayed. They would see Lester praying under his tank and in his tank.

They would come to him and say, "I have a feeling."

"What is your feeling?"

"I have a feeling I'm not going to make it," a young soldier would reply.

"Why do you have that feeling?" Lester would ask.

The man would continue. "You see all these guys dying? I have a feeling I'm going to be next."

And Lester would look him in the eye and speak from his heart, "Did you pray to God that he would save you, keep you, and bring you home?"

"No," would be the solemn reply.

"Well," Lester would say, "Let's pray."

And together they would pray. At night Lester would camouflage his tank by covering it with old logs and shrubs, shove leafy branches into the treads, and then crawl in under the tank. He would light a candle. And they would pray together.

Lester and his Bible would give hope to many soldiers as they fought their way across Europe. Just as his father had given him faith, Lester passed it on to the men he served with. It was this faith in God that gave them hope, lightening their hearts and letting them fight without worry.

Outside the induction center in Pottstown, Lester stayed silent as he listened to his father's words. He would miss this gentle man. He read the words his father had inscribed on the inside of the Bible:

"From Walter H. Groff to son Lester E. Groff. May God watch over you and keep you safe."

Lester knew God was listening.

Cyrus Greenberg always thought of himself as a lousy student at the best high school in Philadelphia. He hated his studies and did poorly on tests in spite of the fact that he was a smart boy. He felt the staff had no rapport with students, and that the quality of teaching was poor. Perhaps he was right; or maybe he was just smarter than most of them.

When graduation day finally arrived, Cy was relieved to put all this frustration behind him. It was wartime and he wanted to go into the service by choice rather than be drafted like most of his friends. He just couldn't see himself in the army, lugging a sixty pound backpack through mud and snow while being shot at. He figured the navy would be more to his liking, particularly since he was used to eating three meals a day and sleeping in a bed at night.

"I will let you go into the navy," Cy's father promised him, "but first you must complete one semester of college."

Frustrated by his father's declaration, Cy reluctantly agreed.

Cy's experience at college was very different from high school. He attended Temple University for a semester, enjoyed it immensely, and surprised himself by doing extremely well. However, by semester's end, and to Cy's great disappointment, his father backed out of the promise and refused Cy permission to enlist. His father had hoped that Cy would change his mind. He didn't, and on the ninth of October, 1943 he enlisted in the navy by forging his father's signature.

Six months later, after surviving boot camp in Sampson, New York, and completing a course in diesel engineering in Virginia, Cyrus Greenberg was standing on the deck of an LST that had just sailed down the Mississippi River. Newly constructed at the Bridge and Iron Works in Illinois, the ship was going to war. But first the officers and crew were headed for a shakedown cruise in the Caribbean. The crew's average age was twenty and they were ready to go. Cy wasn't apprehensive in the least.

There were some men who, in spite of being drafted, refused to go to war.

Red Wells had just arrived back in the States after two years of jungle warfare training in Panama and Trinidad. Now a highly trained infantry soldier, he was stationed at Camp Shelby in Mississippi, awaiting deployment to Europe.

Having been separated from his buddies in Trinidad, Red made quick work of befriending a few guys; in particular, George Vath from Trevose, Pennsylvania. They had a lot in common, especially their interest in raising hell on the weekends in town, dancing with the local girls and getting into mischief. Once they even got matching tattoos.

The recruits at Camp Shelby had just finished their basic training and were waiting to be shipped to Europe as well. Red wondered how they would survive with so little training. He remembered one particular young man who simply claimed that he "wasn't going to war." He was a happy-go-lucky fellow who had done well in basic, but kept telling everyone this. Nobody took him seriously; they thought he was joking. One day he was on his bunk when the others were leaving to eat.

"Let's go," Red said to him, "it's time for chow."

But the young recruit wouldn't budge, "Nah, I'm not going to chow today."

Red looked at him and asked, "What are you going to do?"

"I don't know,' was his reply, "I think I'll stay here and shoot myself."

Red responded, "Well okay, but you're gonna miss chow!"

Five minutes later they heard a gunshot; the young man had killed himself. Red felt very bad about the incident; he regretted not taking the man seriously. *Maybe I could have helped*, he thought. But probably not. The man had made up his mind. He had said it, and he meant it: He was not going to war.

The time for departure was just moments away. Richard Becker could hear steam spewing from the locomotive that would take him to war. In spite of the nip in the air on that crisp January morning, Reading's Outer Station was a hub of activity, filled with the sounds of young men saying goodbye.

Richard had hugged his mother one last time before leaving home; reminding her that he would buy her a new house when he returned from the war. She loved him dearly, yet chose not to see him off at the station, instead staying home that morning with the baby sister he called "button nose." Richard somehow knew that baby Christine, who arrived when he was seventeen years old, was a gift to his mother, born to take his place. God knew that Richard was going away.

Richard's only brother, David, five years his junior, threw his arms around Richard and refused to let go. Their father, LeRoy, and sister, Geraldine, stood close by patiently watching and waiting their turn to say goodbye.

"Don't go, don't go," David begged, remembering the pride he felt when his brother was drafted.

But now, in his brother's arms, David wept.

Growing up, Richard had been more than a brother to David; he had cared for him and looked out for him and their sister, Geraldine, for as long as David could remember. Although both their parents worked full time to survive those tough post-depression years, their father suffered frequent bouts of emphysema and asthma and many days he was too sick to go to work at Jacob's Aircraft in Pottstown. Richard stepped up to the plate by helping to rear his siblings and by bringing home his small salary from two part-time jobs. The strong allegiance to his family did not arise totally from the young man's sense of duty; but more from the deep feelings of love he felt for each one of them.

Whispering softly into David's ear, Richard reminded him again, "You're the man in the family now, you must hold up." Accustomed to his responsibilities for so long, Richard knew the time had come to pass the torch to his only brother. Richard had a much greater calling now, and he would perform it cheerfully, as always, and to the best of his abilities.

Richard loved life. He went to church and participated in Boy Scouts and camping. He loved watching cartoons and movies, and reading the Sunday comics. His lively baseball games with the boys in the neighborhood drove the neighbors crazy, particularly Mammie Wolfgang and her dog Daisy who lived on the corner. She called the police each time a game was underway. But most of all Richard loved the outdoors and enjoyed walking the wooded hills and mountains around his hometown of Reading, Pennsylvania. Even in the coldest months, he brought the outdoors inside by sleeping with his bedroom windows wide open. He could remember waking up in the big brass bed he shared with David, with snow on their blanket, a wonderful down filled "tick" given to the boys by good neighbors who knew there was no coal for their furnace.

Richard's arms still wrapped tightly around his brother evoked memories of their wrestling matches, when Richard would roll David up in a blanket, completely restraining him for the briefest of moments, then releasing him in gales of laughter. Then his reverie took him to a time when David suffered a nightmare and nearly leaped down the attic staircase in his sleep, Richard catching him just in the nick of time. It wouldn't happen a second time, because Richard tied one of David's ankles to one of his own before they went to sleep the next night.

The steam locomotive behind him let out a long shrill whistle and Richard knew it was time to go. He would take with him precious memories of a loving family. Those memories would sustain him through the difficult days ahead, give him strength and courage when he needed it most, and justify the sacrifices he would inevitably be called upon to make.

The time had come to let Richard go. David would remember this day vividly for the rest of his life. He released Richard, but couldn't let go of the feeling inside. He had had a premonition and knew without a doubt that he would never see his brother again. Today was the saddest day of David's life.

3

THE SLEEPING GIANT
EARLY PACIFIC

"We patrolled up there... cold... foggy... can hardly see a ship next to you. In this fog, our task force of battleships and six destroyers picked up an enemy ship. 'Enemy ship, course so-and-so! Stand by to open fire!' That was our exact course and speed. Our captain said, 'Don't shoot, don't shoot! American ship!'"

Lyle Koenig, Aleutian Islands, 1942

"One hundred miles and closing."

Lyle Koenig cringed at these words. *The Japs will be on us like hornets soon.* He'd heard the call to general quarters come squawking over the Aylwin's intercom and had wasted no time getting to his battle station. Now he stood gazing out at the vast turquoise sea before him. It was deceptively beautiful. *The Coral Sea,* he thought; he'd never heard of it before. It all looked the same: endless waves reaching out for three hundred and sixty degrees. All that changed was the weather.

"Sixty miles."

The enemy planes were drawing closer. At least the Aylwin wasn't alone. Dozens of ships lined the horizon, giving him some measure of comfort.

Lyle scanned the sky. *Nothing yet. No movement.* Pearl Harbor had been frightening, but it was nothing compared to how he felt now. At Hawaii nobody had been expecting a fight, but today he knew what he was getting into. The apprehension scared him.

"Twenty miles."

He wished the voice would stop. Glancing over at the number two gun, he thought, *I'll be feeding it ammunition soon.* He rubbed his forehead and suddenly wished he was somewhere else – like at home. But then a flicker of motion caught his eye and he saw planes on the horizon. *Dive bombers!* His sense of duty took hold and he snapped to attention, ready for a fight.

Violent explosions tore through the USS Lexington, spewing fire and smoke from her fractured hull. Lyle watched helplessly from the Aylwin.

"The Lexington's been hit," someone shouted.

No kidding. A pair of torpedoes had just pierced her earlier; now men were jumping to safety, leaping from the deck in an attempt to escape the inferno. They floundered in the water, kicking away from the burning aircraft carrier. Lyle watched in horror. *Just like Pearl Harbor.* For a moment time slowed and he was transported back to his first combat. He couldn't take his eyes off those sailors in the water. *They're abandoning ship,* he thought with horror, *the Lexington is going down.*

For four days a massive air battle raged and Lyle bore witness to the devastation. Dive bombers swarmed through the skies, menacing the ships and striking fear into the men aboard them. Savage antiaircraft fire repelled many of them, but some made it through and wreaked their havoc. The peaceful Pacific was quiet no longer; Lyle saw that firsthand. *At least we're on a small ship,* he reassured himself, *that should save us.* It seemed the larger ships were being targeted first, like the Lexington. This made him feel a little better.

Ed Taggert regretted telling the U.S. Army about his job as a mail boy in a defense factory. His honesty had earned him a spot sorting mail in Camp Hill, Pennsylvania, and he was miserable. He lamented his decision to enlist in a letter to his father who was in the National Guard, and two weeks later Ed was shipped out! He was off to Fort McClellan, Alabama for basic training. Ed never knew if his father had any influence in the decision, but Ed was grateful nonetheless.

Basic training was easy for Ed who was a fit eighteen-year-old sports fan. He had played baseball, volleyball, and Sunday afternoon football at home, and felt as though he could run around the army's obstacle course all day. There were guys in their forties in his unit who had a heck of a time keeping up with the younger men and Ed felt sorry for them.

On the first of September in 1942 he boarded a converted cruise ship, the SS Nordham, and set sail for the U.S. occupied New Caledonia, an island off the east coast of Australia, south of the Coral Sea. No battles had taken place there, but it was occupied by U.S. forces in January 1942 to protect Australia from further Japanese advances from the Solomon Islands. Due to its location to the sea lanes from the United States to Australia, New Caledonia was now a vital air and navy base for the United States.

A destroyer accompanied the Nordham for a short distance out to sea, but the ship was on its own for the remainder of the three-week trip. The Pacific was a shade of blue that Ed could never have imagined, and to his surprise the trip was leisurely and the seas calm.

Ed was assigned to a field artillery battery as a replacement. Here he received a bit of training on the 105mm artillery pieces, but not much at all. Not enough to make him feel comfortable with the equipment. The noise was horrible but after awhile Ed got used to it. It was hot, too, the beginning of their summer season, and the men rarely wore shirts. But Ed was glad to be here, and the first night in New Caledonia the men shared a volleyball game. *So far*, Ed thought, *being in the army isn't so bad!*

Seven weeks after Ed arrived in New Caledonia, he boarded a troop ship for the five-day trip to Guadalcanal. It was late October, 1942. After a couple of days at sea, the men stopped at the New Hebrides Islands, and stayed put for nearly a week. Ed was glad for the break, but the flies were the worst Ed had ever seen. The men were bitten and tormented constantly. The naval battle at Guadalcanal was the reason for their delay. By week's end, word was given to ship out. The men were relieved at the news and pleased to get away from the murderous flies.

Things were relatively peaceful when Ed's ship arrived and unloaded their gear. The men were all issued British Enfield rifles, but Ed had been assigned a Tommy gun, probably because no one else wanted it. Ed was thrilled with the gun; it made him feel like John Dillinger. But he wasn't so sure today as he struggled to carry the gun and the large drum magazines with six canisters of 50 caliber bullets to shore.

There were quite a few troop ships unloading men and supplies; it was a busy place. Coconut palms that grew abundantly in groves lay in devastation from the shelling. Tanks, landing craft and guns were scattered around, more evidence of fighting. Every once in awhile the men encountered a body - some had been missed in the clean-up.

The men bedded down on the ground in the coconut groves that first night. They could hear gun battles in the distance, and feared the Japanese were coming ashore.

The thunderous rumbling of naval fire grew louder in the distant sky. Like a storm drifting low over the water, it rolled across the bay and entered the thoughts of the soldiers lying quietly on the beach. But it was no storm. Cold and unfeeling, the battle raged blindly in the night. To the men in the coconut groves it meant one thing: the enemy was near. This is why Ed Taggert couldn't sleep, why his thoughts ran wild. How could anyone rest at such a time?

The hard-packed ground barely moved beneath his back as Ed shifted position. Around him, writhing like worms upon the sand, his friends stirred restlessly. Nobody could sleep, yet who could blame them? From across the water disaster loomed. War was in the air. And the Japanese, for all they knew, might emerge from the darkness at any moment, bayonets at the ready. Even now the rustling of land crabs met their ears. The little fiends crawled everywhere, scuttling about in the fallen coconut fronds, crackling and crunching like the boots of enemy soldiers.

They were alone at the moment, cut off from support. A hundred-odd men with their artillery in the night. It wouldn't do them any good if the Japanese sneaked up onto the beach. They'd have to fight hand to hand, man to man. Shadows danced beyond their vision and the GIs prepared for an attack. Or at least they did what they could. There was no fortified line, no proper entrenchments, but mentally it helped to be ready. Ed was ready to fight, but he hoped to God he wouldn't have to.

He survived this night without incident, though it was certainly frightening enough. Some time later, he found himself involved in another disturbing incident – this one involving souvenirs.

Ed scrambled up the rocky slope, sweat rolling off his brow, dirt clumping on his boots. Pausing for a breather, he looked back and saw he was about halfway to the top. His buddy, however, was charging ahead in pursuit of a gathering commotion on the other side of the hill. Mopping his forehead with a grimy sleeve, Ed quickened his pace and followed suit. A moment later, gunfire erupted nearby, throwing crackling echoes against the jungle canopy in all directions. It was startlingly close, coming from beyond the crest of the slope. Staying low, he wove his way through a maze of mortar-blasted tree trunks until he caught up with his friend near the top. They huddled close, pressing their bodies into the rocky earth and poking their heads upward just far enough to see what was happening below. In a small valley beneath them, a group of marines were firing their weapons into the hillside. It seemed they'd found a fortified cave and were fighting their way inside. Ed watched with detached fascination as one of the men moved up with a flamethrower and raked the base of the hill with fire. It was mesmerizing, watching the flames flicker and dance along the rocky terrain, rending soil and grass to black ash. But there were men dying inside the cave. He could hear them. Their wails seemed inhuman. Jarred abruptly to attention by the horror, he slid down behind a large rock as the marines finished the job below.

It took only minutes - though it seemed longer - for the commotion to cease. With only a moment's hesitation, his buddy jumped to his feet and began scrambling down the hill in a whirlwind of tumbling dirt and stones. He wanted a souvenir, he shouted back. Ed stayed put, a lump in his stomach, his desire for trinkets lost. It was the right decision, and he was glad for it when his friend soon returned with a gruesome prize. He'd cut off a Japanese ear and was brandishing it like some kind of medal, grinning widely in the jungle light. Half an hour ago Ed had wanted a sword to take home. Now his buddy was dangling a man's ear in his face. Was this war?

Ed smoothed the wrinkled paper between his fingers as he folded it on his lap. Headlines from across the world stared up at him. Things were going well for the Allies, or so it seemed. He realized, however, that each bullet point on the checklist of progress meant untold suffering for both sides. How many had died to secure just this little island? How many had died since the beginning? It seemed absurd.

Looking down at the news, he was suddenly struck with a feeling of great historical significance. *Here I am,* he thought, *on the army's first Pacific offensive.* Someday he'd look back and be able to say, *I was there, on Guadalcanal.* In a strange way he liked that, and he wondered if the men around him felt the same.

A battle was taking place somewhere in Russia, according to the paper. A city called Stalingrad. Ed shuddered a bit when he imagined the fighting there. *I'd rather be here than freezing to death in Europe. I'm glad I came this way and not the other.* If he was going to die, he wanted to do it someplace warm. What he never supposed, however, was that those men fighting and dying half a world away were thinking just the opposite.

In May 1942, the USS Honolulu was given an urgent order to report to the Aleutian Islands for a thirty-day patrol. The ship set sail under full steam from the balmy Pacific, first stopping in Hawaii to take on fuel, some foul weather gear, but no stores. There wasn't time. *No stores?* It made no sense to Ralph Mason. The men were accustomed to the tropics and suddenly they were in Alaska!

Ralph shivered against the chill. It was darned cold and he wasn't used to it. He was on watch on the open bridge in the only warm clothes he owned and the coffee pot was empty. The regulation stocking hat was okay, but his pea coat over his working blue uniform was too bulky, and not nearly warm enough. *It's freezing!* Ralph rubbed his arms hard.

Then he heard footsteps on the stairs. His buddy was holding a coffee pot.

"Hot soup," the man announced. "Extra grease." And tucked under one arm was a loaf of freshly baked bread.

Ralph grabbed the coffee cups from the shelf and his buddy carefully poured out the steaming vegetable soup. It was the only way for the men to keep warm. *Thank God for the guy in the galley,* Ralph thought as he wrapped his hands around his mug and sipped the soup. He couldn't take his eyes off the bread. They'd have to eat it quickly. Stealing bread was definitely against regulations.

Several weeks later, Ralph Mason scoffed down his dinner; not so much because he was hungry, but because he wanted to get it over with. *Rice and navy beans again! With catsup!* Well at least he had rice and powdered milk with raisins to look forward to later that evening. The Honolulu was well into her month-long patrol in the Aleutians, but she was running out of stores. And the men were hungry!

Wham! Greasy sardines went sailing across the mess hall when one of the men tried to open his sardine can with a fire ax. They were given a special treat tonight, sardines! Well, *at least it's not rice and beans,* Ralph thought, digging his pocket knife into the can.   One of the storekeepers found a cache of sardines and each man was given one can and six crackers. That was dinner. Except for one guy who tried to open his can with an ax.

Early in 1944 Ed Taggert was shipped to Bougainville in the Solomon Islands. He performed much of the same functions as on Guadalcanal, fighting the Japanese with his artillery and holding a perimeter. Ed was there for one year.

"Sorry?" Ed thought he'd heard the sergeant wrong. "I really need some sleep."

"No, you're going to a birthday party."

"Who has birthday parties out here?"   Ed was exhausted and in no mood for jokes. He'd just returned from a four day patrol in the jungle.

"Look, I don't know what it's about," the sergeant said with a hint of irritation, "but somebody sent your name and you're supposed to go to this party."

He pointed to a jeep idling nearby and said no more. Ed had little choice but to obey.

Speeding along a narrow jungle road in the jeep, Ed tried to make sense of what he was doing. He'd never heard of a birthday party happening before. The vehicle took him a short way across the island, to a clearing full of young soldiers.

"Is Ed Taggert here?" A special service man swept his eyes across the group of soldiers. Ed stepped forward hesitantly. "Well, it was your mother who arranged this.

She contacted the Red Cross and asked if there was some way to have a party for you. Seems they liked the idea and passed it on to us."

Ed shook his head and laughed. He'd forgotten his own birthday. Amid pats on the back and handshakes, he moved up to the table and saw something wonderful waiting: cake and ice cream. He hadn't seen ice cream in ages. They must have gotten it from the ships off shore just for them. It made him feel like a million bucks, and for the better part of an hour he glowed with happiness as he shared the birthday dessert with the soldiers around him.

The Americal Division (America, New Caledonia Division formed in New Caledonia) was located close to where Ed Taggert's unit was stationed. The island, now under the control of the Allies, had become quite the busy place. Bob Hope and his USO Show made a visit, and the Americal Division cleared just enough jungle to make a football field. Lights, run by generators, were installed for night games, and spotlights were bounced off the nighttime cloud cover to help illuminate the field. *Jungle football?* Ed's antennas went up. He loved sports.

The men were quick to assemble touch football teams, and lacking proper equipment, they played in T-shirts and regular Army boots. A few of the guys scrounged up tennis shoes; Ed was not one of them. He joined the six-man team by playing end, and his buddy Elbow played quarterback. And Elbow was an ace! So we played several games, mostly at night, and since Elbow was so good, we were winning.

Soon a battalion team was put together and Elbow and I were picked for that team as well. Then somebody got the crazy idea to play the navy. *Why not*, Ed thought. His team was winning a lot and it didn't matter much to him who he played, just as long as he played.

The first big army/navy game was scheduled for Christmas Eve day and both teams were up to the challenge. The coach of our battalion team was a former Lehigh All-American named Sparky, a short stubby guy who played with the New York Giants a little bit before the war. He could have played quarterback, but he knew Elbow was the better quarterback, so he let Elbow play instead. But he was a great coach!

When the day of the big game arrived, a violent electrical storm hit the island, striking twelve men. Ten men were injured and survived; the other two were in critical condition. Elbow, a medic, was called to the scene to revive the two men. One was lying in his bunk when lightning struck the tent pole and then struck him. He was unconscious, not breathing, and the change in his pocket had fused together in one solid mass of hot metal. The second man was standing in his tent when he was struck directly. No pulse, he was already gone.

Elbow gave it his all that afternoon fighting to save the two men. The field hospital, where they were rushed, had no luck reviving them either, and they were pronounced dead. Elbow was devastated. So were Ed and the rest of the guys in their battery. So much so that the football game scheduled for that evening was postponed until the next day, Christmas Day.

Christmas Day arrived unlike any other Christmas the men had ever known. Thousands of miles from home, two touch football teams put on colored T-shirts: army, yellow, and navy, white, and readied themselves for their big game. Soldiers, sailors and marines all over the island were gearing up for an evening of fun. This was not their typical Christmas celebration, particularly since they were separated from their families. But on that particular Christmas Day in 1944, nobody seemed to mind. Tonight was special!

Ed found out later that all the guys on both teams had played college football, with the exception of Ed and one other guy who had played in high school. *No wonder they were good*, Ed thought. The only experience Ed had was playing with the Oak Lane Yellow Jackets in the Pop Werner Conference at home on Sunday afternoons. Small time stuff, but he loved it all the same.

The big game would never be forgotten. The weather had cleared, the lights shone brightly against a backdrop of jungle vegetation, and Ed's army team beat the navy team twenty-one to zero. The marines had put teams together as well, and inspired by the Christmas game, issued a challenge to the army. Some things are better left undone. Just one week later, on New Year's Day, the army team beat the marines soundly, fifty-four to six.

Howard Withers first saw combat when his marine unit stormed the beaches of Roi-Namur in the Marshall Islands.

Howard had cooked breakfast for the men on his ship this morning. *I am a cook, but a marine first*, Howard would often say. Cooking wasn't Howard's first choice after boot camp - in fact it wasn't a choice at all. *All men whose last names start with S or W have been assigned to cooks' and bakers' school*, the notice stated. Howard was crushed.

So this morning Howard had cooked, and now he was preparing to be a marine. *Cook breakfast, then storm a beach.* He wasn't sure he was ready.

Howard was proud of the fact that his Fourth Marine Division was the first division to go directly into combat from the United States. And they were also the first division to capture Japanese owned territory.

For two days before the invasion, battleships, cruisers, destroyers and aircraft fired shells and dropped bombs in a relentless salvo on Roi Namur. Howard stood on deck and watched the island exploding. Clouds of black smoke and flames were erupting everywhere. The navy was hitting hard, but no Japanese were to be seen anywhere. Howard knew they were dug deeply into the underlying rock, and lying low in trenches and prayed they were being blown up with the island. Howard wasn't sure the furious bombardment would be enough.

Higgins boats were starting to fill and Howard watched in horror their attempts to approach the island. The island was heavily defended with artillery and anti-aircraft guns. Machine gun fire erupted from everywhere. Some of the boats made it to shore, others didn't.

Howard climbed down the cargo net hung from the side of his troop transport and jumped into a Higgins. Three dozen men heading toward the beach heard the rough scraping sound that meant they had hit bottom. The ramp fell open and the men charged into the water.

Bullets whizzed past Howard, but not others. They were falling, tinting the water crimson.

Howard had hit the beach under fire. He was lucky, he'd made it ashore. *Just keep pushing*, he told himself, *and stay down!* Told they had to secure the island, Howard inched forward on his belly, his M1 by his side, trying to stay alive at the same time.

The fighting was costly and brutal. In a little more than one day Roi Namur was secured and Howard had survived. Soon after the island was taken, Roi was bombed by the Japanese. A few incendiary bombs hit an ammunition dump, turning a chunk of the island into an inferno. *What an eerie feeling to be hunkered down in a foxhole and you're being bombed, and you don't know where it's gonna hit.*

Dead Japanese were scattered everywhere. Hundreds of them. Mutilated by the bombing and shelling, and some self-mutilated by hara-kiri. It made Howard sick. They swelled in the heat, oozing. The dead didn't last long in such weather.

4

LIGHTING THE TORCH
AFRICA & ITALY

"I was sick at heart because I had not seen my family and I knew I was going to be attached to an infantry unit somewhere soon."
Richard Biehl, North Africa, 1943

Dust and sand. Sweltering sun. Parched lips. It felt like purgatory. Retreating, firing blindly, barely holding the enemy at bay while they moved steadily back. Losing ground, first by the yard then by the mile, driving, walking, limping, left, right, left, right... he had to keep moving. *Stay ahead, stay awake,* he remembered. *Stay alive.* How long had it been?

Two years. Twenty four months of hellish back-and-forth combat. And for what? A strip of arid earth, a bombed-out-city, a shell-pocked dune? *What did we gain?* They had fought the Allies for so long, inflicted so many losses. But both sides had suffered. His had just lost more.

The battle for North Africa was almost over, and Tommaso Gentile remembered it all. He recalled a desolate road, stretching from horizon to horizon in an unnamed patch of nowhere. It led from one danger to the next, shepherding an unending line of haggard men towards some uncertain fate. The enemy was behind them, veteran Allied units closing in. *No telling how close they are.* Tommaso had to keep moving. But his Italian army uniform was sweltering, weighed down with sweat and clods of dirt. It stuck to his skin and itched terribly beneath the harsh North African sun. But he wasn't alone. His comrades suffered with him. At least he wasn't wounded.

Lost in his thoughts, Tommaso almost didn't notice the truck approaching from behind. He turned in time to see it race past, trailing a plume of dust as it went. The back was open; a dozen sets of eyes peered out at him. *Healthy soldiers, probably officers.* It seemed that anyone with a shred of importance – or perhaps something useful to offer – got to ride in the trucks. Everyone else had to trudge for miles in the heat. *We aren't worth the fuel,* he thought bitterly. It was probably true. The Italians always seemed to be retreating, and their organization was chaotic. Tommaso recalled some of the officers stuffing their trucks full of frivolous things like furniture and clothing, leaving little room for the men. So they walked.

Another vehicle was moving up now – an officer's car. It drove slowly along the road, its occupants gesturing to the troops. He shielded his eyes with an upturned palm and squinted. Was it somebody important? He could see what appeared to be an escort following the car. *Who the heck would be all the way out here,* he wondered. Then he laughed. *Maybe I'm going crazy and it's just a mirage!* But crazy or not, the vehicle was very real. It continued on its way, moving closer and closer to Tommaso. And when it came within a stone's throw of him, he suddenly recognized the man inside. *Field Marshal Rommel!* There was no mistaking it – the Desert Fox himself was driving past, trying to rally the troops in his own peculiar way. *What is he saying? Don't worry, keep on fighting? Don't give up, we're going to come back?* It was nonsense – empty phrases for desperate times, muttered in German and translated hastily. Tommaso knew he meant well, but there was little weight behind the words. The men had seen the truth, had it hammered into their awareness time and time again by enemy tanks and artillery. Air strikes and mortars, machine guns and bayonets – this was their reality. And the endless retreat. It felt like everything was spiraling out of control. Rommel could keep his words. Tommaso just wanted to live.

The Field Marshal's car passed by and continued on its way, leaving Tommaso alone with his thoughts once more. He glanced back at the long line of soldiers stretching out behind him, then turned ahead.

He let out a long sigh and mopped his brow. Dust and sand. It just kept going.

More than a thousand miles from African soil, an air war was raging in Europe. Waves of bombers, stationed in England, flew daily missions across the Channel in hopes of grinding Axis production to a halt. For most of the airmen who participated in these raids, life was nerve-wracking. And for many of them, it was a very short career.

Paul Gordon sat in the belly turret of his B-17 and watched as the English Channel churned beneath him. The grey water, cold and choppy in the October air, rolled along in great surges. He'd been observing it for a while now. *France must be close*, he guessed, and for a moment a wave of exhilaration passed over him. He didn't know what their target was today, but the thrill of the hunt had been building ever since takeoff. It was a good feeling, and not the least bit frightening. This was technically his fourth mission. The first three were aborted due to mechanical problems, but today was different. *I'm finally in the war*, he thought, *I'm ready to fight!*

It wasn't long before the Channel slipped past and gave way to the French countryside. From this height everything merged together like a quilt. Hedgerows, fields, roads – there were a thousand patches of color locked together seamlessly and dotted with tiny villages. It was a beautiful sight, made even nicer by an apparent lack of Luftwaffe resistance.

Time melted away, the minutes stretching to hours as Paul kept a watchful eye on the sky beneath the plane. There was a lot to see, though most of it looked the same after a while. *Green spot, orange spot, trees, a lake, a cloud...* He scanned it all, looking for something interesting, but the harder he tried the less focus he had. Sighing, he stifled a yawn.

A voice broke the monotony.

"Watch out for bandits," said their pilot over the radio, "We're getting close."

Paul couldn't help but notice that their RAF escort had vanished. Of course they lacked the range for such a mission, but it was nice having them around. *Oh well*, he thought, *we'll make do without them.* The bomber formation was dangerous enough on its own with its overlapping array of machine guns, but a combination of ground fire and air attackers could still overwhelm them. Paul knew this, and it unsettled him a bit when flak activity reports started coming in.

Things grew more and more tense as they closed in on the target area. Though he didn't know it, their mission was to bomb a railroad marshalling yard at Lille, near the Belgian border. It was respectably defended, and it wasn't long before Paul could see dark puffs bursting in the air around the bomber. This sporadic antiaircraft fire grew denser and he began to wonder about the things he'd heard from other crews. *The flak is thick enough to walk on,* a friend had said once. From the look of things ahead, he was ready to believe it.

Within minutes the sky turned dark with smoke and he knew they must be over the target. He could hear the bomb bay doors open over the pop of explosions. But there was a problem.

"We can't release yet," the pilot barked over the intercom, "there's a formation of Liberators below us."

Paul dropped the turret to get a better view. The pilot was right; he could see the B-24s dropping their bombs underneath him. It would be risky to release their own payload with friendlies so close, so they continued on and made a wide turn back over the railroad yard. It was a dangerous move. The antiaircraft fire was hellish by now, and they were essentially circling inside it. But they had to complete the mission.

Paul bumped his head on a piece of metal as the plane bucked violently. It's *like being in a balloon,* he realized, *they're swatting us back and forth.* Shrapnel clattered against his Plexiglas dome and his attention suddenly jumped to something at the corner of his vision. *Smoke!* He swung the turret around. *Some poor bastard is on fire,* he thought. Then it dawned on him: it was coming from his own plane.

"Number four engine is burning!" Voices crackled on the intercom. He couldn't tell whose.

The bomber dipped as it began dropping out of formation; Paul watched the gap widen between them and the other friendlies. It was a dangerous move, but it had to be done. They couldn't maintain speed and even if they could, their crippled plane was a hazard to the rest of the bombers. He gripped his guns with white knuckles, nerves steeled for what he assumed would come next.

"Watch for enemy fighters!"

There it was. His pulse quickened. *The lagging bomber always attracts attention,* he knew, *It's only a matter of time.* He swept his turret around and around, scanning the horizon.

Mal, the tail gunner, noticed them first. "Fighters!"

Paul swung to face six o'clock and saw them closing in from the rear. But they were still pretty far out. At least for now.

"Watch them," he told Mal, "If they start in, call me because I'm going to watch below."

He dropped his guns and looked toward the ground. *Nothing but flak down here.* Dark puffs hung beneath them in vast clouds, spitting shrapnel everywhere. Squinting, he tried to look past them. Then he heard gunfire from behind and realized what was happening. Spinning back into position, he turned just in time to see an FW-190 closing in low from behind. Paul squeezed the trigger and lit up the sky between them. The enemy pilot did the same, his wings flickering with cannon flashes. He was so close; Paul could hear his guns hammering, could see the yellow paint on the fighter's nose. Bullets tore through the air in both directions, paths crossing in two great slicing arcs. *Wham, crack,* they pierced Paul's turret, slamming into his weapon and shattering the gun sight. Jerking back, he brought his hands up as shards of glass peppered his face. *Blood!* The goggles saved his eyes, though he was bleeding. And the German fighter was gone – it disappeared in the blink of an eye. *Did I hit it?* He wasn't sure what had happened. *Did it blow up?* But it didn't matter. Another one was screaming in from the rear. And the tail gunner's weapons were silent.

"Mal, six o'clock, Paul yelled."

No answer. He returned fire, lobbing fifty caliber rounds at the bandit closing fast. The tracers jerked wildly in the sky as they flew. But something was wrong with his guns. They jammed and stopped working. *Think fast!* Mind racing, he swung his turret menacingly, just like they'd taught him in training. It didn't work; the fighter kept coming and by now he was spitting bullets into the Plexiglas dome. Paul didn't have a choice. He had to get out.

The belly turret was shattered but Paul managed to pound the hatch open and drag his upper body into the waist compartment. *Get to the tail gun,* he told himself, *I can knock out that fighter.* He assumed Mal was dead, so it made sense that someone should take over his position. But he never got a chance. As Paul pulled his legs out of the turret, he saw another fighter beneath him. The German was barely fifty feet away, staring up at the B-17 with cold eyes. *This is it,* he realized, *I'm going to die.* Time slowed to a crawl, the sounds of battle slurred, and everything seemed to blur for a moment. *How easy it is to die.* He thought of his mother, closing his eyes and picturing her face. She looked sad. *She'll hear how her son was killed in action.* It broke his heart. *I'm sorry,* he told her, *sorry it had to end like this.* He could hear distant tapping now, like rats on a tin roof. *Tap, tap, pop.* Opening his eyes, he watched the bomber's fuselage light up with tiny points of light as bullets punctured the metal. *This is it...* They couldn't possibly last much longer.

Paul was jarred back to attention by a sudden blast of gunfire just a few feet away. *The waist gunner!* He looked down and saw, much to his surprise, the enemy fighter still hovering beneath him. The pilot, without firing, banked hard and disappeared with a flourish. *He's coming around for a pass,* Paul realized. Scrambling to his feet, he turned toward the rear of the plane and watched in horror as the waist gunner jerked in agony, slammed into the opposite wall, and slid dead to the floor. It was terrible. *Is anyone still alive?* It was hard to tell. The bomber was starting to list and none of the guns were being used. *This is bad.*

The bail-out oxygen cylinders were just an arm's length away. Paul grabbed one and started scrambling towards the tail position, but he didn't get far. A great crash split his ears – a horrendous metallic tearing noise – and he was thrown violently against the fuselage. Face jammed against metal, feet slipping in blood, he flailed his limbs in an effort to right himself. Suddenly he realized that everything was quiet; no engines, no gunfire, no thundering flak. Just the rush of cold air. *My God*, he thought, *we crashed! We crashed and I'm still alive!* It seemed ridiculous but he couldn't explain it. He tried to stand but slammed his head into an upside down machine gun. Then, turning around, he suddenly realized the truth. There was nothing behind him – the bomber's tail was gone. He faced a bright gaping hole and the cold rush of wind.

It took only moments for Paul to grab his parachute and approach the huge rift in the plane. Limping and stumbling, he tried to fasten the straps on his harness. He got the chest buckled but couldn't manage the legs in all the confusion. He knew he had to get out, though. *Just jump!* With a tremendous effort, he managed to hurl himself out into the void.

Falling face first, half unconscious and bleeding, Paul grasped his parachute's D ring and tugged with all his strength. The canopy opened, the chest strap pulled up to his armpits, and the buckle slammed him in the jaw. He blacked out.

Wake up! Paul thrashed in his harness. Only a moment had passed. *You're choking!* He couldn't breathe – the straps were against neck. *Pull yourself free... pull yourself...* Grappling at his throat, he clawed at the buckle. It gave, snapping free and dropping him even lower. He struggled to hang on, locking his fingers to avoid slipping out completely. Its balance upset, the chute began swinging him wildly as he fell. Back and forth, back and forth – he felt his blood-slick hands losing grip. *I should be dead!* He could barely hold on, but the ground was coming up fast. *Just a little longer!*

Wham! Paul's boots dug into soft-packed dirt and he keeled over, dragged along by the billowing parachute. Letting go, he crumpled to the earth, gasping for breath. Just above, a German fighter zoomed down and started circling him. He struggled to his feet and, on some inexplicable impulse, gave a big salute and a wave. The pilot responded with a wag of the wings before climbing out of sight.

It was suddenly rather quiet. Paul groaned and looked down at his body. *So much blood... is it mine?* Now that his adrenaline was receding, everything throbbed agonizingly. He wasn't sure he could make it out of the field on his own. So, exhausted and gravely injured, he kneeled in the dirt and weighed his options. *At least I'm alive*, he thought, *though I shouldn't be.*

He sighed. A figure was approaching in the distance.

Paul's injuries were extensive. He had a machine gun round in his foot, another in his elbow, several leg wounds, and shrapnel cuts on his face. He was nearly killed in his ball turret, again in the plane, and came close to slipping out of his parachute on the way down. In short, it was a miracle that he survived. Five of his buddies didn't.

After landing, Paul was taken in by French civilians who made him comfortable but were unable to hide him from the enemy. For two hours he was visited by curious men, women, and children, but ultimately a German car arrived and he became a prisoner of war. It would be a very long time until he knew freedom again.

Jerry Schoener was aboard the destroyer USS Mayrant when the Allies bombarded Casablanca for the African invasion. Along with the battleship USS Massachusetts and various other vessels, the Mayrant poured fire into the harbor, targeting enemy ships and installations.

Jerry was regularly a torpedo man, but at the time he was serving as sight-setter on one of the big guns. It was his job to make targeting adjustments and focus the shots when their aim was off. Thanks to this, he was able to observe first hand as the Allied flotilla poured fire into the city over the course of two days. It was quite an experience for the teenager from Pennsylvania, getting to watch the great big guns spit fireballs skyward. *My first action,* he thought as he looked inland, *I won't soon forget this.*

Tommaso Gentile opened his eyes and the dusty road faded away into memory. Trucks and dirt, retreating men beneath the African sun, his glimpse of Rommel – it all seemed so long ago. *Was it really just months?* He could still picture the vast terrain, still smell the earth beneath his boots, still fell the scorching heat. The same uniform clung to his weary frame, now hundreds of miles from where he started. But it was dirtier, more ragged - the boots scuffed and the jacket hanging open limply. He felt more like a refugee than a soldier, and for good reason. It had been weeks since he'd arrived in Tunis, exhausted from the long retreat. His unit was decimated, his officers demoralized, and this was the end of his third year in the army. That meant he could go home to Italy – or at least that's what they told him.

In reality, Tommaso had spent his recent days in ramshackle quarters near the airport at Tunis, waiting for planes that never seemed to arrive. It was his understanding, and that of the several hundred men with him, that they were waiting to go home. But that dream was yet to be fulfilled. The few airplanes he saw were either badly damaged or needed for other duties. So he waited. And waited.

Life at Tunis was dull, but at least he was alive and relatively healthy. Many of his fellow Italians hadn't been so lucky. *It could be worse,* he realized, *I could still be walking back there.* He recalled a day, not long ago, spent trudging through the Libyan countryside beneath the unforgiving sun. He'd been nearly dead from exhaustion, dehydrated, and burdened with the idea that he might never see his family again. So he did something sneaky. Watching truck after truck pass by, each bristling with weary Germans, he was struck by a thought. *They don't see how miserable we are. If they knew, they might help us.* Pulling a ragged cloth from his pack, he tied a makeshift sling and tucked his arm inside. And before long, a rickety truck came sputtering along and slowed down beside him.

"Comrade," a soldier shouted down in broken Italian, "what's the matter?"

Tomasso didn't even need to answer. His appearance said it all.

"Come on then, get in the truck. Jump up here!"

The Germans reached down and helped him climb into the back of the vehicle. He was relieved. After days of walking he could finally rest his legs. *Maybe I'll make it home after all,* he thought. It was a good feeling. Then he noticed a peculiar smell and caught a flash of movement in the corner of his vision. *Pigs!* It was a farm truck. It seemed the Germans had taken the vehicle from a civilian in their hurry to retreat, and had liberated some livestock as well. Tommaso smiled for the first time in a while. *Everyone is desperate, even our well-equipped allies.* With this thought he closed his eyes and let out a deep sigh. It was going to be a long ride.

Tommaso was abruptly jarred back to the present by a commotion nearby. He shielded his eyes with a hand and listened. The officers were talking.

"They're almost here," they said.

He knew what that meant: the British were in the city. He'd been expecting this as time wore on – they all had.

One of the lieutenants came walking down the line. "Don't shoot," he ordered, "Don't give them any reason to fire on us."

What a joke. What are we going to shoot with? Most of the men had weapons but no ammunition. Even if they wanted to fight, the most they could do was bludgeon the Brits at close range. *No,* he admitted, *it's over now.*

Within minutes the Italians were flying a white sheet and the silhouettes of Allied soldiers were visible in the distance.

"Strip your weapons," the lieutenant shouted, "Break them apart if you can."

The weary men followed his order to the word, and before long the sound of splintering wood and clattering metal filled the air. Tommaso pulled the bolt from his Carcano rifle and hammered the fore stock against a rock. *At least the enemy can't put it back together again,* he thought. Then he wiped the sweat from his brow and waited to be captured. It was his final bittersweet act as an Italian soldier.

For most of the men who had fought in defense of North Africa, the long war was finally over. Tunis' capture by Allied forces in May of 1943 forced the surrender of more than a quarter of a million Axis soldiers and ended the African campaign. Many of these men were passed into American hands and shipped to various POW camps. Some even ended up in the United States. Tommaso Gentile was taken to Casablanca before making the trip across the Atlantic with his fellow prisoners. There, admiration for his new host country would lead him to an unexpected and fascinating future.

Meanwhile, American soldiers fresh out of training were being shipped to North Africa in preparation for an entirely new campaign. Little did they know that, within a few short weeks, many of them would be fighting on Italian soil.

Nightfall in the North Atlantic. Cool breezes, salty air, and creeping darkness. Edward Zabinski leaned against the ship's railing and took in the sights. There was just one, really – the endless rolling expanse of water stretching out in every direction. It was the same every hour of every day; the only thing that changed was the light. *And the feeling,* he thought. Glancing west, he watched the last traces of sunlight slip below the horizon and couldn't help but feel a little bit nervous. *This is when they come out, the submarines.*

Edward was a Navy Armed Guard aboard the civilian tanker SS Dillworth, which at the moment was en route to Tunis with a belly full of gasoline. It was only one member of a large convoy, but its cargo made it a prime target for German Wolfpacks. The twilight hours at dawn and dusk were the worst; occasionally an explosion would flicker on the horizon, signaling the death of a ship. He'd seen this more than once, and it never felt good. He always wondered if maybe he'd be next.

The chilly breeze picked up and Edward shivered a little. *It's too eerie out here,* he decided, moving away from the railing. He looked along the length of the ship. Its deck was littered with miscellaneous cargo: crates, army vehicles, and even a few airplanes with the wings removed and boxed up. A bit farther down a 20mm gun was welded to the deck. That was his battle station, though he hoped he'd never have to use it. *That might change once we get to the Mediterranean,* he realized. He would find out soon enough.

For just a moment, Richard Biehl thought back to his journey across the Atlantic Ocean. He remembered being there, halfway between continents aboard the cruise ship SS America. He closed his eyes and recalled when he'd been told of his destination. *You're going to Casablanca,* they'd said, *in North Africa.* Relief washed over him as the news made its way through the hundreds of soldiers aboard the ship. The African campaign was over, so he wouldn't have to fight – at least not yet. It was a good feeling.

Then reality returned. He opened his eyes and flinched a little. The African sun glared bright and hot, unfiltered by the cloudless sky. *Casablanca.* He was finally here – a part of the war at last. But the fighting had passed him by. He could see the lingering signs: long faces, armed guards, and of course, soldiers everywhere. There were some startling sights as well. Along one of the docks, across from a long row of tattered warehouses, a huge ship sat low in the water. It was the French battleship Jean Bart, which had fought under Vichy control against the American invaders. It looked especially helpless, and was missing some of its guns. *What a waste,* he thought. It was his first glimpse of destruction and he'd barely set foot onto the continent. What else was in store for him?

Just then, Richard noticed something unexpected. Across from the harbor, on the edge of town along a boulevard, a long row of trees poked into the sky at neat intervals. *Palm trees,* he realized. He'd never seen palms before, as they certainly weren't native to Pennsylvania. Yet here they were, very much alive and real. A smile crossed his face as he drew near them, and for the first time in a while he felt that old familiar sense of adventure. But then he saw the army trucks waiting ahead, and reality sank in once more. It seemed he wouldn't be staying in town for long.

Back in Europe, the air war continued relentlessly. And some men learned that, while in the skies, they were never safe. Danger could come from anywhere at any moment.

Clouds rolled by like cotton balls outside the plane, flashing sporadically in the dense mist that clung to everything. *Thick as soup? Is that the expression?* Rotating slowly in the top turret of his B-17, sighting down the sleek lines of twin fifty caliber guns, Vincent Miller tried to recall the classic fog analogy.   It was going on seven in the morning and the weather over the English Channel was dismal. He could hardly see the bombers around him. *Pea soup*, he suddenly remembered, *it's thick as pea soup!*   It really was. Since taking off, visibility had been extremely poor. This was normal for England; in fact, they'd all come to expect it.   And as usual, the fog was slowly dissipating as they gained altitude. *Should be clear by the time we hit France.*

By now the bomb group was in tight formation and well on its way. He looked around. The squads were stacked high, medium, low - staggered in three dimensions to provide maximum firepower.   He imagined the overlapping fields of fire, the invisible cones that stretched out from each gun and spelled death for enemy fighters. *It must be intimidating,* he thought, *to jump out of the clouds and see us flying along. So many guns...* Something flashed in his peripheral and drew his attention. The squadron ahead was above him, poking out of the fog. Their visibility must have been – H*ey! The fighter escort!* Vincent let out a sharp gasp as a P-51 Mustang came screaming out of a cloud bank and intersected the formation in front of his.

The pilot tried to veer away but it was too late. With a violent flash, the tiny fighter sliced into one of the B-17s and disintegrated. The tangled fuselage, ruined and on fire, spewed wreckage in every direction and began plummeting. A second bomber caught a chunk of metal on the way down, tore a wing off, and joined the first. Vincent could hardly believe his eyes. It was a horrible chain reaction – the sort of thing he'd heard about but never expected to see. Men were bailing out of the bombers, parachutes flickering and smoking, refusing to open or crumbling to ash as they fell. They wouldn't make it. And even if they did, there was nothing but water beneath them. How many miles lay between them and the English coast? Twenty? Thirty? He shuddered at the idea. *Poor bastards*, he thought, *it's not even their fault.*

As the doomed planes sank smoking beneath the clouds, Vincent said a silent prayer for the men. This was the scariest thing he'd witnessed to date and they weren't yet in enemy territory. *If this can happen*, he wondered, *what's in store for us ahead?* The question weighed on his mind, tugging at the edge of his consciousness as he rotated in the turret. Around and around, he kept spinning, scanning the horizon until France peeked out from beneath the clouds. Everything would be answered soon.

Richard Biehl let out a low groan. *Trucks. Always with the trucks.* It was his eleventh day at Casablanca and the time had finally come to move out. To be more accurate, it was his eleventh day staying on the *outskirts* of the city in a makeshift tent city full of strangers. *Good times.* He reflected upon the past week and its array of activities. Calisthenics, running, guard duty, training... On the plus side, most of their work was done in the morning hours to escape the heat. That left enough time to visit Casablanca and see the sights properly. Of course, this being the army, the GIs were left to find their own transportation. He remembered getting passes with his buddy Wilbur and hitchhiking the ten miles into town. *Lovely city, wide boulevards.* He closed his eyes and pictured it. *Palm trees, snake charmers, and mansions.* One of the larger homes had been converted into a Red Cross Club and he'd spent an afternoon there drinking Coke and eating Hershey bars. *Hershey's chocolate in Africa,* he mused, *who'd have thought?* It brought a tiny smile to his face. Much like glimpsing his first palm tree at the harbor, exploring Casablanca had filled him with an interesting sense of wonder. Adventure, excitement, new people and places – the army wasn't so bad after all. But there was one thing, something that gnawed at him endlessly.

Richard was sick at heart. Despite the distractions, he couldn't quell the sense of dread that had been slowly building since day one. He knew that, ultimately, no matter what he did he'd be attached to an infantry unit soon. It was only a matter of time until he'd be thrust into combat. And there he was, sitting in a truck, speeding across North Africa with an untold number of nameless replacements. He had no weapons, no rations, and very little sense of purpose. That morning they'd had an early breakfast before rushing back to the docks to begin their epic convoy across the continent. The trucks were waiting for them, brand new and shiny – not entirely different than the men they now carried. *How many of us, a month from now, will look back and remember these as the good days,* he wondered. *How many of us will still be alive?*

Richard sighed and turned his gaze to the featureless terrain rushing by. From the position of the sun he could tell they were moving east. *But towards what?* Pushing the apprehension from his mind, he thought about the family waiting for him back home, and how long it had been since he'd seen them. But somehow that only made it worse.

Spending nights in rural North Africa was certainly an interesting experience for Richard. His convoy, having driven practically nonstop for several days, had been stopping to rest each evening. In an unusual twist, the trucks would circle into a defensive formation while lookouts were posted to keep the scavenging locals at bay. *We're like the pioneers with their covered wagons,* he mused, *except the pioneers didn't have people trying to forcefully trade chickens for cigarettes.* The local inhabitants, no matter where they stopped, would inevitably appear with their wares, looking to barter live animals, eggs, and various other things. It was strange, to say the least. The GIs had few cooking implements on hand, so their uses for raw foods were limited. And, of course, what would they do with animals? Tonight's offerings were different, however. Richard and his temporary buddies were camped on the fringes of an old French Foreign Legion training center, so the community members were used to having soldiers around. This meant that instead of food and trinkets, prostitutes were waiting. As soon as the trucks stopped they emerged from everywhere at once. But of course no one bothered with them. It wasn't allowed, and it certainly wasn't a good idea. So the women just watched and waited before slipping back into the shadows.

As he moved steadily east, spending long hours in the army vehicles, Richard began to notice more and more signs of war. At first it was the soldiers – American and British troops in the towns or passing in trucks. Then it was prisoners. Just a few hours ago, they'd passed a long line of uniformed Italians repairing the road. They had stretched out their hands and pleaded for cigarettes as the GIs went by. Near them, behind a tall wire fence, German POWs had watched in silence. Now, as they approached Tunisia, the sights were getting interesting. Burned out tanks, abandoned vehicles, blasted scars in the land – it made him glad that he'd missed the fighting.

On the outskirts of one small community, the convoy went bumping past a series of low buildings, and as Richard looked out the opposite side of the vehicle he saw something unexpected. A cemetery, marked with American flags and row upon row of graves, lay not far from the road. It was a solemn reminder of the war's true price, and he felt a twinge of sorrow in his heart as he watched it pass by. *An entire war's worth of battles has been fought before my arrival here,* he thought, *How many more will there be?* What a depressing question. *How many will I see?*

The cemetery wasn't the only thing that caught Richard's eye. One day, at the end of his long drive across Africa, he found himself looking at something quite remarkable. Shading his eyes with a free hand, he let out a low whistle. There before him, stretching out as far as he could see, a gigantic field of captured German vehicles and equipment lay shimmering in the hot African sun. Tanks, trucks, and scout cars lined up; helmets and rifles stacked in great pyramids; everything was stamped with the palm and swastika emblem of the Afrikakorps and neatly arranged. It was one of the strangest things he'd ever laid eyes on, and perhaps the most succinct testament to the Allies' victory in Africa. Here was the technological backbone of an entire German army, severed and abandoned in the middle of nowhere, caged behind walls of barbed wire and guarded by the enemy. *To them*, he realized, *we are the enemy. How strange it must feel to be defeated.*

With a sudden spring, Richard leaped onto the hood of a nearby truck and stood quietly for a short while. He wanted to remember this moment, to burn the image into his mind. It was a truly symbolic representation of those who had died and of the war's most recent chapter – now ended.

Though he suspected the worst, in truth Richard was only days away from the front lines. To the north and east, across a narrow stretch of Mediterranean waves, the island of Sicily lay bristling with enemy defenders. It wouldn't be long before Allied boots set upon its shores.

Blue skies dawned wide over Gela as Sam Scales struggled to keep his balance aboard the lurching LCT. He stood on the main deck of the tiny craft, gripping the side rail with both hands in an effort to keep upright. The Sicilian waters were still churning from a storm that had blown in overnight and wreaked havoc on the invasion fleet. The *Mussolini Wind*, as some of the GI's called it, had tossed the smaller ships like toys. Now, hours later, its aftereffects were still present in the shape of rough seas.

Sam's landing craft was loaded to the gills with men and tanks. With each large wave, the heavy vehicles shifted slightly, tethers groaning under the stress. Earlier, a chain securing one of the tanks had snapped like twine, whipping viciously against the deck and sending its cargo sliding. A handful of men were nearly crushed, but they managed to scramble out of the way just in time. *What a trip,* Sam thought, *an amphibious invasion is a heck of a trick to pull off.*

Just then a loud crack thundered in the distance. *They're firing at us again.* The German coastal defenses were obviously on full alert, but they hadn't put up much of a fight yet – just some artillery and air resistance. A great wet pillar shot up not far from his boat as an enemy round struck the water. He flinched instinctively. Then another shell burst on the opposite side, but much closer. *Do they have a bead on us?* Anxiety was growing in his chest. Everyone expected to fight today, but actually getting shot at on the water was a frightening experience. *Well,* he said to himself, *at least they haven't hit us.*

In chilling response to Sam's thought, a tremendous blast abruptly rattled his senses. He wheeled around and witnessed, much to his horror, the landing craft next to his erupt in a shower of fire and steel. It had been struck directly. Men and tanks lay dying and ruined on the deck, smoke billowing from a tattered rift as the GIs raced to extinguish the flames. He was stunned for a moment, but there was nothing he could do. So he said a prayer and turned back to watch the rugged Sicilian coastline approaching. *Just get to the beach,* he thought. More enemy fire was coming in now; little jets of water popped wildly at the edges of his vision. *Keep moving and we'll make it.* But as the morning grew louder and more violent, he began to have his doubts.

"I swear to God I'm going to go on a cruise here someday."

Edward Zabinski muttered to himself as he looked out across the Mediterranean. He was in awe. The water was perfectly calm and the deepest shade of turquoise he'd ever seen. *Gorgeous,* he thought, *just beautiful.*

The tanker ship SS Dillworth was moving west on its way out of the Mediterranean. It had just delivered fuel to the Allies in Tunisia so Edward was guarding a more or less empty ship. While this fact made him feel a little better, it didn't lessen the danger they faced from the Germans. He just tried to ignore his apprehension and enjoy the sights.

The sun was dipping low in the sky; Edward gazed ahead into the glare and pictured Gibraltar waiting for them. *We'll pass it soon enough, then it's on to the Atlantic.* A lump formed in his throat at the idea of making another trip through the great open ocean. *If it's not one threat, it's another,* he thought. Planes, ships, submarines – it made little difference. It always felt like something was lurking just out of sight.

For now Edward was happy enough to push the dark thoughts from his mind and enjoy the approaching evening.

"Beautiful," he repeated quietly.

It really was.

Richard Biehl paused for a moment, catching his breath and turning to look back at the beach and the LSTs. His overnight trip on the Mediterranean had been disorienting. *What happened here?* He wasn't aware that, just three days prior, amphibious landings had taken place and the Allies had clawed their way onto the island of Sicily. But he could see that something major had occurred. Shell craters, ruined equipment, and other debris littered the area. Whatever the battle, he was glad to have missed it.

He craned his neck. What was that off in the distance? Artillery fire? It sounded like thunder but the skies were clear. *So they're still fighting, then.* The troops were engaged not far from where he stood, steadily pushing their way inland. It felt strange to think that he'd be joining them soon.

Richard moved about fifty yards before coming to a road running parallel to the shore. There were buildings on the other side, padded by trees and grass. And beyond, crawling higher and higher, craggy green hills receded into the distance. *Look at this terrain,* he thought, *it must be a heck of a fight out there.*

Just across the road, some of his fellow replacements were hard at work setting up mosquito netting. *Just like in Africa.* He took this as a bad sign, but continued nonetheless. The men were busy passing rumors back and forth, and as he approached them he caught the gist of the conversation. There had been a German counterattack nearby, a fierce thrust by the Hermann Goering Division. *Tanks and artillery,* they said. *Lots of tanks.* Richard wondered how the GIs had managed to repel such an attack. But someone already had the answer: *Naval fire.* He grinned a little. It felt good to have that kind of support. However, it dawned on him that by the time he hit the front, he'd be well out of naval range. They'd just have to do it the old fashioned way.

The next morning Richard was loaded into a truck with half a dozen other men and driven through rugged terrain to division headquarters. He knew what this meant: an assignment. As an advance replacement, he was immediately placed in a regiment and sent to the front as a scout. This worried him, but at least he had the support of competent GIs. The first time he met his squad was just before moving out.

"How much training have you had?" The squad leader asked with a blank expression.

"Nine weeks," Richard replied.

The man shook his head. "Look," he said, "you just keep your eye on me and you'll be okay." Then he smiled and turned to move out.

Something in the words made Richard feel better about things. He would be fighting soon, but at least he was with good people. And as he marched along the dusty road with his squad, sweat beading on his forehead, his mind was at ease.

Sam Scales was hungry and tired from fighting his way across Sicily. So far, the mountainous terrain had treated them poorly and the Germans had treated them even worse. *It's a small miracle we made it,* he mused. From his perch atop the radio cabinet in his halftrack, he looked out across the Italian countryside as it glowed in the morning sun. It was very green and cut with long shadows. *Beautiful but dangerous.* A haze clung to the land, obscuring the distant hills and limiting his vision. He knew Palermo was close, somewhere just on the horizon. *But what's waiting for us there?* The choices were limited: either Germans or Italians. *Or maybe both,* he thought.

A noise caught Sam's attention and he turned to find a jeep tumbling along the dusty road behind them. *Uh oh,* he thought. He recognized the vehicle's markings and the distinctive figure riding in it. *Patton.*

The jeep approached to within several yards and screeched to a halt. There, in the passenger seat, sat General George Patton with a sly expression on his face. He gripped the windshield and pulled himself partially upright.

"What's the matter, soldier?" The words were directed at Sam. "Didn't you have any breakfast this morning?"

This hit a sore spot.

Most of the men respected the general at the very least. A lot of them even liked him. But Sam was in a strange mood today and the question had rubbed him wrong. *What a foolish thing to ask,* he thought with a scowl. *When you're in battle, you don't just stop for lunch. We don't have servants to make us food.* For all he knew, their kitchen truck was still in North Africa. Maybe it was the hunger talking, or perhaps the fatigue, but he was in no mood for banter. So he crossed his arms and turned his back on the general without saying a word.

An awkward moment of silence ensued. Patton glanced from one man to the next. Then, dropping his weight back into the seat, he waved an arm.

"Drive on," he said to his driver.

With a kick of dirt and a dusty puff, the jeep continued on its way. Sam watched until it was a speck in the distance, then looked at his buddies. They were grinning from ear to ear. *Did I just snub the general?* He almost couldn't believe it. *Yes... yes I did.*

Sam chuckled sheepishly and the men in the halftrack erupted in laughter.

Jerry Schoener felt the Mayrant shudder violently – felt the deck rattle beneath his feet as a savage plume of water burst off the port bow. *That was a hit*, he realized, *they got us!*

The destroyer was patrolling near Palermo, Italy when it was overtaken by German dive bombers and forced to defend itself. The crew did what they could to keep the enemy planes at bay, but inevitably a bomber got through and ditched its payload. Hitting only a few yards from the ship's bow, it burst hard enough to rupture the hull and allow water inside. Jerry was topside when he heard the news. *Engineering is flooding*, they shouted, *we're taking on water!* It was a scary moment.

With help from several other vessels, the Mayrant managed to avoid sinking long enough to limp back to harbor and stabilize. It would eventually be towed away for repairs.

Life as a scout in Sicily was grand for Richard Biehl. Or at least that's what he told himself to keep going. A hundred yards ahead of his company, lurking in the bushes with an outdated rifle, just waiting to get shot – it was certainly an interesting job. He was supposed to find the enemy, but most times they found him first. *It feels as if the eyes of the world are on me*, he thought, *that's what this is like*. The best way to describe how he felt was with one word: exposed. The rugged Italian terrain offered some concealment but little protection, and the weapon he carried felt less than adequate. His unit didn't have enough M1s to go around, so he was given an old bolt-action Springfield rifle. And while this technically fired bullets like everything else, it just felt weak in his hands. It would have been nice to have an M1 for those times when the enemy saw him and opened fire.

Still, Richard managed with what he had, and by the time he reached Troina he had very much settled into the scout role. But by then the fight for Sicily was coming to a close. This early combat was not a waste, however. Rather it prepared him for even tougher days to come.

With Sicily liberated, the Italian army was no longer a threat. Their capitulation was a milestone for the Allied advance, and it looked like mainland Italy would be the next step in the campaign to free Europe.

Richard stood on a high slope in the Italian countryside as dusk approached. For three hundred and sixty degrees, everything in sight lay draped in green and gold. Rugged hill lines, silhouetted by tall poplar trees and dotted with ancient villages, jutted up and caught the sunlight as it fell. It was magnificent. In the gentle valley below, draped in deep shadows, the airfield's runway lights were starting to flicker. They were fuel drums, he realized, filled with gasoline-soaked sand and ignited. He'd seen them earlier that day as he passed by the tiny airstrip, though it hadn't dawned on him until now what they were for. Quick and efficient, the hallmark of military improvisation. He wondered from how far away they could be seen.

Richard flicked his gaze to the sky. He thought he heard an engine. Was it the Italian air force, surrendering their planes as they'd promised? He'd been told, as many of them had, that the former enemy was prepared to 'donate' what remained in their possession. It seemed dubious, but he wasn't one to question orders. All he knew was that the airfield in the little valley below was some kind of rally point, and that it had to be kept safe from German interference. Maybe the Luftwaffe would drop some paratroopers in an effort to sabotage the exchange. Or maybe they'd come in from the hills. He thought about the tiny contingent of air corps personnel waiting patiently down there. They were in no position to fight, so it was Richard's job to protect them. So far, so good. But there was always tonight. And tomorrow.

Richard cleared his throat in the cooling air and stretched his arms. It was going to be a long night.

As far as Richard saw, the Italians never delivered their planes to the airfield. But neither did the Germans interfere. Much later, after returning to the United States, he learned that a soldier from his hometown of Temple, PA - a man named George - had been with the air corps down by the runway. The two never met in Italy, yet crossed paths without realizing it.

Farther north, the fighting still raged.

"Hold your fire! Do not shoot!"

Edward Zabinski's heart pounded madly in his chest as he manned an antiaircraft gun aboard the liberty ship Marcus H. Tracy. They were docked in the harbor at Ancona, Italy, where the ship's cargo was being unloaded. But the operation had been rudely interrupted by an air raid.

"I said hold your fire!" An officer repeated his order.

The skies were dark enough to mask the approaching bombers, but Edward knew they were coming. He could see the shore batteries firing already, kicking a storm of tracers into the air. *They look like fireworks,* he thought, though he knew better.

"They'll see the muzzle flashes if we shoot back," the officer said, "so we'll just sit tight unless they give us no choice."

Edward wondered if it was true. *Is it dark enough to hide us?* The water was almost black at night, but what did it look like from the air? *Are we invisible to the enemy?*

To his horror, flares began to appear over the city ahead. It seemed the Luftwaffe was dropping them in an effort to see what they were hitting. But this made the planes easier to spot, too. All Edward could do was watch, wide-eyed and tense, as the flickering tracers and sputtering flares sped through the sky. He heard explosions – bomb strikes. Fire danced on the horizon. And it wasn't long before the sound of engines drew close overhead. *Please don't see us,* he prayed. Sweat beaded on his brow. *Just keep going...*

It felt as if ages passed before the raid ended. Edward could finally breathe a sigh of relief. It had been a close call, or at least it seemed that way. Sitting in the dark, trigger-finger itching and scared out of his wits, he realized just how random and terrifying war could be. Bombs were anonymous and deadly, and he couldn't even fight back. *With any luck,* he hoped, *I won't have to go through that again.*

He was wrong.

A fitful night of sleep passed and Edward found himself off duty in the morning. Still shaken from the bombing raid, he thought a bit of exploration might clear his head. So he joined a group of sailors and went ashore. Ten men strong, they passed through Ancona and headed north.

Edward was struck by the amount of activity in the city. *It's so busy,* he thought, *trucks, troops, weapons...* Everything was in constant motion; men walked or rode around in every direction, tanks rolled by, and civilians went about their lives. Here and there he caught glimpses of cargo in transit; some of it from his own ship, no doubt. It seemed that most of the movement was focused away from town, so the sailors followed along. A few of them wanted souvenirs, and it seemed likely that loot could be found near the front lines.

The main route north was jammed with vehicles, so transportation wasn't a problem. Edward and his buddies split into groups and prepared to hitchhike. One by one, they hopped in the back of supply trucks and spent the better part of an hour squeezed between featureless crates, bouncing up and down on the bumpy road. The longer they drove, the more disturbing the landscape became.

Hopping down from the moving truck, Edward joined his group at the side of the road and tried to get his bearings. The front was close – they could hear thundering in the distance. *This must be the Canadian sector*, he realized, noting the uniformed men around them.

"If it's trinkets you're after, you'll find them ahead."

He turned to find a grinning soldier staring at him. Edward suddenly realized how strange they must have looked – a group of unarmed sailors standing on the roadside in infantry territory. *Of course he knows we want souvenirs.*

The man spoke again. "Look, you can come along with us and we'll show you where you can find some German rifles."

It seemed a nice enough offer, so the sailors joined them.

"But I'm warning you," he added, "it's not pretty up there."

He wasn't kidding. The sights got worse as they moved. Burned-out vehicles and unidentifiable pieces of junk dotted the road and shell craters appeared more and more frequently. Edward and his new Canadian friends had only been walking for a few minutes when artillery fire started booming beyond the trees.

"Get down!" The Canadians scrambled for cover.

Wham! An enemy shell struck the road ahead, kicking dirt into the air and rattling Edward's teeth. *No! Just like last night!* Quaking, he dove headfirst into a ditch at the side of the road and covered his head with his arms. *Bam!* Another blast. Then another. He wasn't sure what to do; there wasn't anything he *could* do. They just waited for it to end.

After several minutes, the dust settled.

"All clear, let's go!"

Edward rolled onto his back and tried to steady his breathing. *That was way too close,* he thought, *I'm not sure a souvenir is worth this.* But he was already committed; he'd come too far to turn back. So he got to his feet and dusted himself off. Then he spotted something awful. A man – or what was left of him – lay only a yard or two from where he stood. Tattered Canadian uniform, bloated frame, ruddy discolored skin; he must have been killed days ago. It made Edward's stomach turn, but that wasn't what really got to him. Scattered about the dead man were letters and photos flecked with dirt and blood. It looked like he'd taken them from his pocket in his dying moments. Edward looked at one; it was a picture of a young smiling girl. *This must be his sister,* he realized. Then it hit him: *They probably don't even know he's dead.* He felt a lump in his throat.

"Don't touch our dead," one of the soldiers said, noticing Edward's focus. His eyes were sad and weary. "But do what you want with the Krauts."

Edward couldn't bear to look any more. *So this is what it's like.* The price of war finally sunk in. *This is the front.*

Head low, he climbed back onto the road and followed his friends deeper into danger. It was a while before anyone spoke again.

There was a bombed-out farmhouse very near the fighting where the Canadians took the sailors. Inside, the soldiers were boiling water and brewing tea in big five gallon cans. Edward and his buddies each accepted a cup and sat for a while before leaving. True to their word, the cheerful Canadians saw them off and pointed out where they could find German rifles. It wasn't a difficult hunt; bodies were everywhere and most of them were still armed. But after the day's events, Edward was less enthusiastic about the whole thing. Still, each of them took a rifle before heading back to Ancona.

I'll remember this day when I look at it, he decided as he rode south in the back of a truck. *It would take a lot to forget.*

England wasn't the Allies' only staging ground for bombing runs. Italy itself served as home to countless airmen during the war, as its proximity to German soil made it an ideal launch pad for attacking enemy assets.

"What are you doing? Open the hatch!"

George Stauffer's nose gunner was yelling over the rush of engines and air in the cramped waist of his dying B-24 bomber. George, the crew's bombardier, was trying not to panic. They were in Romanian airspace, just a few miles from the expansive mass of oil refineries at Ploesti. The sky outside was thick with flak and smoke, and he was trying as best he could to bail out before the crippled plane drew any more attention. The pilot had given the jump alarm only moments ago, but George was having mechanical trouble.

"I can't open it," George shouted back, tugging at the hatch lever, "it's jammed!"

The bomber's hydraulic systems were badly damaged from the hellish flak over Ploesti, and he was starting to wonder if they'd be able to get out. The plane was slowly spiraling over the ruined countryside, spraying fuel and smoke from its mangled engines.

"Here, take hold of me!"

George had a plan. He grabbed his parachute ring and braced his elbows against the hatch, motioning for his buddy to get behind him.

"When I give the signal, kick as hard as you can!"

The gunner nodded and slid into position, jamming his back against the fuselage and placing his feet on George.

"Get ready!"

The plane bucked violently as a flak round burst outside. It sounded close. George took a deep breath.

"Okay, go!"

He felt a sharp kick against his chute and a slam as his arms struck the metal hatch. Then his body compressed against it and it gave beneath his mass. With a great snap it popped free and he went tumbling out into weightlessness.

The air outside was cold. It rushed by at almost two hundred feet per second, howling in his ears and whipping the fabric of his flight suit. *One, two, three...* He counted in his head, measuring the length of his free fall. *Get clear of the plane,* he remembered being told. *If you have enough altitude you can afford to wait.* So he did. And when he felt that the tangled mess of bombers and flak clouds was far enough above him, he gave the rip cord a tug and braced himself for the jolt.

So far, so good. George was floating under the radar, so to speak. The antiaircraft guns were still focusing on the planes overhead and he was probably still out of small arms range. *Uh oh!* Maybe not. He looked down and noticed little puffs of smoke. *They're definitely firing at me,* he realized, tipped off by the whiz of bullets passing nearby. But there was nothing he could do; he was at the mercy of the breeze. So he said a little prayer and waited, drifting closer and closer until, at long last, he crashed into the ground with a thud.

"Amerikaner kaputt!"

That can't be good, he thought, unhooking his chute harness and whirling around.

"Kaputt," the German repeated, raising his submachine gun.

George let out a sigh and put his hands in the air as a weary-looking group of enemy soldiers fanned out around him. *I'm a prisoner of war.*

What is your position in the plane? Where did you come from? George could still hear his interrogator's questions. The German colonel had been so emphatic. The words churned over and over in his mind, amplified by the throbbing pain at the back of his skull. One of the guards had hit him – smashed him in the head with a rifle butt and knocked him unconscious. Now he was lying in a tiny dark room, his senses reeling from the trauma. *What is this, a closet?* Everything was black except for a faint glowing sliver beneath the door. It was yellow and sickly. *Perfect lighting for a Nazi hideout.* He thought he heard a noise. *There! A voice!* Was someone talking outside? *What is your position,* it asked. No, it was in his head, that damned voice again and again. It wouldn't stop, yet he couldn't even remember all of it. It wasn't the only thing that was fuzzy. Before being brought to this building, he'd been forced to walk through Bucharest with other prisoners. He recalled the civilians throwing things at them – cans, stones, garbage. He could still see their tormented faces. *But how did I get here from Ploesti?* The Germans must have brought them in trucks. He'd been grilled for what seemed like hours in a dingy little room down the hall. He remembered a chair, some guards, the officer... *And the questions.* They wanted to know about the Allies' invasion plans. *Invasion plans? What was he talking about?* All he'd given the colonel was his name, rank, and serial number. *And that thing about the Luftwaffe – how cowardly it was to shoot at men parachuting down.* This had upset the Germans to the point of screaming, and for a moment George was certain he'd be shot. *Maybe that's why he hit me,* he realized, raising a hand to the back of his head. He felt blood crusted in his hair, and he winced at the touch. His body hurt, too – how long had he been crammed in this closet? George shifted his weight and tried to stand but his legs started to shake and a flash of dizziness washed over him. Disgusted, he dropped back to a sitting position. Then a noise caught his ear. *What's that?* Somebody was approaching; boots clacked against the floor outside. *Don't tell them how you feel,* he said to himself, *Don't let them see you weak.* He felt his chances were better if he appeared strong. *If they think I'm sick they'll take me away and I'll just disappear.* He wasn't going to let that happen.

Ken Hart was probably the first to notice his navigator's mistake. Tucked in the ball turret of his B-17, he watched helplessly as they approached the Anzio beachhead at a thousand feet. *Uh oh,* he thought, but there was nothing he could do. Before the pilot realized what was happening, ground fire started pouring in.

"Get us out of here!" The crew was in an uproar.

Bucking violently, the bomber banked hard and pulled up. Ken winced as bullets popped through the fuselage and pieces of metal clattered on his turret dome. *We're supposed to be thirty miles from here,* he realized, *this is suicide!*

Something in the plane banged loudly and he started to sweat. If they were going to die, this seemed like a silly way to do it. *We aren't even in enemy territory.*

"We're hit pretty bad," said a crew member over the intercom.

No kidding, Ken thought. They'd taken direct fire from less than a quarter mile. Frankly, he was surprised they hadn't lost anybody.

After a few minutes it became clear that they couldn't make it back to base, so the navigator decided to land the plane at an airfield near Naples. It didn't take long to reach, yet as they approached another problem reared its head: the landing gear was damaged. Its hydraulics had failed and the wheels refused to lock down. Fortunately,

Ken's turret was functioning, so he was able to climb back into the B-17's waist compartment.

The plane came in fast and sloppy, teetering from side to side as it rushed toward the runway. Bracing himself, Ken gripped a strut and waited for impact. *Will the landing gear hold?* There was no telling, but he had a bad feeling.

Wham! The bomber landed hard, wheels smoking on the tarmac. The landing gear, weakened from gunfire, buckled and dropped the plane with a jolt. Ken lurched forward, stumbling through the fuselage, and slammed into the ball turret's upright support. He felt his ankle twinge. Metal grinding, the plane skidded along the runway on its belly, shearing off metal and kicking up sparks before finally coming to rest in a dented, bullet-riddled heap.

Well that wasn't so bad, Ken thought, though his leg was starting to throb. *At least nobody got killed.*

And he was right. Despite the miscalculation, the fierce ground fire, and a violent crash landing, his crew suffered little more than bumps and sprains. Except for the navigator, who was thrown through the nose on impact and lost a leg.

5

OVERLORD
D-DAY & NORMANDY

"D-Day, we were standing on the ship watching these airplanes fly. It was nothing but ships all over... What was I thinking? Well, what an experience for me, at twenty years old, to stand there and see all this."

Lester Groff, Normandy, 1944

In the months approaching D-Day, Allied forces worked feverishly to prepare for their much-negotiated second front. But despite the success of similar operations in Africa and Italy, Normandy would require far greater numbers and superior coordination. It would pose the ultimate challenge: the amphibious invasion of Fortress Europe. Small-scale practice runs were planned, and in April of 1944 – more than a month before D-Day – an exercise codenamed "Tiger" took place off the coast of England near the town of Slapton. It would end in tragedy.

Cold, unfeeling waters churned ceaselessly just off the English coast. It was after two in the morning - the darkest, most desolate hour to be awake and on duty. And in the surging Channel eight ships loaded down with Allied troops and sailors prepared for maneuvers. They were LSTs – large landing craft bristling with men and equipment. Their job, though unknown to some of those aboard, was to complete an amphibious landing. It was Exercise Tiger. They were practicing for D-Day.

Charles Brubaker could feel his LST pitching as he stood in the engine room. Up, down, up down... it was enough to make a man sick. But he was used to the motion, as most sailors were. What bothered him now wasn't the sea. It was the activity coming in over the radio. He gripped his headset with both hands, pressing the microphones into his ears and listening closely.

"Full right rudder." The captain was giving odd commands. "Full left rudder."

Strange chatter had been coming through for a few minutes now, coinciding with puzzling maneuvers and sounds. In fact, he could have sworn he'd just heard gunfire. Was it part of the exercise? *It can't be,* he thought, *there's nothing out here – what are they firing at?* It was worrisome, though not a definite reason for alarm. At least not yet. *I don't know what they're planning, I'm just stuck down here for now.* But then the word *flares* chirped over the radio and his pulse quickened. The captain sounded serious, maybe even worried. Something was happening outside.

There! The guns again! Charles cocked an ear to the ceiling and listened. Something was hitting the ship – he could hear the metallic ping of projectiles reverberating through the hull. *This is serious,* he realized. And it was. Voices were starting to filter in from above: shouting, upset cries, and confused yelling. It sounded bad, but there was nothing he could do. So he gritted his teeth and continued his work as the tense minutes ticked away.

Charles left the engine room as soon as he could. *How long was I down there,* he wondered, *fifteen minutes? Twenty?* He'd lost track of time in the frantic rush of activity, his senses overwhelmed by mechanical sounds and radio chatter. The engine room station made it difficult to tell what was happening, but he had a pretty good idea. *Now to go see for myself,* he thought.

Feet pounding onto the slippery deck, he emerged topside and braced himself against the blast of cool air. He stopped dead in his tracks. There were wounded men ahead, and visible damage to the ship. One of the crew members went scuttling past and Charles caught his attention.

"Hey, what's going on?"

The man paused for a moment, then shouted something as he moved away. His attention was elsewhere but he got the message across. There had been an attack – the Germans saw them and fired torpedoes at the convoy. Now at least one of the LSTs was gone, several were damaged, and his own had been hit by friendly fire in the confusion. *That explains the mess up here, and the noises I heard,* he realized. But he couldn't grasp the full scope of the attack, for the darkness concealed it. All he could do was stand there in the dark and listen to the distant cries of stranded sailors bobbing in the water.

The enemy had gotten lucky. Though Charles couldn't possibly have known at the time, nine German patrol boats had happened upon the Allied convoy and launched torpedoes into its midst. Three LSTs were hit; one sank and two were badly damaged. Flares were sent up, and in the ensuing chaos the landing craft captains maneuvered as best as they could to avoid the enemy fire. Poorly escorted and caught off guard, they had little time to react. And despite their best efforts, more than seven hundred men died that night.

Exercise Tiger would long be remembered as something of a mystery. Because of its secret nature, little was acknowledged until after D-Day itself. Yet it wasn't the Allies' only clandestine endeavor. On the English mainland, quite a bit to the east, a very different sort of activity was taking place. This one had another important objective: disinformation.

Back and forth through the grassy field. Always back and forth. Lester Groff was starting to wonder about these exercises. He'd been doing this for nearly a month and it was usually the same. *Five tanks one way, five the other. What's the point?* They were supposed to race the Shermans around in a clearing near the English Channel, and the only requirement was that they make a lot of noise. *It's obviously some kind of decoy,* he thought as he made a tight turn and sped between a pair of large trees. *Just like those dummy paratroopers the guys were talking about.*

Lester's suspicions were correct. In an attempt to confuse the Germans, the Allied nations had been using misdirection. It was no great secret that a Norman invasion was imminent, but at least they could keep the enemy guessing.

Hah! Spotting a little tree ahead, Lester was suddenly reminded of his training back at Fort Knox. The sergeant there had drilled certain things into their heads – first and foremost the invulnerability of the Sherman tank. He remembered driving though walls, over logs, and even through houses. And of course, he'd plowed over his fair share of trees.

He was suddenly struck by the urge to run something over – namely the tree in his view port. *Do plants count as collateral damage?* Responsibility got the better of him, however, and he swerved hard to the side.

"Alright, Les. We're going around for another lap." The tank commander sounded bored.

Well at least it's not just me, Lester mused, shifting gears and punching the gas.

Life in England was beginning to get interesting for some of the men stationed there. As summer approached, duties increased and training became more frequent. Something big was on the horizon.

Richard Biehl stood just beyond the barracks with his company, looking out at the English hedgerows and green fields beyond the edge of the base. It was a familiar sight – he'd been here for months - but something in his company commander's voice was different today.

"This is the terrain you'll be in soon," he said, and his tone betrayed a twinge of apprehension.

Richard knew it was a clue, but nobody let on. *It's not a very good secret,* he thought. *We're shipping out.* He was going to France; the only question was when. It certainly felt soon, though.	Training had ramped up lately and there was a strange feeling of *imminence* in the air.	An invasion was coming – this much was certain.

That night, Richard was put in charge of guard duty and given an unusual task.	Along with four GIs from the platoon, he was told to wait for Captain Carney, who would escort them to an undisclosed location.	So he stood quietly in the dark and wondered what he was in for.

Before long a pair of figures emerged from the murk. *That's the sloppiest GI I've ever seen,* he thought as he eyeballed the man with the captain.	The soldier was certainly disheveled.	Five o'clock shadow, dirty trousers, unbuttoned pocket flaps, an untucked pant leg – the list went on and on.	It was suspicious to say the least.	But he didn't say anything; it wouldn't have been appropriate.

The two men led Richard and his buddies to a desolate corner of the base where a small windowless shack stood alone and unguarded.

"No one is permitted inside this hut," Captain Carney addressed Richard directly, "except for this gentleman."

The mysterious stranger moved over to the door.

"You're in charge of guard duty," the captain said before turning and vanishing into the night.

With this, Richard and his men were left alone.	The strange GI entered the hut and closed the door firmly behind him, leaving the guards little to do but stand and wait.	It was Richard's duty to escort him wherever he needed to go, and to make sure nobody else entered the building.	*Strange indeed,* he thought.	But he did what he was told.	There was something weighty about the captain's order – it felt oddly important.

The true nature of his guard assignment was later revealed to Richard. The unkempt soldier was no army man. Rather, he was a naval fire control officer in disguise. While Richard stood guard, this man was inside the secure hut studying a mockup of Omaha Beach, memorizing targets for D-Day.

Gabe Fieni sat in his pup tent, listening to the rustle of wind in the grass and the soft murmur of voices nearby. He was somewhere in the English countryside, very near the southern coast, in an enormous field full of tents. His unit was shipping out soon - though he didn't know where to - and had therefore been moved some hundred and fifty miles away from their usual base of operations. This meant, among other things, that Gabe would no longer be able to see his girlfriend, Doreen. Though he was in active service, he and his buddies had been allowed to travel into town each night. So they did, piling twenty deep into the back of a truck and mounting an invasion of the local dance hall. On one such outing, a beautiful girl sitting alone had caught his eye. He asked for a dance and the rest was history.

Of course, now that Gabe was in a different place and destined for Europe, he would probably never see Doreen again. This thought had him in a glum mood, and as he sat in his tent he tried his best not to think of her. It didn't work, though; rather it made things worse.

"Hey, there's someone here to see you."

"Huh?" Gabe poked his head out of the tent. A guard was standing over him, looking down with a bored expression.

"Some girl wants to see you," the man repeated, pointing a finger off toward the front of the encampment.

"But I don't know any girls around here."

Gabe was puzzled, but the guard said nothing more. He simply sighed and walked away. *Who's looking for me,* he wondered, *could it be? No, there's no way.* Was it possible? He scuttled out of the tent and took to his feet, moving quickly in the dusky light. He counted his strides on the trampled grass, trying to calm his mind. The trains were so slow, and it was so far away. *Even if she did find out where we went, she wouldn't make the trip.* Or would she? His heart was racing as he rounded a corner and saw his girlfriend standing there. *Doreen! She found me.*

With a great smile he embraced her and they both started talking at once. There was so much to say and so little time.

"Can you stay long?" he asked.

She nodded. And for the next three hours the time flew by.

Gabe's unit didn't stay in the tent city for long. When he was told they'd be leaving one night at eleven, he knew he had to see Doreen again. It would probably be the last time, so he sneaked off to bid her farewell.

On the way back into camp, Gabe checked his watch. Nine thirty - plenty of time still. He crept back toward his tent, confident that he'd gotten away with it. But his heart sank as he neared the tent and saw his sergeant standing there. Gabe approached with a sheepish gait.

"Fieni," the man began, "as long as I'm first sergeant of this outfit, you'll never amount to anything."

His gaze held a contempt that Gabe had never seen before. It stung. But the admonishment was worth seeing Doreen one last time.

For most of the men who would end up in France, the time spent in England was happy enough. Apart from frequent training, there was little to worry about. They were well-fed, often well-entertained, and above all they were safe. Yet a sense of impending action grew in their hearts as the weeks wore on, until, in the final days before Normandy, many were convinced that an invasion was inevitable. So it was with little surprise when the orders came through to pack up and move out.

Richard Biehl was ordered aboard a ship at last. June had barely begun and the time for invasion was drawing near. He was given all manner of items – seasick pills, long underwear, a new uniform, a gas mask, and grenades among other things. Then, along with a great mass of soldiers, he was taken to an English harbor and placed aboard an LCI.

The next day they set sail, entering the English Channel and reaching their rendezvous point. But the weather was too poor to continue so they returned. By now it was certain: the officers told them exactly what was happening. *You're going to a place called Normandy,* they said, *to be part of an invasion.* It reminded Richard of his first journey to North Africa, except now he was getting bad news. There was nothing he could to change this fact, so he simply prayed. They all did.

Eventually the weather cleared and the ships returned to the Channel, where they joined up with an armada unlike anything he'd ever seen. All night they sailed, creeping slowly towards France through choppy seas. And when they reached their destination, they waited, for there was still one last task to be done.

Though the men in the ships weren't aware of the fact, as they huddled in seasick apprehension upon the water, paratroopers were passing overhead. Theirs was to be the opening move.

Ed Stallman eyed the light next to the open door in the C-47, waiting for it to change. *Come on*, he thought, *let's get the hell out of here.* A flak round burst in the darkness outside, close enough to punch shrapnel through the fuselage. Someone behind him yelped painfully. The plane bucked up and down, buffeted by ground fire, but Ed kept his balance. Between the hundred pounds of gear and the men wedged around him, it would have been difficult to fall over completely.

Ed was a paratrooper and an engineer, and at the moment he was flying low above Normandy, waiting for the signal to jump. But the Germans were wise to the sneak attack and were putting up thick clouds of flak in an effort to stop them. So far it hadn't worked, but the men in the plane were starting to worry.

"We have to get out of this plane," one of the paratroopers shouted, "They're cutting us to pieces!"

He was right. Flak shrapnel clattered everywhere, growing worse by the minute. There were pieces all over the floor. The plane's fuselage was full of tiny holes that glowed against the explosions outside and whistled madly in the wind. *This is crazy*, Ed said to himself.

Suddenly the C-47 jumped sideways and the pilots started shouting to one another. Something was wrong. Then the light by the door went green and all Ed could think about was getting out of there. *That's it! Let's go!* One by one the men shuffled forward and tumbled into the night. When it was Ed's turn he didn't hesitate.

The chute deployed automatically and Ed quickly found himself dropping through a hail of antiaircraft fire. It was terrifying. He swung back and forth in the harness, tossed about by the wind, straining to keep stable. *Are they shooting at me*, he wondered, *can they even see me?* There was no way to tell, and it was maddening. He could do nothing but wait.

The ground came crashing up and Ed rolled onto his side. *Clear the chute*, he thought. The shroud lines were tangled but he managed to free himself from the buckles and ready his rifle. He looked around carefully. Tall hedgerows blocked his vision in every direction. The night was alive with distant gunfire, but he didn't hear anyone nearby. *Good.* Now he just had to rendezvous with his unit and get to the objective. Except... *Oh no*, he realized, *this isn't where I'm supposed to be.* They had jumped early; in his rush to unload the plane, the pilot had signaled them too soon. Ed was miles from where he should have been. He couldn't be angry, though. *The pilot probably saved our lives by getting us out.* Still, it was a problem.

Ed was supposed to be near Carentan, so he made some quick calculations and started heading in the right direction. As he crept through the countryside, he was awed by the scene unfolding above him. Tracer rounds rose into the air like ropes, weaving around in tight columns and raking across the sky. Flak bursts popped everywhere at once. And the parachutes – hundreds of tiny canopies drifted down from the planes in great clusters. *I wonder if I know any of those guys,* he thought.

There was an intersection ahead and an open space in the hedgerows. He could see a tree poking over the tangled foliage. It was quiet; he advanced carefully. He had a clicker in his pocket - the guys called them *crickets.* They were supposed to use them to identify friendlies in the dark, but he didn't trust it. *What if the Germans take one off a body? No,* he decided, *I'll just do it the old fashioned way.*

Ed rounded the corner and saw something that made his heart sink. Just ahead, tangled in low tree branches, a dead paratrooper hung from his parachute lines. His throat had been cut – Ed could see it clearly in the moonlight. *Alright,* he thought, *I'm not going to end up like that.* So with a deep breath and a glance behind him, he pushed on towards Carentan and his friends. It was going to be a long night.

As Ed was making his way through the maze of French hedgerows, the invasion fleet waited patiently just off the coast. When morning broke, they were ready.

Happy birthday, he thought to himself, *this is one heck of a party.* Sitting just off the Normandy coastline, perched upon his Sherman tank on a lurching LST, Lester Groff mused at the timing. Twenty years old on D-Day. What a milestone.

"You've got a hell of a birthday, Les," one of his buddies said.

Happy birthday, indeed. But what's this all about? Today seemed momentous, like it would go down in history. And while he was glad to be a part of it all, he couldn't help but feel overwhelmed. Planes, bombs, naval guns – it was exciting and terrifying all at once. Ships stretched out upon the horizon as far as he could see, moving in toward the beach from all directions. *What if we get hit?* Enemy shells were landing sporadically among the flotilla, some of them frighteningly close. He thought back to his training at Fort Knox, to what his sergeant had said. *You're invincible. Your tank will protect you.* He'd believed it until now. But watching the men dying out there, seeing enemy shells tearing into the ships, he began to have doubts. Would the tank protect him from that? A pit was growing in his stomach.

Paul Wolfinger gazed intently at the mass of ships crowding the English Channel. He was aboard the USS Swivel, manning a twenty millimeter gun and watching the invasion progress. So far, it was quite a show. Too far away to see the men on the beach, he was close enough to absorb the sheer scale of the operation. The air crackled with nonstop gunfire, much of it from the larger ships nearby. *What a sound,* he thought, *such noise!* It was like thunder and firecrackers all at once, a terrifying cacophony that never ended. He wondered what effect all the firing was having on the enemy. It must have been terrible.

Closer to shore, men were landing on the beach in waves.

The sound was unlike anything he'd ever heard. Artillery, mortars, naval fire, airplanes; they mixed with the lapping of seawater upon metal, the groaning of engines, and the desperate screams of dying men. And the unceasing machine gun fire in the distance; it never relented, not even for a moment. What the hell was happening out there? Richard Biehl tried to fight the anxiety rising in his chest and wished, just for an instant, that he could see over the edge of the landing craft. But then he felt a bump and someone started shouting. And he realized that, though they weren't yet close enough to unload, they had stopped moving.

The engines revved loudly in protest, coughing up a plume of acrid exhaust.

"I can't go in reverse. I can't go forward. We are a target!" A young Coast Guard lieutenant was shouting bluntly at Captain Seatnum. "You've got to get your troops off the ship now!"

Richard's heart hammered against his ribs as he heard the words. This was, by far, the most terrifying thing he'd ever experienced. Beached off the Normandy coastline with enemy fire pouring in like rain and a belly full of troops, his tiny landing craft was helpless. If they didn't do something soon, odds were they'd all be killed. So the captain, with just a bit of grumbling, gave the order to disembark. It was better to get out now and take their chances in the water than to stay here and get shot to pieces. Everyone knew it, even if they didn't like the fact.

With a quick shudder, the Higgins' front ramp dropped and the men shoved out. Richard was first in line on the port side; he dropped into the frigid water and sunk in up to his chest. The air kicked its way from his lungs as the cold engulfed him. Shivering and gasping for breath, he tried desperately to move forward. But the water tugged at his body, surging up and down and slamming him randomly about. He dug into the soft sand with his boots, legs pumping, eyes focused ahead. *Left, right, left right.* He had to move. *Faster! Get to the beach!* But it was so far. About a hundred yards lay between him and the shoreline, a football field's length filled with gunfire and thrashing debris. Behind, he could hear splashing and screams. The short guys, weighed down and panicking, couldn't keep their heads above the water as they jumped off the landing craft. They were drowning, dragged beneath the waves by the weight of their gear. They wouldn't even get a chance to fight.

A mortar round slapped into the surf nearby, drawing Richard's attention. Just beyond the splash, an unoccupied jeep floated like a cork flanked by dark shapes in the water. Bodies. They were everywhere, bobbing wildly in the tide. A lot of the landing craft were still there, too, some of them smoking or engulfed in flames. They jutted up out of the water like bullet-riddled teeth, a grim counterpoint to the tangle of tank traps and pylons that lined the sand ahead. He squinted through the salty haze and suddenly realized how many men were on the beach. Sprinting across open sand, huddling behind obstacles, jerking under devastating gunfire; there was simply no order to what he saw. Hundreds of GIs swarmed about in utter chaos, doing whatever they thought would keep them alive. *Get to the bluffs,* he recalled the officers telling them, *and you're home free.* As he slogged his way ashore, weaving past mounds of shattered steel and severed limbs, past weeping men and cratered sand, he knew what a fallacy that was. But it stood as an objective, a concrete goal. And in the sheer terrifying madness that was Omaha Beach, it was all he had. *Get to the bluffs,* he told himself. It was the only thing that made sense.

George Vath broke onto the beach at a dead run, boots slapping into the wet sand and pulling up clods of muck. He was driven – determined to make it through the hell that lay before him. Bullets bit into the ground at his feet and clattered off the tank traps beside him. Shrapnel shredded the air in front of his face. *Move, run,* he thought, *don't stop for anything!* It was working. A lot of the men were stalled out of fear or desperation, clinging to any obstacle they could find. They were targets, sitting ducks for the mortar fire that saturated Omaha beach. He saw them dying, screaming, bleeding. Wailing in agony as their insides twisted into the sand. Trembling as the bullets poured in like sleet. He couldn't help them. They couldn't help themselves. It was every man for himself – everything or nothing. *You're going to make it!*

George almost did. But almost wasn't close enough. As he sprinted boldly along, weaving between obstacles and dodging enemy fire, fate threw him a curve. An artillery round - or perhaps a projectile from one of the shore batteries covering the beach – burst directly in front of him. The last thing he saw was a violent flash of sand

and debris rocketing skyward. Then everything went dark and he was gone. His journey ended halfway up the beach.

Boom! Another battleship gun fired inland, supporting the men storming the beach. Charles Brubaker stood on the deck of LST 511, looking out through the sea salt haze that lay between him and the Normandy coastline. From the scale of things over there, he guessed they were about two miles offshore. That was close enough for him. The armada of Allied ships – large, small, and everything in between – was taking a pounding. The nearer the beach, the worse it was. He could see landing craft burning off shore, apparently beached in the tumbling waves. It was a shallow coastline, a fact that was clearly making things difficult. *I'm glad I'm out here*, he thought.

A short distance away, the battleship USS Texas was blasting away with its main guns. It had been firing at the coast for some time, or at least that's what it sounded like. It was hard to tell from below deck – a lot of the noises mingled together and took on a distant character. For most of the day Charles had listened as the invasion fleet fired ceaselessly and the Germans fired back. It was terrifying and amazing all at once. And the ships – the sheer number of vessels in the water around him was mind boggling. No matter where he looked, no matter how far in the distance, the English Channel teemed with activity. Battleships, cargo ships, landing craft, supply vessels – they were everywhere. Three hundred and sixty degrees of overwhelming naval superiority. The only thing he could compare it to was something out of ancient history – the Greek invasion of Troy.

Suddenly a small craft came sliding up alongside the LST and men began shouting. He couldn't make out the voices over the thundering naval bombardment, but as some of the other sailors passed by, he overheard them talking.

"They want to know who we've got on board," said the first.

"Headquarters Company, that's who."

"That's not what they're looking for."

Whoever was in the little boat wasn't interested. The man shook his head and pointed towards another LST behind 511 before shoving off. *What a mess*, Charles thought, *what a logistical nightmare*. Then, with a final glance at the beach, he moved below deck. He was needed in the engine room.

Lester Groff, knuckles white, gripped the controls of his Sherman and waited for the signal to go. They were close to shore... any second now. He thought about the ship he'd seen take a hit earlier, how the enemy shell had ripped through the men and the tanks on the deck. It frightened him terribly.

Suddenly the LST gave a lurch and the doors swung open ahead. The line of tanks revved their engines and bolted forward. Lester followed, moving the Sherman forward, down the ramp, and into the water. It was deeper than he'd expected, maybe four or five feet. *Thank God for the waterproofing*. Peering through his periscope, he saw they were still a good distance from the shore. So he

drove. It was all he could do, move forward and just hope
nothing hit them. Bullets popped into the water ahead,
rattling against the tank and kicking up plumes of salty
froth. He felt the treads dig into soft sand and the water
suddenly grew shallower. *Good, let's get on with this.*

The waterlogged truck churned slowly through the
surf, belching dark puffs of exhaust as it moved. Gabe
Fieni, sitting in the driver's seat, gripped the wheel with
white knuckles and prayed they wouldn't get hit. The
Germans were still throwing shells at the beach, and
though the machine gun fire had eased up somewhat,
bullets bit into the waves at regular intervals. Some of
them were very close – too close for comfort.

Gabe's truck was fitted with benches in the rear, and
upon those benches sat an extremely worried surgical
team. They were trusting Gabe's driving skills to see them
safely ashore, though with each passing shell strike it
seemed less and less likely they'd make it. Still, he was
doing the best he could. As he drove out of the shallow,
choppy surf and up onto the sand, it occurred to him that
luck more than anything would keep them safe. It was up
to him to weave around craters and tank traps, past
burning vehicles and clumps of soldiers, but whether or
not he got shot was up to the Germans. *Just keep going,* he
told himself, *We'll see how my luck holds.*

The sun hung low in the west, obscured by a rocky
peninsula jutting out into the Channel. From the bluffs
above Omaha Beach, Richard Biehl looked down at the
chaos below. LSTs were lined up as far as he could see,

front doors open and disgorging all manner of men and vehicles. Behind them others waited patiently for their turns. The sand itself was a mess of activity as trucks, jeeps, halftracks, and everything else imaginable pushed steadily inland. It was the largest traffic jam he'd ever seen, and it was growing by the hour.

What a sight, he thought. It was awe-inspiring and gruesome all at once. They had made it, though the fighting had been brutal. *Was it worth the effort?* He thought it was.

The D-Day invasion opened the way for the Allies, giving them a route into France and a chance to reclaim territory from the Germans. Thus, Normandy became Europe's front door, and for the remainder of the war men would cross its threshold on their way to the fight.

Leroy Renninger's LST stopped with a bump as it ran aground on the sands of Omaha. Doors swinging wide, a symphony of truck engines revved and pushed forward into the choppy sand behind a cluster of infantry. Leroy was a passenger in the front of his artillery truck, which was full of men and towing a howitzer. He held onto the window frame as the vehicle slid down the ship's ramp and dug into the beach. *Here we go,* he thought, *I'm finally here.*

It was exciting to be on the continent after long weeks of anticipation. He knew, however, that he'd be in combat soon enough. This worried him, and as he rode ashore the thought hung in his mind.

Many of the men who participated in the invasion never set foot on the beach. The navy sailors who had manned the ships, coordinated support fire, and run salvage operations could only wonder at the horrors experienced by the infantry.

Paul Wolfinger looked astern at the crippled LST towing behind his salvage ship. It sat low in the water, damaged from D-Day activities. A long way behind it, the misty sands of Omaha Beach were shrinking into the distance. Only a few weeks had passed since the day when Paul had stood in the Channel, watching and listening to the invasion bombardment. *I was about the same distance from shore then.* He couldn't get the memory out of his head.

He was aboard the USS Swivel, heading back to England on the latest of many trips across the Channel. *It won't be the last,* he thought. For the past few days his ship had been hard at work clearing the Normandy beaches of obstacles. He was amazed at how many small boats and landing craft were still scattered along the coastline. *We'll probably be doing this for weeks.*

Even months later, the simple act of unloading and passing through the Normandy beaches stirred emotions in soldiers' hearts. It was a rite of passage – a common bond between the men who came later and the men who had fought or died during the invasion. As time wore on, the scenery changed but the feeling stayed the same.

Richard Hiller slogged through the wet sand, boots soaked and reeking of salt water. His pack was heavy; just walking up onto the shore was a chore. *This is it*, he thought, *Omaha Beach. I don't know how they did it under fire.* As he moved, he thought about the men who had died here just a short while ago. It almost didn't seem real. In the evening dusk he could just make out a scattering of shapes all along the sandy slopes. Vehicles and men, crates and construction materials – Omaha was alive with activity. It was surprising how clean everything looked. No bodies, no blown up limbs or fallen helmets – it resembled a supply depot more than anything. *Certainly not a battlefield.* But perhaps he was wrong. *It's high tide,* he realized, *for all I know the terrible sights are hidden beneath the water.*

As he stood looking back over the scene, Richard felt a sense of pride. This was more than a beach – it was a monument to the Allies' determination and to the men who had died here. *We're the good guys,* he thought with a smile. The salty Channel breeze was growing chilly in the dark. Richard turned and started inland.

6

LIBERATORS
FRANCE & BELGIUM

"When dusk fell, the Luftwaffe attacked and hundreds of ships offshore opened up with antiaircraft fire. It was the grandest Fourth of July celebration you've ever seen. Greens, reds, oranges, explosions in the sky; little bits of metal would trickle down on your helmet. We were soaking wet, cold and frightened."

Richard Biehl, Normandy, 1944

"Here he comes again."

Richard Hiller motioned toward the sky above the beach. From the sandy hilltop where he sat with his buddy Nolan, Richard could look down to the shoreline and observe what was happening in the twilight. He checked his watch. Nearly eleven at night. It was a bit disorienting being in Normandy with the time difference and the later sunset. France's time zone was an hour ahead of England's, but the geography didn't quite match.

Just to the north, across the English Channel, it was approaching ten o'clock. But down here it was later, even though the sun was in the same position. Thanks to this fact, there had still been traces of light in the sky less than an hour ago. The end result was that, though he felt tired, it didn't seem like he should.

"Yep, that's him alright."

Richard watched the little German plane come screaming over the beach, guns blazing. What was he even shooting at? "Bed Check Charlie," as they affectionately called him, made his nightly flyby around the same time each evening. His objective, it seemed, was to harass anything he saw on the beach by firing wildly and repeatedly into the sand. Whether or not he destroyed – or even hit – anything was still up for debate. In fact, Richard wasn't even sure if it was the same plane every night. For all he knew, Charlie flew off and got shot somewhere out of sight, only to be replaced the following day. The guys down on the beach were certainly trying to see to this. The sky above them was alive with antiaircraft fire, tracers flashing and dancing as they nipped at Charlie's heels.

"You know, Dick, this is better than the Fourth of July." Nolan grinned, eyes glittering happily in the glow of flickering gunfire.

Dick smiled a little too. It really was festive in a morbid sort of way. But then Charlie passed out of range, unharmed as usual, and the sky went dark once more. *Oh well*, he thought, *there's always tomorrow.*

Gabe Fieni let out a low whistle as he watched the bomber spiral down in the distance. It was pretty far away, probably near Saint Lo, so he couldn't tell what it was exactly. But it was definitely one of the Allies. It smoldered as it fell, leaving a dark trail of smoke and debris. He felt bad for its crew, though he could see some of them bailing out. They were tiny specks in the sky, dropping through the air like gnats. *At least they're landing near our lines,* he realized, and the thought made him feel a little bit better. But he knew some of them wouldn't make it. *About ten men to a plane. That's a lot of casualties.* And this was the ninth crash today, at least that he'd seen.

It was a strange feeling to watch the battle raging ahead and know that he'd be entering it eventually. What would be left when he got there? He was a driver so he probably wouldn't be holding the front line, but danger lurked everywhere. He never felt safe. They'd likely have him cruising around on his own, delivering supplies and picking up passengers like usual. Except the farther east they went the more perilous it seemed. It was only a matter of time, he felt, before he'd come under fire. Would it be a surprise? An ambush? Or would he see it coming? There was no way to tell.

A swarm of fighter planes had joined the bomber group ahead. He watched as they engaged the Luftwaffe. *We have great pilots,* he thought, recalling that for as long as he'd been here, he'd never seen an American fighter shot down. And then it dawned on him. *They won't let me carry a weapon, but that's just too bad.* He was going to have to find a way to defend himself, and soon. Looking ahead, he weighed his options. *I'm going to find myself a gun*, he decided, *We'll see what's left at Saint Lo.*

More than a thousand miles from Normandy, downed airmen were being held at a POW camp in Bucharest. Their experience was similar to those held in camps elsewhere, but with the added danger of Allied bombings.

George Stauffer huddled in the basement of the Romanian school building he called home. It was dark, but he could feel dust fluttering down from the ceiling as bomb strikes thundered in the distance. The whole building rattled and he wondered if it might collapse one of these days.

He was a prisoner of war, guarded by both German and Romanian soldiers and kept in a converted building that just happened to sit near an Allied bombing target. Nearly every day the planes would roll overhead and unload on the city, and each time George and his fellow inmates were ushered into the basement. He was beginning to think he'd spent more time down here than anywhere else.

Life as a prisoner was difficult. George thought about some of the things they did to get by. Making playing cards out of soap cartons, whittling chess sets from scrap wood, cobbling meals together from meager rations – it was an unpleasant and strange existence. They weren't exactly mistreated, though the German guards could be harsh, but he was always hungry. Cabbage soup was their staple food, along with some fish parts and the occasional potato. He supposed it could have been worse. *At least I wasn't in the Pacific,* he often thought, *those guys have it bad.* He shuddered to imagine what torments the Japanese prisoners must have been enduring.

Before long the raid ended and the guards began shepherding the men upstairs. But it wasn't going to be simple today; some of George's buddies were going to play a trick on the Germans. As the prisoners filed up the steps, two of them slipped away and hid in the basement shadows. In a few minutes, the guards would finish their head count and realize they were missing. Panic would ensue as the Germans shifted blame for the escape back and forth, and a search would be called. *Then it's out with the guns and flashlights, and those fools will be distracted for another hour,* he thought. It was a risky prank to pull; men had been shot for hiding. The trick was to make your way back into the prisoner area before the guards caught you. Most of the time it worked and the head count ended up plus or minus a few, which infuriated the commanders. Of course it wasn't a huge deal, but it was the airmen's tiny contribution to the war effort. *Stir up some trouble and keep them guessing.* George smiled. He was near the end of the line; it wouldn't be long before confusion set in. *Maybe I'll hide with them next time,* he thought, *It'll give me something to do.*

"Nine hundred ninety eight..." Richard Hiller's gaze was fixed skyward at the veritable swarm of aircraft flying overhead. "Nine hundred ninety nine, one thousand." He was starting to lose count.

He stood with a small group of fellow GIs at the edge of a replacement depot in the sunny French countryside.

After days of training and lectures, it was nice to see some action, even vicariously. And the squadrons passing above them were certainly more exciting than anything he'd seen in the past week. They were headed towards a place called Saint Lo, or at least that's what some of the guys were saying. It wasn't very far away; he could hear the bombs thundering just out of sight. *The Germans must be putting up one hell of a fight,* he thought, *if we need that many planes to push them out.*

What he didn't know, but could probably guess, was that Saint Lo was being obliterated before his eyes.

"Watch your heads!"

Someone was shouting from the next hedgerow over. Combined with the noise of an approaching engine, that could only mean one thing. Gabe Fieni let out a small sigh. "Twilight Charlie" was back. He'd heard of enemy planes coming in at odd hours, harassing the infantry and doing just enough damage to be a nuisance. In fact, it seemed common enough for the guys to have a good laugh about it as they swapped stories. But having his own German Charlie to worry about dulled the humor somewhat. And here he came, right on schedule. It was just before dusk, as usual, and Gabe could see the enemy plane coming in low and fast. His normal routine was to make a few passes at top speed, spitting gunfire into the hedgerows. Sometimes he shot across them, but most times he would aim between and spray bullets up and down the narrow lanes. He did a fair amount of damage and even managed to kill a few guys. Thanks to this, a lot of the GIs were determined to knock him out of the air. Some of them bragged about how they would shoot Charlie down. But no one had managed it yet. *Well, maybe today*, Gabe thought.

As Charlie neared his target, Gabe heard the usual crack of machine gun fire erupt from the plane. Then, in response, rifles and antiaircraft guns opened up from all around, throwing a hail of bullets into the air. Charlie stayed on course, determined to do whatever it was he set out to do. But then, much to Gabe's surprise, something unexpected happened. He heard a tremendous bang – a big explosion – and the soldiers around him began to cheer.

"We got the son of a bitch!"

Men were shaking their rifles in the air, jumping up and down.

"We finally got him!"

Gabe, a bit surprised, started moving towards the sound of the explosion, ushered along by a throng of his buddies. They moved down a narrow lane, past several intersections, and around a corner. Then, barely fifty yards from where he had stood before, he laid eyes on a piece of smoking debris. It was Charlie's engine – or what remained of it – resting in a hedgerow. Sizzling and charred, its propellers were bent and broken, and tattered pieces of fuselage hung around it.

We really did get the guy, Gabe thought, *or at least someone did.* And with this he started back, happy that Twilight Charlie would claim no more victims.

The town of Saint Lo was ruined beyond description. Houses, shops, churches – for as far as Gabe Fieni could see, nothing remained but smoldering piles of brick and stone. *What a mess.*

Gabe moved slowly along past waves of debris which choked and narrowed the street. As he walked he couldn't help but stare at the devastation around him. It was everywhere. The street, or at least the center pathway, had been mostly cleared of bodies. Corpses still lay scattered along the edges here and there, and many were half-buried in rubble. Tattered limbs poked out from the ruins, and Gabe couldn't help but wonder how many were buried that he couldn't see.

I wonder if any of these guys have a pistol I could use? He slowed his pace and approached a dead man lying off to the side of the road. The medics hadn't gotten to him yet, hadn't moved him with the others, so his uniform was intact. He was a German officer; an Iron Cross hung lifelessly from his neck. But that wasn't what drew Gabe's attention. Rather it was the fancy double holster he wore, and the twin Lugers inside which caught his eye. He hesitated for a moment. *I could really use those,* he thought, *and he certainly doesn't need them anymore.* He wasn't allowed to carry a gun, so the notion that he might no longer be defenseless was tremendously appealing. And of course, there was a certain irony in wielding the enemy's own weapon against him. Gabe quickly glanced around, then bent down and unfastened the officer's holster. *Now I have something to protect myself with.* He smiled and buckled the Lugers beneath his jacket before turning and starting back towards his truck. There was no more time for sightseeing. He had to move on. But at least now, he felt a little bit safer.

Back in the driver's seat, Gabe started the engine and gave the truck some gas. And as he rolled past rubble piles and left the town behind, he said goodbye to Saint Lo. Maybe he'd return someday.

Leroy Renninger wasn't sure he'd heard his sergeant correctly. "Do what, now?"

"I said would you be interested in going along and picking up dead? We have a ceasefire. Nobody shoots. We just go out and collect our casualties."

It sounded gruesome, but something made Leroy agree. So he left his artillery piece and walked out into a French field along with medics and other volunteers from the line company. There were dead men everywhere and more than a few wounded. Over the course of several hours he helped collect the bodies, but as the day wore on it became harder and harder to continue. The hot sun, beating down on the fields for days on end, had a terrible effect on the dead. *You and I are no different from a rabbit or a deer,* he realized. Some of the bodies were too rotten to recover easily, so he had to roll them up in a blanket or a shelter half. It was awful. As he was carrying one back to the line, aided by another soldier, he heard a voice.

"Here you go, you son of a bitch." It was one of the volunteers. He was gingerly placing a severed head back on its body. "You might want this again." Then he laughed.

That's pretty hard boiled, Leroy thought, wondering how anyone could joke about such a thing. But as he walked through the heat, corpse in tow, it suddenly dawned on him. *Maybe that's just how you cope. Laughing helps you get through it.* It was a strange thought, but it made sense. He made sure to remember that for the days to come.

"Get up there! Do it!" The lieutenant repeated his order, shouting over the deafening crack of machine gun fire.

Nick Phillips, hunkered down behind a tree, stared at him with wide eyes. *That's crazy,* he thought, *we'll never take it like that.* But his officer was adamant that someone jump out and draw the Germans' fire. They were pinned down by a pillbox just ahead in the woods, and one of them was going to have to run up there and take care of it.

"No way," Nick refused the order, "We're going to do it the right way. I'm not just going to walk into a hail of bullets."

The lieutenant seethed, but gave in. Some of the men gathered behind Nick and raised their rifles.

"Alright, let's button it up!"

Within seconds the MG42 was silenced by withering rifle fire from the GIs positioned behind logs and trees. Its gunner, either wounded or terrified, abandoned the weapon and moved out of harm's way. This gave Nick the chance he was looking for. Jumping from behind a tree, he sprinted madly across the uneven terrain separating him from the bunker. As he ran, he fingered the grenades on his belt and hoped the Germans didn't see him coming. He was lucky. They didn't.

Climbing up onto the pillbox's roof, Nick popped a pair of grenades off his belt and jammed them into a small air vent protruding from the concrete. Just like every other time before, he listened for the explosion inside the room beneath him. When he heard it, he gave the signal and the waiting GIs moved in for the kill. But the Germans didn't come out, so someone brought up an explosive charge and blew the door off. A handful of dazed enemy soldiers ran out into the smoking doorway. They were cut down in an instant.

"Now *that's* how you take a pillbox," Nick said to himself. He was pleased.

Gabe Fieni was in awe. Let's *go to Paris*, Lieutenant Hanson had said, but Gabe wasn't prepared for this. *I heard on the radio it's been liberated.* He wasn't kidding. They were on a wide boulevard, inching along in the jeep with the top down. Parisians choked the street, jumping, shouting, and cheering in every way imaginable. The crowd was jammed shoulder to shoulder in all directions. There was simply nowhere to move, so Gabe pulled the jeep to the side of the road and let some women drag them across the sidewalk and into a bar. *Where are the other soldiers?* He and the lieutenant were the only GIs around, but he wasn't about to complain. There were women everywhere, and as much wine as they could drink. *We don't need anyone else*, he thought, *this is our party!*

Willard Bickel was a guest in the home of an extremely friendly French family. Along with some of his buddies, he'd accepted their dinner invitation, though it went against his better judgment. Seven courses and a few bottles of wine later, everyone was in a lovely mood and the hour was growing late. So, taking advantage of the

French hospitality, the GIs cleaned up and went to sleep on the third floor of the large house. They slept well.

But during the night, Willard heard a disturbing commotion downstairs. He bolted awake and crept to the window, only to discover that some German soldiers had arrived and were emptying the house of its occupants. Unsure of what to do, the Americans stayed quiet and watched as the soldiers dragged the French men out into the front yard. It seemed they were looking for someone.

While this was happening, one of the ladies ran up from downstairs and tried to warn the GIs.

"Get out fast," she said, her voice trembling, "while you still can."

It was a stroke of luck that the Germans hadn't checked the third floor. But they were still out front, so Willard and his friends gathered their belongings as quickly as possible and went sneaking out the back. As he ran through the fields behind the house, he looked back and realized what a close call he'd just had. Unfortunately, it wouldn't be the only one.

A few days later, he was marching with his unit along a road in the middle of nowhere. They'd been warned not to stray from the path because of the presence of minefields. But one of the men couldn't help himself. Needing to urinate, the soldier ventured off the road and dashed behind a barn to relieve himself. Then Willard heard an explosion. Assuming the worst, their chaplain rushed off to attend to the dying man, but he was gone for a long while. When he finally returned, he was white as a sheet.

"I knelt down to give him last rights," he said, "and right between my knees were the prongs of another mine."

Willard made sure to remember these events, for they illustrated the random and violent nature of war in a way that needed little explanation.

"Red Dragon" bounced along in the turbulent skies over the English Channel, shaking its crew as it bucked up and down. Standing in the top turret, Vincent Miller cursed his bladder. He and the others had urinated in the grass before boarding the B-17 but – like usual – he had to go again. *I swear, as soon as we get up here,* he grumbled. Of course, the bumping didn't help matters. He made up his mind to find an empty ammo can when he had the chance. *The tubes are probably frozen anyway*, he mused, referring to the official makeshift bathroom solution aboard the plane. They rarely worked, thanks to the freezing high altitude temperatures. Similarly, drinking water was available but generally unusable.

Vincent's missions had been getting longer and longer lately, and a lot more dangerous. It seemed every time they went out the plane returned with a few extra holes. He was a little bit worried that, unless something changed, he might end up dead or a prisoner. *Hopefully I'm wrong,* he thought, *Now where's that ammo can?*

The path wound through the French woods ahead, meandering between rocks and trees and eventually passing out of site around a shallow bend. It was quiet in the morning forest, save for the noise of the GI squad marching along. Richard Hiller was with them, bringing up the rear as one of the last patrol members. He was the new guy, so they gave him this position. He wasn't sure if it was a good thing or not.

Moving quickly along, the men paid little attention to the scenery. By now they'd seen enough of trees and fields. It was Germans they were watching for. They wouldn't be disappointed.

"Get down!" Richard's buddy Martinez shouted from the point position, waving his arms as he dropped to the ground.

In sudden unison, the rest of the squad followed, pressing their bodies to the earth and keeping their heads low as they scurried into the underbrush just off the path. Ahead of them, not very far away, a group of Germans started firing wildly at them with rifles and machine guns. Richard couldn't tell if they were aiming at them specifically or just hosing the area with bullets. It seemed the latter was likely, but it made little difference. The GIs were pinned regardless.

"Return fire!"

A volley of rifle reports erupted from the men huddling in the bushes, doubling the confusion. Bullets whizzed back and forth, left and right, snapping twigs and kicking up dirt, slamming into trees and showering the men with wood splinters. The man on Richard's left yelped in surprise as his canteen and haversack took hits, spilling water and shredded canvas. And the man on the right dropped his rifle as a round pierced the stock. Then an explosion rocked the battle. Martinez was up front throwing grenades. Three, four, five... he lobbed one after another towards the enemy muzzle flashes, and with each came a thunderous crack and a plume of debris. It was overpowering. And it worked. For a moment the Germans stopped firing. Were they disoriented? Wounded? Richard didn't want to stick around to find out, and neither did anyone else. So they grabbed the opportunity and retreated into the woods.

Back where they started, the patrol members looked around and made sure the Germans hadn't followed them. It looked safe enough. But then Richard noticed something: their sniper was missing.

"Did anyone see him after the firefight?" Martinez was worried.

No one could remember, though. And they couldn't go back or they'd likely lose someone else. So they waited.

Wow, Richard thought, realizing something, *that was my first combat. My baptism by fire.* It was terrifying and exhilarating all at once. But he felt bad for the sniper. *We shouldn't have left him there.*

Late that night the sniper returned. As luck would have it, though he was wounded in at least four or five places, none of them were fatal. And over the course of many hours, he'd been able to slowly drag himself through the woods on his stomach. It was more than a mile back to the camp from where he was shot, yet he'd made it alive. It was a small miracle.

There was something strange about that hole in the side of the hill. It looked like a small tunnel with doors, but it was set back from the road out in the middle of nowhere. Gabe Fieni, towing a water tank trailer, couldn't let it pass by without satisfying his curiosity. So he drove his truck right up to the entrance and threw the doors open. *I probably shouldn't be doing this,* he thought, but he had to know what was inside.

Driving into the tunnel, Gabe flashed the truck's headlights and let out a low whistle. *Wine. Lots of wine.* The room was huge and lined with vats, each labeled with a year and some French words. *1896, 1904...* He read them one by one. It was impressive. Suddenly, he was struck with an idea.

"Hey, I'm going to take some of this wine," he said, eyeballing the tank behind his truck.

"Uh, we probably shouldn't do that," his buddy replied nervously, "We'll get caught."

But Gabe's mind was made up. He was already opening the seal on the tank. "I don't care. I just want some of this."

With a grin, Gabe backed the truck up to one of the vats and began calculating how much he could fit in the tank. *Two hundred gallons at least,* he thought, *that'll do nicely.*

The enlisted men back at camp had their happiest night in recent memory thanks to Gabe's efforts. While he was supposed to have brought back water, no one complained when he returned with a tank trailer full of vintage French wine instead.

A dying man's moans floated through the sleeping forest and tormented Nick Phillips as he lay huddled behind a tree. It was tragic; the GI was slowly bleeding and no one could reach him. He'd been cut down by shrapnel and his leg was in tatters. Nick had tried three times to crawl out and pull him to safety, but each time a hail of bullets stopped him cold. All he could do was hide in the underbrush and watch as the wounded man thrashed weakly upon the ground.

I can't save him, Nick realized, *he's going to die right there.* It was the worst feeling in the world.

"Nick... Nick..." The man was calling his name.

He closed his eyes.

"Help me... please..."

I'm sorry, he thought, *I'm so sorry.* He vowed, right then and there, not to make any more friends in the army. It was just too hard to lose them.

Damn, that was close! Vincent Miller flinched in the top turret of his B-17, gritting his teeth as shrapnel clattered against the Plexiglas dome. Something loud snapped right near his head; he turned to see a jagged sliver of metal sticking out of the gun sight. *Closer than I thought... this must be the same group we hit coming over.* They were approaching Belgium at twenty five thousand feet, returning from their factory target in Germany, and the flak was unusually hellish. He thought back to a few hours earlier, when they'd been shot at while approaching the Rhineland. The German antiaircraft batteries had knocked out the lead bomber; as they dropped out of formation Vincent's B-17 was instructed to take its place. Now here they were, mission accomplished but trying to make it home in one piece. And the sea of flak around them certainly wasn't making things any easier.

Another burst rocked the plane, bumping Vincent off balance. As he righted himself and spun around to look forward, he noticed something disturbing: one of the engines was on fire. He could see it clearly from his turret position – flames spewing from the outside engine on the right wing. He started to say something, but the pilot – his buddy Howard – already knew.

"Alright, let's get ready to bail out." Howard dipped the plane and banked, dropping them out of formation and away from the other bombers.

He must know something we don't, Vincent thought as he watched his squad mates recede into the sky above. But he wondered if they might still be able to save the plane.

"How about banking to the left," he radioed up, furrowing his brow at the burning engine, "Try and get the gas away from the flames. See if you can blow it out."

There was a moment of silence. Then the pilot responded with a wag of the wings. Vincent braced himself as they rolled to the left, and for a moment he saw the flames dwindle. *It's working!* But then the bomber righted itself and the engine flared up again. His heart sank.

"No good," Howard said, "Get ready to go."

Vincent had never had to bail out of a plane, but he knew what to do. There wasn't enough room to wear his chute in the turret, but it was just a few feet away. So he dropped down into the waist and grabbed it. Strapping it to his back, he scrambled over to the door and pulled the emergency panel. The hatch flew off, blasting him with cold air and jarring his senses. *Looks like I'm really going to have to do this*, he thought. But even though he'd never jumped before, he was strangely unafraid. Perhaps he didn't have time to worry in the face of such a crisis.

Clearing his mind, he dropped to a sitting position and dangled his legs out into the void, bracing them against the rush of air. Then he hesitated as a thought struck him. The pilot had given the order to jump, but something was keeping him from taking the plunge. He looked around for the rest of the crew but didn't see anyone. *I'm not going to jump if nobody else is coming*, he thought. For some reason, he pictured himself bailing out, parachuting into foreign territory, and then looking up to find that the others had fixed the engine and were flying home without him. It seemed silly but it was a legitimate fear. However, a clatter nearby caught his attention and he turned his head to see the bombardier and navigator crawling up from the nose section with their parachutes.

"Go," said the navigator, motioning at Vincent.

Reassured, he took a deep breath and leaned forward, tumbling out of the plane and into weightless nothing.

The rushing air froze his senses momentarily. *One thousand one, one thousand two, one thousand three*, he counted in his head. *I have to get away from the plane.* He tried to look up, to catch a glimpse of the B-17, but he couldn't see it. Ten seconds was enough though. When he reached the count he pulled his rip cord and hoped for the best. With a violent jerk, the chute opened, tugging at his harness and knocking the wind from his lungs. His boots, tied to a chest strap, kicked up and slammed him in the face. Then the laces tore and his footwear went sailing out into the void, trailing a glittering splatter of blood from his battered nose. It was a minor indignity; he was just glad to be safely floating to earth. But the landing was another thing entirely. Looking down, he saw the terrain rapidly approaching, so he gritted his teeth once more and braced for impact.

Hitting the ground felt like jumping out of a two story building: it hurt. Vincent came crashing down onto a planted farmer's field and rolled head over heels before coming to a stop. Then, tugging dizzily at his chute cords, he stood up and freed himself from the tangle. He looked around, trying to catch his breath as he surveyed the area. A field with some kind of bushy crop, wooded hills in the distance, a cluster of houses nearby; Belgium certainly looked different from ground level. Then he had a sudden thought. *The plane*, he remembered, casting a glance upward, searching for motion. But only the clouds stared back.

An abrupt noise caught his attention and he wheeled around to find a pair of teenage girls scampering towards him. *This is probably their farm*, he realized, *they know I'm here.* He took a step back and unhooked his parachute harness but the girls barely acknowledged him. Instead, they grabbed the chute and gathered it up without a word before turning back toward the house. *They must want the silk.* As he watched them jog away, the gravity of the situation sank in. He was alone in hostile territory and at the mercy of the locals. *Where am I*, he wondered. *Maybe I should hide.* So, scanning the field for some kind of concealment, he wracked his brain and tried to decide what to do next.

Ten minutes passed. Then twenty. Vincent lay still beneath a brush pile, peeking out at intervals to watch for new developments. Should he wait until dusk? He wasn't sure. Thirty minutes came and went without incident, and he began to grow uneasy. Then he heard a whistle and his pulse escalated. *They're looking for me!* He could see them now, a small group of civilians carrying something. They were heading right for him; it seemed they knew where he was. So having nowhere to hide and little else to do, he took a deep breath and stood up. *I'm ready for them,* he thought, *no matter what happens.*

Cookies! Freed from visual obstructions, Vincent suddenly realized that the approaching civilians were wielding baked goods. *They have cookies and they're not shooting at me,* he rationalized. *That's probably a good sign.* And it seemed he was right. After a quick exchange of smiles and sweets his heart felt lighter. They were friendly after all. But right in the middle of their introductions, one of his hosts abruptly turned away with a worried expression. *Does he hear something?* He cocked an ear in the direction of the houses and thought he heard an engine. They heard it too, and before he knew it he was back in the brush pile, watching the civilians scamper back to where they came from. His heart sank a little.

Vincent remained hidden for another quarter hour. Then, sensing the coast clear, his hosts returned and brought him into the village. There, in a small house, a few of them who spoke English prepared him for what lie ahead. They took his uniform and gave him civilian clothing.

"Can you ride a bicycle?" a tall man asked.

Vincent nodded in affirmation, and before he knew what was happening they had him pedaling along towards another house. This one was larger – it was a doctor's residence. The Belgians hid him upstairs while they prepared his fake passport. Airmen carried photographs and a packet of currency for this purpose, and the locals knew just what to do. They whipped up a set of documents in no time flat.

The doctor's house was comfortable enough, but it wasn't a safe place to hide. Two days after Vincent's arrival, a large German car rolled up to the door and deposited a small group of officers. They needed medical attention.

"We have to move you," one of the Belgians whispered to Vincent, "You can't stay here."

"Yeah," he replied, "I realize that."

Later that day, Vincent was ushered from the house, placed on a bicycle, and led to yet another hiding place. This one was the home of a friendly couple who had three children – a young son and two older daughters. They let him hide with them for a week, and things went smoothly save for one inconvenience. Their outhouse was on the other side of the main road that cut through town, which meant that every time Vincent needed to use it, someone had to escort him across the exposed thoroughfare and stand watch. It seemed a little silly, but they couldn't take any chances.

One day the couple approached him.

"We're going to move you again," they said. Something was up.

That evening Vincent hopped on another bicycle and followed the man along a winding network of paths laid out in the surrounding fields. Between rows of crops, through tall grass, and even through narrow cuts in fences, they pedaled for at least an hour before finally arriving at an unfamiliar farmhouse. Then, disoriented and tired, he went to sleep. But the next morning he made an amusing discovery. Looking out a window, he recognized the house he'd just left sitting a short distance up the road. It seemed the Belgians had taken him on a roundabout bicycle ride, doubling back and forth in an attempt to shake off anyone who might be watching. They were truly serious about keeping him safe.

The rest of Vincent's stay with the Belgian underground was spent in relative peace. The Germans came and went without getting too close, and he never felt they were looking for him. In truth, he lived rather than hid at the farmhouse. When his hosts knew the enemy was gone, they would invite him outside for makeshift soccer games in the orchard. Some of his fondest memories were kicking their little makeshift ball around with the townspeople and their kids. But it wasn't all fun and games. As night fell the Belgians' tone grew serious, and from out of nowhere weapons would emerge. Each evening the men and women girded themselves with rifles and revolvers, slung grenades on their belts, and went about their duties. He didn't know exactly what it was they were doing, but they certainly looked fierce. *These underground guys are almost scarier than the Germans*, he found himself thinking on more than one occasion, *I'm just glad they're on our side.*

As the weeks wore on, more and more reports came in detailing the Allies' advance. The temptation to try and meet up with them was strong, but the Belgians insisted that all downed airmen stay where they were. *Your troops are advancing quickly enough*, they would say, *it's safer just to stay put. They'll reach you soon.* So Vincent waited, not scared but restless. He felt safe but the thought of going home gnawed at the edge of his mind day after day.

Finally, after several months as a guest of the Belgians, Vincent's chance arrived. The Allies were close and the underground was more active than ever. They took him to an office in town and laid out their plans. A young fellow at a desk spoke to him.

"We're supposed to get you up to the capitol, to the Hotel Metropolitan," he said, "Would you mind coming with us and staying with me overnight?"

Vincent expressed his enthusiasm.

"Good," the man replied, "Tomorrow I'll take you up."

And he did. Within twenty four hours, Vincent found himself at the hotel in Brussels. He walked through the door, smiling wide, and discovered a pair of familiar faces waiting for him. His radio operator and waist gunner were sitting in the lobby. How that was arranged, he never knew. But it was the best feeling in the world to see them.

The very same day, Vincent and his crew were driven to France in an army truck. They ultimately ended up in Paris, where they were interviewed and looked after before being shipped back to England.

Hill 340. That's what they were calling it officially. Or at least he thought that's what they'd said. Richard Hiller wracked his brain, trying to recall what number they were defending this time. *I guess it doesn't really matter. They're all the same – just some mound of dirt in the forest.* It had just gotten dark, and from where he sat away from the trees he could clearly see the stars. They had their backs to the woods, thick foliage obscuring the approach behind them. These were German holes, leftover from some earlier battle. But to the Americans occupying them now, it felt strangely backwards, like they were facing the wrong way. *Oh well,* he thought, *at least we didn't have to dig for a change.* Still, he felt odd being at the end of the line. Everyone else was hidden under tree branches, but he and Whitey were out in the open. And even though he knew that a canopy of leaves offered little protection, he would have been glad for the visual cover. It was mostly psychological, but it still bothered him.

Whitey yawned and shifted in the hole next to Richard. They were both tired, and an opportunity for sleep was approaching. "You sleep," Richard said, "I'll take first watch." With that, the other man closed his eyes and nodded off almost instantly. Richard sighed and looked out across the barren landscape ahead. He suddenly felt very alone.

Richard woke with a start. Was that a rustle in the bushes ahead? He bolted upright and listened. Pitch black. Dead silent. Nothing to see or hear. Then he heard a rumble beside him and noticed that Whitey was snoring.

"Dammit, Whitey." He gave him a kick and Whitey twitched awake. "Stop falling asleep!"

Whitey mumbled something and adjusted his helmet. Then Richard heard it again. A twig snapping. He looked up slowly, and in the darkness he saw a face looking down at him. *Germans!* There he was, eyes glinting fiercely in the moonlight – an enemy soldier less than two feet away.

Richard let out a yell and grabbed for his weapon, then lashed out with the rifle stock. Nothing – no impact. He bolted upright and looked out of the hole. The German had vanished. How was it possible? He'd been there just a moment ago. Richard swung his weapon across the horizon, but he could barely see a thing. *It's so dark,* he thought, *he must have jumped back into the shadows.*

Shaken, he dropped back into the foxhole and tried to steady his nerves. He had a feeling he wouldn't be sleeping much more tonight.

Robert Mest listened intently to the engine noise coming over the tree line ahead. It was a familiar sound; he knew exactly what was making it. Closer, closer... it grew louder by the second. Then abruptly it stopped.

"Buzz bomb! Get down!"

He looked up; there it was, just above the trees, falling quickly – a little winged fuselage laden with explosives. It was coming down close. *Run,* he thought, *get some distance on that thing!* It hit fifty yards away and sent a shudder through the earth. Robert's feet lifted a few inches off the ground and he stumbled, nearly falling. *Wow! What a blast!*

Life at the engineer supply depots was never dull, especially with buzz bombs coming in daily. A lot of them continued overhead and struck somewhere behind the lines, but more than enough dropped down within sight. Sometimes they hit close. *Like this one,* he thought. *I just hope I'm this lucky all the time.*

"Incoming!"

Leroy Renninger stood frozen, eyes glued to a smoking artillery shell sticking out of the choppy soil only ten feet away. It had landed just a moment ago with a great thump. *A dud,* he realized, *that would have killed me.*

A moment later, more shells started coming in. He flinched with every impact. Some of them were close, but not close enough. *That first one was free,* he thought, *I might not be so lucky again.* There wasn't anything he could do about it, though, so he just kept manning his Howitzer, setting the sights and blasting away.

Whatever they did, it seemed to be working. The enemy fire let up somewhat and the GIs grew more confident. *This is a good sign.*

Suddenly a message came chattering over the radio. The sergeant relayed it to Leroy's gun crew.

"One of our spotter planes got hit," he said, "Not sure exactly what happened."

Leroy's heart sank. He wondered if it was friendly fire. The plane had been flying just above the treetops, spotting for their artillery. In fact... *What if it was us?* What a horrible thought. The odds of hitting their own Piper Cub were slim, especially with a Howitzer, but somehow he felt guilty.

"It might have been me," he told the sergeant, though no one else really thought so.

But Leroy couldn't shake the feeling, and for the rest of the day each time he fired a shell he thought of the men in the plane.

Lester Groff jammed the Sherman controls forward and stepped on the gas pedal.

"You're almost at the top, watch it."   His tank commander was helping navigate a steep hill near the town of Stolberg.

The Germans were waiting somewhere down below, in amongst the trees and buildings at the edge of town.

"Twenty feet, then we're over."

Lester peered through his periscope but couldn't see much. The tiny slit offered little visibility. *At least I'm protected, though.*

He felt the hill flatten out and eased up a bit to give the commander time to get his bearings.

"Uhh, I don't see anything down there."

That's odd, he thought.

"Wait, scratch that.   There's..."   The commander paused, then, "Oh shi-"

He didn't get to finish. *Bang!* The Sherman lurched violently as something struck the underside and exploded. Lester slammed his head against metal. *They got us!* The engine was still running but he couldn't move. *The treads are jammed up*, he realized, *and we're stuck with our belly exposed.* They were sitting ducks.

Smoke was billowing up past his viewport and a charred smell filled the compartment, so he opened the hatch and started sliding his way out. He could see the rest of the crew doing the same. Together they flopped down into the dirt and took cover behind the tank. *Ping!* A bullet ricocheted off the side of the vehicle. Lester flinched and moved back, staying low to avoid gunfire.

"Let's get back and find another ride," he shouted as he scurried away from the hilltop.

He knew there were replacement tanks waiting behind the line. *We'll grab one and try again*, he thought, *and this time we'll go around the hill.*

Robert Reeser found himself driving north along the Moselle River one night, squinting into the darkness from behind the wheel of an ambulance. He was a medic, and he'd been ordered to drive to a little riverside town to evacuate some wounded soldiers. It didn't sound like a bad mission.

But when Robert arrived he discovered that things were worse than he'd been told. An officer was waiting for him along the roadside.

"Is anybody else coming to help you out?"

"Not that I know of," Robert replied, "I just took off on my own."

The officer sighed. "Well, we're going to need about three or four ambulances."

"Can you call back and get some more? I don't really know what to tell you."

"We had a river crossing earlier. About three hundred guys went over and ran into German resistance. Now they're stuck on the far side with twenty two wounded GIs."

It sounded like a rough situation, but Robert didn't see how he could help. The officer had an idea, though.

"Hey," he said, "did you ever drive on a pontoon bridge?"

Robert shook his head.

"Well you're going to tonight. Take off your shoes and let's go. I'll find someone to guide you.

A few minutes later, Robert was inching his way across the Moselle River on a bridge made of floating pontoons. He had to creep along in low gear to avoid slipping, and a man walked in front of the vehicle to provide visual cues. It was nerve wracking, but in twenty minutes he made it across the river and located the injured men on the far bank. There wasn't enough room for them all, though. So he crammed a handful of litters into the back of the ambulance and stuck one of the "walking wounded" up front. The ride back went a little quicker.

After unloading his cargo, Robert turned around for another load of men. But much to his surprise, the Germans threw flares up and started lobbing mortars into the river. Either they were firing blindly or their aim was inaccurate, because they didn't manage to hit the bridge in all the time it took Robert to make three back-and-forth crossings. By then he was exhausted and stressed from the constant pop of enemy rounds crashing down around him.

At that very moment, a second ambulance showed up, apparently summoned from some far-off location. Robert asked the driver to go pick up the rest of the wounded, but the timid man refused. Even after an argument, there was no convincing him. So for a fourth time, Robert steeled himself and drove across the pontoon bridge, this time certain that he'd be killed. Ironically, it was one of his passengers who would not survive, though Robert's driving had nothing to do with that. The man simply died while waiting for his ride.

Frank Lashinsky fell in exhilarating silence. Pulse racing, eyes wide, he careened earthward at a tremendous speed. The only sound penetrating his thick flight helmet was the rush of air as he plummeted through the sky. Reaching for the D ring, his fingers closed around the metal handle and he gave it a pull. But nothing happened. No jerk. No sudden pressure on the harness like he'd been told to expect. What could be wrong? His mind raced, searching for an answer. But despite the fear creeping into his chest, he remained calm. *The pins must be bent,* he wagered, *they didn't pull free.* Craning his neck, he judged the distinct absence of a parachute canopy above him and hoped that his guess was correct. He'd never done this before. Maybe it was supposed to be reckless.

With a great rush of adrenaline, Frank took the handle with both hands and pulled with all his strength. He braced for the jerk. He wasn't disappointed. The chute opened hard, knocking the wind from his lungs. He felt the harness straps tighten against his body, straining like cables under the immense pressure. And above him the canopy billowed fiercely, slowing his fall and bringing him upright. Relief washed over him and he looked up. The plane was gone, little more than a memory now. It had vanished quietly in the night. He had survived his first jump. Now he just had to land.

Frank was floating through the skies over Yugoslavia. His B-24 had been mortally damaged by flak and the airmen were forced to bail out. Now Frank, the crew's tail gunner, was alone and disoriented, gliding down towards an uncertain future.

Squinting toward the ground, Frank tried to calculate his landing trajectory. There was a steep hill covered in trees coming up fast below him, and he winced at the thought of tumbling through a tangle of branches. But there was little choice, so he crossed his legs and shielded his face, bracing for impact. Three, two, one... he smacked into the earth. There was no snap, no crunch. Just the flapping of leaves and a great jolt as he slammed into the hillside. The damp soil sagged beneath his boots. Scrambling to untangle his chute, he jumped to his feet and looked around. It wasn't a hill after all. Nor were there trees. Instead, Frank stood in what appeared to be a gigantic sinkhole covered with the largest ferns he'd ever seen. The fronds were at least as tall as he, and some towered even beyond his own height. It was, to say the least, surprising.

Frank had only a fleeting moment to marvel at his landing before voices began creeping down the slope. He couldn't make out the language, but it didn't sound like German. Still, he wasn't certain where he was and for all he knew, the enemy could be anywhere. Crouching low beneath the fern canopy, he took off his helmet and loosened his .45 pistol in its shoulder holster. *Better to be ready just in case,* he thought. But if the people up there were friendly, he didn't want to appear hostile. In any case, his nerves were fired up. He just hoped he'd make it home.

Frank crept to the top of the sinkhole, listening to the voices all around it. He knew he'd been spotted. *They must have been watching us come down.* It probably wasn't the first time for them. He knew they'd find him before long. There was no way they could miss his chute tangled in the fern grove. Given the predicament, he decided to appear as friendly as possible. So, mustering all his courage, he scrambled up onto level ground and waited.

A small group of women and children were approaching from one side. They stopped and fell silent when Frank emerged from the depression. He heard more voices behind him, and he turned to find a cluster of men armed with rifles. *Uh oh*, he thought, *are they hostile?* For starters, he was pretty sure they weren't German. The Germans wouldn't dress like locals and sit around waiting for Americans to drop from the sky. Or would they? He furrowed his brow and remembered the gun in his holster, trigger finger tingling. *If they rush me, what should I do?*

He had an idea. Figuring they wouldn't shoot at him if he was near the women, he approached the group of ladies and held out his identification card. It contained his photograph, an American flag, and some phrases printed in numerous languages.

"Amerikanski," he said with a smile.

But they didn't respond.

He repeated himself, "Amerikanski."

By now the men had approached and, seeing what he was doing, softened their expressions. One offered a handshake and spoke in broken English.

"The Germans must have seen you come down. You must leave here quickly."

Frank nodded and followed them to a barn in the distance. Moving quickly, he turned back to see the women collecting his parachute and carrying it away. *Good*, he thought, *they're erasing my tracks.*

Over the next few weeks, Frank's B-24 crew was collected from various parts of the countryside. Together they lived with the partisans in the Yugoslavian town of Sanski Most, where they spent their days laying low and longing for home.

Richard Hiller's heart was racing. He wiped a bead of sweat from his brow with a grimy sleeve and squinted into the darkness. The street looked clear ahead. Not a German to be seen. But he knew they were hiding somewhere. He'd been "volunteered" to go on this mission, tasked with distracting the enemy long enough for a rescue operation to be carried out nearby. *Distraction,* he thought, *is just another word for bait.* And indeed it was tonight. There was murder in the air; he could feel it pressing at his temples and tingling along his spine. Someone was going to get killed. He felt a tap on his shoulder and turned to see a lanky GI scuttling up behind him. It was the translator. The guy who'd grown up in this area and whose job it was to do recon. *What the hell is his name again?* It didn't really matter. It was too quiet to talk. The nameless man slithered ahead into the darkness, flashing a gesture that said *follow me.* Richard didn't really want to, but he didn't have much choice.

The street was deserted after all. But the next block down wasn't. Richard could hear German voices chattering quietly as he hunkered down and crept along a low stone wall. There was some distance between them and the enemy, but not enough to feel safe. So they moved as silently as possible. A large house suddenly appeared around a bend, looming dark and empty above them. Their guide stopped, looked around, and darted into the side yard, motioning to them with a wave of his hand. Richard took a deep breath and followed.

The house was deserted, its previous occupants having left in a hurry. Furniture lay strewn about and ransacked, books littered the floor, and a thick layer of dust covered everything in between. As he passed through the foyer toward the front staircase, Richard noticed something unusual. A gigantic stained glass window, perhaps twenty feet tall, adorned one wall, its intricate panes illuminated by the moonlight streaming in from outside. He paused for a moment to let his eyes adjust and was spellbound. Pale rays, filtered through soft sheets of fluttering dust, shone through the colored glass and shimmered across his body. It was a beautiful oasis in the inky monochrome of the dark mansion, something wonderful and unexpected. But he couldn't stop for long, and before he knew it the man behind was pushing him forward up the staircase. As he rounded a corner and stepped out of sight, he glanced once more toward the stained glass window and saw that it had darkened.

The room in which they stood was small and bare save for an empty bed frame. No furniture, no mattress, no rug... just a lonely metal lattice crusted with hints of rust and neglect. A floor to ceiling window, standing open, looked out onto a small balcony and the sleeping town beyond. Whitey was kneeling next to the opening, his rifle propped against the wall. He fiddled with the grenades on his belt, popping them off one by one and lining them up on the floor. Richard moved next to him and readied himself. It was almost go time.

"Fire!" A machine gun opened up from the next room over, spitting bullets into a house across the courtyard. Richard watched as the windows violently shattered and brick chips flew about wildly. Then, on his cue, he and Whitey launched grenades through the front windows. They exploded almost instantly, pushing plumes of debris through the holes in the bullet-torn wall. The Germans were inside, shouting and running about in confusion. But there were more in the houses on either side, and they started to return fire. Bullets were flying both ways, slicing into the walls near Richard and biting into the plaster. Then he heard glass shatter in an explosion somewhere behind him, and he realized the stained glass window had been hit. *Damn shame*, he thought, *it was the only nice thing left.* But he didn't have long to regret the loss.

"Grenade!" Whitey shouted, panic in his voice.

He jumped up and rushed from the room, leaving Richard alone with a sergeant. Confused, Richard backed up and quickly swept his eyes across the floor. There was an American grenade rocking back and forth where Whitey had stood just a moment before. No pin. No arm. Just a rapidly cooking fuse. The sergeant saw it and repeated Whitey's alarm. *Grenade!* With no time to act, Richard did the only thing he could think of. With all the strength he could muster, he threw himself as far across the room as he could, bashing his face on the metal bed frame as he fell. Then he covered his head with his arms and braced himself just as the grenade exploded barely ten feet away. There was a terrible crack and a jolt as his teeth rattled in his skull, and for an instant he thought he was dead. Then the dust settled and he rolled over onto his back, dazed and shaken.

Staggering to his feet, Richard looked toward the door and saw Whitey's head poking out from around the corner. "Where the hell were you?" He moved out into the hallway, helmet gone, blood trickling from his nose. "Whitey, Whitey, Whitey... what are you doing out here? You left me in there."

"Well," Whitey replied sheepishly, "I said 'grenade' and I beat it." He exchanged a meek glance with the sergeant.

Richard just groaned and doubled over to catch his breath. He could barely hear over the ringing in his ears and his head was throbbing. He'd been lucky.

After several minutes the firing outside had ceased, so the GIs gathered their gear and moved downstairs. As he passed the ruined stained glass window, Richard felt a little sad. *What a waste,* he thought.

Their mission accomplished, Richard and the others retreated into the town and laid low at a civilian's house for a short while. Then, when the coast was clear, they returned to their lines.

Paul Fett was resting in his tent near Rouen when he heard a gunshot nearby. It startled him. *We're far enough behind the lines,* he thought, *who would be shooting?* He poked his head out of the low tent and put on his helmet to shield against the rain. Voices were coming from a few rows over. *Shouting.* Glancing around, he scrambled out into the wet orchard they called home and started slogging through the mud. *Let's see what's going on over there.*

It was one of the GIs, a rookie who'd been cleaning his rifle and accidentally fired. The bullet pierced a nearby tent and killed another soldier. *What a tragic accident.* Paul suddenly realized something: *this is our first casualty.*

Richard Walton was at the same orchard that day. He heard the shot, found out what had happened, and was deeply saddened. A lot of the men were shaken by this event; it was their first glimpse of death. The guys who'd been resting near the dead man's tent were especially upset. They knew that, with a tiny adjustment in aim, the bullet might have hit any one of them. It was a sobering wake up call, and a tragic introduction to the random brutality of war.

Frank Lashinsky could hear something in the Yugoslavian night, off on the horizon. A low rumbling. It had to be the rescue plane. The partisans were already in position; they began shouting to one another, passing orders down the line. Frank couldn't understand them, but he suddenly realized what they meant to do. Standing in two long rows upon the dusty field, the citizen soldiers lit torches one by one until they formed a series of illuminated lines. From the ground it didn't look like much, but from the air it must have been impressive. The partisans had made a runway.

As the plane approached Frank began to appreciate the gravity of the situation. A lone C-47, deep in enemy territory, flying a long night mission to pick up downed airmen and POWs – it was quite a feat. The pilots must have been tremendously brave.

The plane touched down in the grass and braked hard, tires squealing. As it passed each pair of partisans, the men quickly extinguished their torches. In this way, the ghostly runway vanished piece by piece, following the trail of the taxiing aircraft and erasing all signs of the rescue mission.

Richard Hiller crouched behind a hedge and looked out at the scene before him. The morning sky, overcast and grey, barely illuminated the muddy churchyard where gravestones jutted out from the mud like teeth. A stiff breeze cut the air, scattering dead leaves and fluttering the brown grass bunched around his knees. And except for the sporadic gunfire rattling in from the hills, the cool November morning lay quiet. No birds. No children laughing. Just the rustling of trees and the crack of artillery in the distance. It was eerie.

"Watch your heads," someone whispered, "I heard there's a sniper up in that tower." Richard poked his head around some branches and squinted. Past the graveyard, about a football field's distance from where he was kneeling, the steeple of a church rose up from a small cluster of buildings. It was the highest point in town, the perfect location for an observation post. Or, if they were unlucky, a German marksman. He thought back to other towns, most of them nameless, and recalled the trouble they'd had again and again. *These damn steeples*, he thought, *they're always in the steeples*. But there wasn't much he could do about it. He was one of the scouts, so he had to move forward.

Richard glanced at his watch. Almost eleven thirty. "Alright, let's do this." He took a deep breath and stepped around the hedge, keeping his head low as he darted towards the first large gravestone in sight. It was big enough to duck behind, so he took cover and paused. Nothing. No shots. *What's he waiting for?* He looked back. The others were following, scurrying from stone to stone, advancing on the church. Gritting his teeth, he moved out and plotted a path forward, keeping one eye on the steeple. His heart was pounding. The anticipation was killing him. *Is he watching me? Is he even up there?* Not knowing almost made it worse. But he had to keep moving.

When the shot came, it was quieter than he'd imagined. Maybe it was the pulse rushing in his ears, or the fact that his attention was diverted momentarily. Or maybe he just wasn't ready for it. The bullet struck him in the right side, near his waist, and spun him around completely. As he hit the mud his mind jammed up, a torrent of thoughts storming through his head. He was stunned. Then he felt the damp cold creeping through his clothes into his flesh and everything became clear. He wasn't dead, but something inside him was wounded terribly. He could feel pain in his side, but he was too weak to do anything about it. So he just lay there, frozen and contorted in the muddy cemetery, unable to move. Eleven thirty on a November morning and he was dying. It was a terrible feeling.

Perhaps an hour passed as Richard drifted in and out of consciousness. He heard shots, or thought he did. His senses grew hazy. Then a face appeared above him, silhouetted against the low-hanging sun.

"Who are you with?" The medic's voice was muddy, distant.

"Comp..." He struggled to reply. "Company I." Then he saw there were two of them. One was injecting his arm with a needle. Morphine. It felt warm in his veins. It made him groggy even as his senses returned. There was shouting nearby. Gunshots rang out and the medics ducked down. The sniper was firing again. Then he heard explosions, and as he craned his head towards the town he saw the church steeple explode in a great burst of mortar fire.

"Let's get the hell out of here," one of the medics said, and they dragged him roughly onto a litter. As they carried him back to the aid station, he watched the ruined steeple smoking in the distance. Then he closed his eyes and fell under the trance of the bumpy ride, and was soon unconscious.

Stan Blazejewski held his breath. There before him, less than twenty feet away in the darkness, a cluster of German tents sat grouped in the woods. The men inside were talking, but what were they saying? He flashed a glance at the GIs beside him. They looked equally puzzled.

"Alright, that's close enough," someone whispered, "Let's get out of here.

Stan couldn't have agreed more. The men turned and hustled back toward their lines. As he walked, he thought back to what they'd seen over the previous few weeks.

They were in Luxembourg near the Sauer River, and it was quickly becoming obvious that the Germans had an interest in the region. He'd seen artillery, tanks, weapons, and equipment. And men – lots of men. *They're up to something,* he thought, *but what exactly?* From his nightly forays into enemy territory, he knew that trouble was brewing. It was clear to anyone who saw it firsthand that the Germans were preparing for some kind of operation. He and his buddies had been reporting this to their superiors for at least a month now, but the higher ups didn't seem to take it seriously. *We're very well informed, yet nobody is using the information we gather.* Or at least it seemed that way.   Regardless, it bothered him tremendously. *I just hope I'm not here if things go south and the Germans roll through.* There were only about a hundred men with him on the ridge, and he knew they couldn't hold back an assault.

He shivered a little as he climbed the steep path that led back to the foxholes. December was just around the corner and the weather was getting colder by the day. It was good that they had the holes dug already, because the ground was too hard to dig easily. With any luck, they wouldn't have to move, or if they did it would be back into friendly territory.

Stan crossed the top of the ridge and paused to look down the slope. It was thickly wooded below. He couldn't see the Germans anymore; there were too many trees between them. But they were around, lurking quietly in the dark forest. *I hope they stay down there.*

He took a deep breath and coughed in the brisk air before starting in the direction of his foxhole.

7

THE LONG WINTER
THE BATTLE OF THE BULGE

"I can remember... during the Bulge... seeing the dead bodies in the cold weather. The body turns black. Bodies were piled on top of each other like logs, because there were so many people getting killed at that time that there was no place to take them. German and American and others. One shoe is taken off the dead body and a tag is put on the toe, and here you saw these tags hanging from what looked like black logs. 'Oh my God, that's a soldier.' If you ever saw where a tank ran over a body, oh... that's hell. The part that gets me is, the mother of this boy gets a telegram: 'your son has been killed in action,' and that's all she knows – that he was killed. But if you saw what his body looked like at this point, it would make you sick until the day you died. Thank God mothers didn't have to see that."

Charles Gryniewich, Battle of the Bulge, 1944

There was the sound again, like a truck passing overhead. It had to be artillery. But it was coming in from the German side of the woods and hitting somewhere down the line. Stan Blazejewski tried to swallow the sinking feeling in his stomach as he crouched in his foxhole. If the Germans were attacking, they'd picked a hell of a time to do it. With the supply halftracks miles away and their gear stowed with them, the GIs had little support at the moment. To make things worse, Stan's unit wasn't even supposed to be there. In a few hours they'd be moving back into France. Or at least they were supposed to.

Something loud and rumbling echoed in the distance. "Sounds like an ammo dump exploded," a nearby soldier said, frigid hands tucked into his armpits. The artillery rounds were passing nearly overhead now. Stan looked up, imagining freight trucks flying by. It was unsettling.

A small group of men came shuffling in from the rear, fresh from breakfast. Stan noticed them and remembered how hungry he was. *Our stuff might be gone,* he thought, *but at least I can still get a hot meal.* With a quick glance toward the cliff ahead of his foxhole, he turned and started towards the kitchen truck at the rear. As he walked, he couldn't quite shake the feeling that someone was watching him.

Stan thrust his hands into his pockets and inhaled deeply as he wove between the trees. Breakfast had been ordinary, but at least he was a little bit warmer now. Spotting a man standing alone, he stopped shoulder to shoulder and looked out beyond their foxholes. It was a strange morning, and his nerves were on edge. The

Germans were up to something, that much was certain. But what exactly? *If they're shelling the rear, something must be going to happen,* he thought. And there was the issue of what he'd seen during the previous nights. He remembered the troops and the vehicles, the tanks and artillery, just sitting across the river not far from where he stood. *They're massing for something, but where's our support?*

Nearly lost in thought, Stan let his mind wander for a minute. But then he noticed something. The morning had changed somehow. He rolled his gaze skyward, then it dawned on him: Silence. The artillery had stopped.

A sharp crack pierced the chilly air. A gunshot. Stan twitched instinctively, just a fraction of an inch. His adrenaline shot up.

"Wow, that sounded pretty close." Turning his head, he saw the man next to him on the ground. It took a moment to register the scene. He was lying in the snow, face up, a small round hole above his eye. But before Stan noticed this or the ruddy stain expanding beneath the dead man's skull, a misplaced thought entered his head. *He's the fellow who brought the mail.* Then the sound of running and shouting overtook his senses, and he found himself sprinting toward the front.

Gunfire erupted in the distance, popping viciously like firecrackers in the frigid air. Stan's boots pounded against the ground as he raced for cover. *This is it,* he thought, *we were right all along.* At the edge of his foxhole, he kneeled to jump in. But fifty feet away, in the next hole, he saw a soldier manning a machine gun by himself, struggling to solo a two man job. Stan dashed over and jumped in beside him.

"Here, I'll help."

"Alright," the man replied gratefully, "you fire and I'll feed the belts."

Eyes on the iron sights, Stan gripped the weapon with sweaty palms. His heart was racing from the adrenaline, but an odd serenity had washed over him. And when the first German helmets poked their way above the cliff in front of him, he was ready.

"What are you waiting for? Shoot them!" His buddy sounded nervous.

"Haven't you ever heard that expression?" Stan tried to remember the words, "Don't fire until you see the whites of their eyes."

But his partner was worried. "They're going to get us!"

"No they're not." He turned his head for a moment and gave a reassuring whisper. "They're not going to get us."

He didn't know why, but he felt confident, almost immortal. Nothing could happen to him now. He just knew it.

Almost in affirmation of his mood, the Germans began filing up the hill completely unaware of the Allied foxholes. Many of them held their rifles by the muzzle, slung over their shoulders or poking along like hiking sticks. He couldn't believe it. Only a few yards farther, and they'd be in for a surprise. No – he wouldn't give them the chance.

Stan squeezed the trigger and watched them drop through the muzzle flash.

"Ughhh…" James Angert stirred in his foxhole. "What was that?"

A thunderous crack echoed through the trees. He sat up and rubbed the sleep from his eyes. It was coming from pretty far away. There, again. It sounded like artillery. Wet snow gently plopped down beside him from a pine branch overhead. Something was happening out there.

"What's going on," a GI inquired, poking his head above the frosty ground.

"Maybe the Germans want their hill back," another replied.

James thought back to the skirmish three days earlier, when they'd taken control of a small hill that overlooked their lines. Had the enemy rolled out the big guns in an effort to reclaim it?

His answer came an instant later as a nearby tree exploded into thousands of splinters.

"Incoming! Get down!"

Dozens of helmeted heads retreated into their foxholes as another round struck overhead. Then another. Before they knew it, the forest was ablaze with artillery and mortar fire. Tree bark, splinters, and razor shards of metal sliced through the air, slamming the ground and kicking up great jets of snow. A haze of ice and dirt billowed madly, nearly blinding the soldiers even as they huddled in fear. And James, in the middle of it all, didn't know what to do. In truth, there was nothing he could do. The firepower was overwhelming.

It seemed like hours, but it could only have been minutes. The artillery ceased and the soldiers emerged into the shattered woods one by one. They seemed dazed, wandering about in confusion. James stepped out into the snow and looked around. Barely fifteen yards to the side, he could hear moaning drifting out from a hole. It was his buddy; he was bleeding from the neck and a medic was grappling with the wound. James looked ahead past the mangled trees and churned-up dirt, into the thick forest ahead. There were shapes moving out there. Then word came along that the Germans were moving in force, and he realized what he was seeing. The line company GIs were retreating towards him. This could only be bad news.

John Gallagher gritted his teeth and shivered in the frigid air. What was happening? As he trudged through the packed snow, following a tiny road that was cratered with frozen mud, he listened to the commotion all around. Someone was firing artillery, and it sounded like they were hitting German positions. But rumors were filtering in that it was the other way around – that the enemy was shooting them. This didn't seem logical to him. The weather was freezing, the woods were covered in snow, and it was a just a horrible time and place to mount an assault. So what were the Germans up to?

As he pondered the question his unit came upon a group of prisoners moving in the opposite direction. They hugged the side of the rood to make room, but it was so narrow that John passed within just a few feet of them. He was shocked. The German POWs looked terrible. They were frozen, haggard, and downtrodden, and many of them seemed either too young or too old to be in the army. John was twenty three, and to him some of them looked like boys.

A particularly loud salvo rocked the woods ahead. John shivered, mostly from the cold – but his apprehension was growing. As they walked, he couldn't quite shake the feeling that they weren't prepared for whatever it was they were getting into. *I hope I'm wrong,* he thought.

Only a few hundred yards ahead, Martin Dorminy was already experiencing the brunt of the Germans' fury. Crouching in a foxhole, he flinched as something pounded into a nearby tree and exploded in a cloud of splinters. *Was that a tank round?* His heart was racing. *Where the hell are they coming from?* Gunfire cut through the air, shattering tree limbs and kicking up a storm of wood chips. It was chaos.

"They're behind us," someone shouted in a trembling voice.

Martin swept chunks of dirt from his helmet and squinted back into friendly territory, but couldn't make anything out through the haze of snow vapor and debris raining down.

"Look out!"

Another tree burst just out of lethal range, peppering the snow with shrapnel. Martin's heart leaped into this throat. *It was a tank!* He could see it now, a silhouette prowling in the woods ahead. There were other shapes too – infantry rushing back and forth. It almost looked like... *No, it can't be. Are they advancing?*

"Back! Get back!" The men up front had reversed and were storming in the opposite direction.

What's going on? John Gallagher was terrified by now. *First one way, then the other!* He flinched as a tree exploded overhead.

"They're coming through! Fall back!"

John was being overtaken by the men ahead of him as they scrambled to avoid being shot. Bullets flicked through the air, and he thought he saw muzzle flashes just above the ground. He turned and started shuffling backwards, retreating in his own footsteps. *Are those Germans?* Silhouettes were rising out of the icy haze – menacing figures bristling with weapons. They had to be Germans. He quickened his pace.

John and his buddies retreated to a safer position, where they were ordered to dig in. But even after they'd cleared the snow away, the soil was frozen solid. As he stood there, cracking the ground with his entrenching tool, listening to explosions in the woods around him, he couldn't help but feel guilty. Some of his unit had been cut off. *Because we didn't get there in time,* he thought. *We failed them.*

His hands ached from cold and from the impact of the shovel. He just kept digging.

"Take along what you can," the order stated clearly, "and destroy anything you leave behind." James felt strange scuttling the materials he'd so carefully kept an eye on before. Here he was, aiming his rifle at a large spool of communication wire as if it were the enemy. At least it wouldn't shoot back. He squeezed off a few rounds, tearing the wire apart, then turned toward the rear. The radio jeep was well on its way already. Looks like he'd have to walk.

The retreat was going smoothly except for one thing: nobody seemed to be in charge any more. James didn't know where any of the officers were, and neither did anyone around him. So they simply walked. They pointed themselves back towards where they'd come from and began marching through the snow. Their destination was a place that began with a K. *Krin... Krinkelt?* He tried to remember the name. It rang a bell, but James couldn't place it on a map. He just hoped it was on the way.

James paused to catch his breath. They were digging again... always digging. Tired as he was, he had little choice but to obey orders. A lieutenant he didn't know had gathered them up and ordered entrenchments dug facing the town church. If and when the Germans came through here the GIs would need some protection. So there they were, chipping away at the frozen soil once more. Looking around, he realized how sparse their forces were. Infantry with rifles composed the bulk of what he saw nearby. If the enemy decided to roll tanks into the line, there was little to stop them. He hoped this wouldn't happen. He wasn't sure he could stand to retreat again.

A bitter chill cut through Stan Blazejewski's clothing, and even in the windless shelter of his foxhole, the night air was intolerably cold. He sat alone, listening to the creaking of trees and the howling breeze, a snow-packed canteen beneath his legs. It seemed logical that if he was going to lose body heat, at least he could put it to some use. By morning he'd have something to drink, though that was little comfort at the moment. Wincing through chapped lips, he looked down to pick at his soggy socks and tried to take his mind off his fluttering nerves. But somehow it only made him feel worse. How many days was it now? Six? Seven? He could hardly keep track any more. They were all the same – sitting and waiting, shooting Germans, dodging grenades, then more waiting. And there was the cold, ever present, slowly draining their will to fight. He hated it more than the hunger.

A sharp crack caught his attention and he risked a peek above the edge of his foxhole. There were lights in the distance, moving slowly between the trees. Red, yellow, green, jittering back and forth as they went. The Germans were always on the move and there was nothing he could do about it. He had learned quickly to be discreet; unless the enemy was right on top of him, it was better not to draw fire. With a nervous sigh he settled back into the hole and brought a hand to his helmet, fingering a crease on the side where something had struck him earlier. *Probably a bullet,* he thought. *Lucky.* They were all lucky, in a way. Lucky to be alive still, no matter how miserable it was. But the enemy was out there, pushing slowly forward. And from his lonely foxhole in the dark forest night, Stan wondered how much longer they could endure.

"Shh, stay down!" There was an engine idling nearby. It sounded like a tank, and it sounded close. James could feel his heartbeat against the grimy material of his shirt. It almost threatened to give him away, to alert the enemy of his presence. But the rush of blood was only in his ears, of course. For all he knew, the Germans didn't even know he was there.

Someone muttered something, the words muffled and unintelligible as they passed overhead from a nearby hole. Straining to hear, James poked his head a tiny way above the frozen soil. Silence. Only the wintry night sounds met his ears. And, of course, the grumbling purr of the German vehicle sitting barely 200 yards from his hole. He squinted into the darkness and swallowed the rising lump in his throat. It was certainly some kind of enemy tank, though he couldn't make out what type. Of course, he realized, it didn't really matter. It was perched upon the road over by the church, its barrel aiming somewhere over their heads. It wasn't moving. Did it see them?

James slunk back down into his hole and gripped the rifle by his side. It felt useless, and of course, it nearly was. If that tank moved up any farther, they'd need something bigger to tackle it. It seemed unlikely that anyone had a bazooka lying around. He had barely finished this thought when a startling crack pierced the calm. It was jarring and horrible in the still night. Nearly jumping out of his skin, he realized that the tank had fired its gun. But there was no impact, no shuddering vibration as the shell struck its target. Could they be aiming at something beyond the town? His heart was pounding again, harder than before. Once more James risked a peek over the edge of his hole. The German tank hadn't moved an inch. It was just sitting there like a dumb metal beast. It fired again and he flinched. But the shell went screaming past into the woods. He dropped back down and cracked a trembling smile. The nearsighted tank was firing over their heads at a target outside the town. It didn't see them, at least not yet. James closed his eyes and said a quiet prayer.

Joe Yourkavitch took another step backwards into the wet snow, boots slipping on the packed layers of dirt and ice beneath the surface. Rifle shouldered, he focused past the iron sights and squinted into the chaotic mess before him. A vast sheet of icy mist, kicked up by relentless mortar fire, hung between him and his targets. Mixing with the low storm clouds and swirling snowfall, it obscured his gaze and made friend and foe look alike. He could see shapes in among the trees, but it was impossible to tell to whom they belonged. All he knew was that the Germans were coming, and they were moving fast.

Cut off from support, Joe's unit was hopelessly lost and surrounded. Stumbling backwards through the winter-torn forest, firing desperately as they retreated, they were bleeding men and supplies by the minute. They were encircled completely, gunfire and terrible sounds rushing in from everywhere at once. Everything was cold, loud, and confusing. Joe didn't even know who was in charge any more. Medics ran about madly, doing what they could to retrieve the wounded left behind in the retreat. The dead and dying were everywhere. It was horrible. The Germans were pushing in from all sides, chipping away at the Americans' little pocket of control. Inch by inch, yard by yard, they lost ground. This should have been a fighting retreat, but it felt more like a massacre.

Suddenly everyone stopped moving. The men began jamming together as those in the rear turned and shuffled aimlessly back and forth. Confusion swept through the line and Joe felt a chilly pit in his stomach. This could only mean one thing. The Germans had come up behind them. There was nowhere left to go now, nowhere to retreat to. Bullets whizzed between the trees, kicking up splinters and dirt. A few yards away, a GI dropped bleeding into the snow. *This is it*, Joe thought, *they've got us*. Only one question hung in his mind: would he live through the day?

"Strip your weapons! Bury them!" One of the officers was barking orders nearby. He couldn't be serious. On all sides, frightened GIs looked around with wide eyes. Some of them obeyed, removing clips from their rifles and tossing them into the snow. Others hesitated, unable to accept what was happening. Some watched with shock and confusion while others seemed willing to fight to the end. But before long, they all followed the orders until every last man had surrendered his arms. And Joe stood with them, shivering and squinting into the woody distance, watching silhouettes bear down on them through the haze. All he could do was wait and pray.

Nick Phillips paused for a moment, dropping a knee to the snow in an effort to catch his breath. His heart was pounding, more from fear than from anything else, and he felt sweat soaking through his shirt. It was a hell of a thing to be sweating and freezing all at once, lost in the forest and hunted by the enemy. Staying alive was priority number one, and that meant avoiding the Germans at all costs.

Where was he? Was this Clairvaux? It looked familiar, but in the dark and from this direction he couldn't be certain. They'd been on the run for hours. Or was it days? He hadn't slept in so long, he couldn't tell. Adrenaline was the only thing keeping him going. The men behind him were whispering. He thought he heard the word "German," and immediately tensed up. Creeping low along the frozen mud, his little band of fugitives moved forward to a Y in the road. They were on the low side of the path; the other cut sharply away and up an incline, leading away from the town. It was definitely familiar. The edge of town was just ahead, past a clump of trees and around the bend. The little pub where they used to go at night was there, too. Or at least he hoped it still was. He closed his eyes and tried to remember what it looked like. The tables, the chairs, bottles of wine... but it only reminded him of the hunger gnawing at his gut.

"Shh, listen!" One of the GIs suddenly hissed at the others and the group fell silent. Something was coming at them on the road. He could hear an engine not far off. Then a pair of lights rounded the bend ahead and his heart skipped a beat. *Germans!* It was a convoy – a truck, a few smaller vehicles, and some other shapes he couldn't make out in the dark. They were heading right for Nick's group, and there was nowhere to hide. So they did the only thing they could – they jumped off the road into the shadows and pressed themselves up against the dirt incline. And there they waited.

As the German convoy approached the intersection, Nick said a silent prayer. At best, they would take the high road and pass by the Americans, provided they didn't see the men huddling in the darkness. At worst, they would turn onto the lower path and run directly into them. There was no way the GIs could fight, and nowhere for them to run. So they waited, barely breathing, not daring to move as the enemy approached. Closer, closer... would they take the high road? Nick wanted to run, to just give into the adrenaline and bolt for the tree line. But he knew he wouldn't make it. They'd shoot him in the back before he got halfway.

The Germans dove up to within a few meters and paused. Nick held his breath. Then, wheels crunching in the snow, they turned and continued up the higher road. He gave a deep sigh and gave quiet thanks to whoever was watching out for him.

The German tank sat quietly in the frozen mud. It looked mostly undamaged and its unhappy crew was standing nearby under Allied guard. *Must have run out of ammo*, James Angert thought as he passed, *maybe it's the one from last night.* As he made his way down the pitted dirt road, he surveyed the men around him. Nobody familiar anywhere. Still no sign of his officers. Little military discipline remained as the GIs plodded along listlessly. They were cold, tired, and hungry. And since they were still retreating, it stood to reason that the enemy was on their heels.

"Hey!" A man came jogging up from behind James. It was Charles Vaughan, bleary eyed and shivering. They exchanged greetings and kept moving with the others. It was nice to see a familiar face, but there was little to be said. So they walked and walked. *Will it ever end?*

"So what do you think?" James Angert looked down at the sleeping bag stretched out on the floor of the hay loft. It looked tiny and sad in the flickering lamp light, but it was all they had to keep warm.

"Only one way to find out." Charles Vaughan bent down and poked a foot into the bag. "Come on."

Thirty seconds and a few frustrated grunts later, the two men found themselves with three legs and half a torso wedged inside. It seemed their grand plan to share the single bag would have to be abandoned.

"It's   not   going   to   work."   Charles   looked disappointed. "Guess we'll take turns."

So they chose their shifts and laid down on the floor, one cold and the other colder.

"G'night, buddy."

"Night."

The wind howled in the darkness outside, blowing specks of snow in through the cracks in the barn. *At least I'm under a roof tonight,* James thought as he lay there. And he suddenly felt bad for the thousands of men who, at this very moment, were shivering in the frigid night, slumbering fitfully in their holes. Maybe having to share a sleeping bag wasn't so terrible after all.

Martin Dorminy's clothing was soaked and caked with ice. For the third night in a row, he was lying in the snow, shivering uncontrollably. It was as much from the cold as it was from the fear. Determined to keep the doomed Americans from moving, the German machine gunners fired sporadic bursts over their heads. Anyone who stood up was dead, so there they lay. Splintered tree chips and dirt rained down hour after hour as sleep eluded them. It was the worst night of his life.

"Martin?" A hushed voice, its Southern drawl unmistakable, drifted in from the darkness nearby.

"Yeah, buddy?"

"My bag," It was his friend, Tennessee. A boy from the hills who stuck with Martin through thick and thin. His voice held an eerie calm. "I have a lot of cigarettes in my bag," he whispered, "if you want to take them."

"You hang onto those. Might come in handy." Martin swallowed a lump in his throat.

"But if something happens, you should take them."

The crack of an MG42 cut him off. Martin felt pine needles tapping against his helmet as the sound of the gun faded away.

"Tennessee?"

"Yeah?"

"When we get out of here, maybe I'll take just a few." He closed his eyes and tried to block out the cold.

The next day was brutal. Gunfire. It never ceased. Martin scrambled through the icy mess of shell craters and debris, keeping his head low in an effort to avoid the bullets hissing past. He was going the wrong way. As everyone else steadily retreated, he was running towards the enemy into the hellish wasteland between the front lines. It was a corpse-strewn nightmare.

Martin dropped to his knees next to a wounded GI. Another medic was already there, administering aid to the thrashing man. Beside him, lying crumpled and bloody in the snow, was a makeshift litter fashioned out of two field jackets zipped together. It was crude, but there wasn't much else they could do. Most of the medical equipment was long gone, captured or destroyed in the retreat. So they did what they could, grabbing the man and pulling him onto the jackets. But it was too late. He wasn't unconscious, he was gone. The other medic swore and moved on. Martin frowned. How many was it now? How many had died in these woods? He couldn't even keep count. Another mortar round burst, spewing dirt and snow into the air. Screaming, a soldier fell to the ground nearby.

Dodging gunfire, Martin sprinted up to the fallen man and slid feet first into the snow beside him, kicking up a heap of bloody dirt and ice.

Tennessee! No! It was his buddy, his best friend. He was badly hurt, his chest heaving with great shuddering breaths. Blood oozed from the tattered cloth covering his stomach, and he winced at Martin's touch.

"Martin," he wheezed painfully.

"Yeah, buddy?"

"Pull me up." His eyes were focused on something out of reach, and it seemed he was searching the sky with his gaze. He tried to lift an arm, tried to grasp Martin's hand, but he couldn't find the strength. "Pull me up so I can see the trees."

"Alright, Tennessee," he choked on the words. "Here we go." His voice was a whisper as he tucked his arms beneath the dying man and lifted him up onto his lap.

"Trees," Tennessee sputtered feebly, "look at the trees." Martin craned his neck, following his friend's eyes, and as he did time itself seemed to melt away. For a beautiful instant the war was invisible; the chaos pulled back like a curtain and in its place serenity bloomed. The forest lay silent and inviting beneath a blanket of snow, its trees stretching like fingers toward the heavens. A breeze billowed through the canopy above, tossing the branches in gentle waves as powdery snow flitted and glistened in the air. But the moment was fleeting. With a final shudder, Tennessee went limp in his arms and was gone. A tear rolled down Martin's cheek as the wails of battle came rushing back all at once. He lowered his friend into the snow. Nineteen years old. He loved the hills and the trees, and now he was with them.

Someone was screaming nearby. Martin moved on.

Tennessee was dead. The men were broken. Germans surrounded them. Martin was having the worst day of his life. When it became obvious that there was no hope of escaping, the remnants of his unit grouped together and prepared to be taken prisoner. *Or worse,* he thought, *what if they kill us?*

Four of his buddies approached him with a plan.

"We're going to break loose, sneak through the lines, and escape on our own."

It sounded like suicide.

"No way, they'd kill us for certain," Martin replied.

"We could really use you as a medic. You won't come with us?"

He refused and they left. Back in training Martin had been taught that, if you were captured, your odds of survival were about fifty-fifty. *I'd rather take that chance,* he decided, *than get shot in the back running away.*

One of the sergeants came trudging by. "I want you, you, and you," he ordered, "We're going over to talk to those Germans."

Martin was too tired and scared to obey.

"With all due respect, you're crazy, sir. I'm not going over there. Look!"

He pointed off into the haze where GIs were still being picked off by sporadic gunfire. The sergeant huffed and stormed off. They never saw him again.

Within hours the entire regiment – or what was left of it - was lined up and disarmed, waiting for the Germans to come. As Martin stood there in the snow, sweating despite the cold, he could only imagine what was in store for them all.

Cold. Bitter, unceasing cold. It crept in on the breeze and chilled to the bone, cutting through wet clothes and soggy socks. Joe Yourkavitch, walking on frigid, unfeeling feet, gritted his teeth and tried to endure. How long were they walking? How long since the order to abandon their weapons? He couldn't even tell any more. Everything since then was a blur, a single unending event marked by cold and misery. Now here he was, marching through the snow in an endless column, surrounded by armed Germans and unable to rest.

A shot rang out ahead, piercing the relative calm. Joe flinched and sunk his hands deeper into his pockets.

"Ugh..." A sickly, skinny guy, Private Lengel, let out a low moan nearby.

Joe turned and grabbed the man's arm.

"Come on, buddy, you'll make it."

He draped Lengel's arm over his shoulders and helped support him as they walked along, stumbling on the uneven ground. There was another shot ahead, and he felt the weak man beside him shudder at the sound. A body lay at the side of the road, blood steaming in the cold as they passed it by. *They're killing the stragglers*, he realized, and he gripped Lengel's arm tightly.

"Whatever you do," he whispered, voice trembling, "keep moving. Don't stop for anything."

The captured Americans hadn't eaten for at least three days and they were miserable. Now the Germans were shooting anyone who couldn't keep up. It was an awful thought.

Joe suddenly heard someone singing ahead. A man's voice, wavering but beautiful, drifted back on the breeze. He was singing a Christmas carol. *Silent night, holy night...* Someone else started in. *All is calm, all is bright...* A tear rolled down Joe's cheek and he joined them.

As the song carried down the line, the prisoners started singing one after another, their voices soaring with emotion. The Germans didn't try to stop them.

James Angert swallowed hard. Following the Colonel's orderlies on foot, radio strapped to his back, he wondered if volunteering had been a dumb idea. Battalion headquarters wanted to know the situation up front, so the Colonel decided to personally observe the fighting. He'd asked for a radio man and, naturally, James had volunteered. It seemed like a decent idea at the time, but now he wasn't so sure. They were still a football field away and already bullets were whizzing by. He tugged nervously at the chin strap on his helmet and made a mental note to keep his head down.

Twenty yards from the front line, the Colonel stopped and took cover behind a hedge while his orderlies dug in. Thick as it was, the hedge was no match for bullets. So with this thought, James followed suit. Grabbing an entrenching tool, he began chopping away at the frozen soil as shells poured in around them. Then, when it was just deep and wide enough to crouch down inside, he jumped in with the radio. The top of his helmet was a few inches beneath ground level. Ten feet away, the Colonel took similar cover as he assessed the situation from his own hole. Poking his head up a bit, James could see him staring ahead through the hedge. Following his gaze, he noticed the line of GI's barely a stone's throw away, fighting from cover in their foxholes out in front. Bullets were flying in both directions, but it seemed the Germans had a leg up in the mortar department. Enemy rounds popped through the trees at random, exploding violently and with little warning.

A tiny voice came over the radio and James brought the handset to his ear. It was Charles Vaughan. He and

Leonard Sharbaugh were manning the radio back at headquarters, waiting for the Colonel's observations. But he gave none. James made small talk for a short while and waited. There was little he could do except keep his head down. Before long the sound of artillery hammered loudly in the distance, so he squeezed down as far as he could and reported back to Charles. But the line suddenly went dead. He checked the radio. No damage. It must have been something on their end.

"Hey, answer me!" James broke protocol and began shouting into the radio receiver. "What the hell is the matter back there?" But there was no reply. Not even static. Granted, there wasn't much to say – the colonel didn't seem to have anything to relay to the rear – but that wasn't the point. Something was wrong back there.

After an eternity of frustrated shouting, a wavering voice came over the radio. "This is Simoneit," it said, "You and I are in communication." James felt a pit in his stomach; something must have happened to the other guys.

A mortar round suddenly slammed into the hedge less than six feet from James' hole, tearing a ragged breach in the wall of brambles. Dirt flew into the air and rained down on him, pebbles clinking as they struck his helmet. Brushing snow and earth from his shoulders, he poked his head up and cast a sideways glance. The colonel, visibly agitated, was gesturing to his orderlies. Then, without so much as a word, he climbed out of his hole and began retreating from the front. James, left behind, suddenly felt very alone. So with little else to do, he hurried behind the others.

Back at headquarters, a very concerned looking Simoneit intercepted James.

"What the hell happened to the radio back there," James asked, "Why wouldn't anyone answer?"

Simoneit just shook his head and took James by the arm. Without speaking a word, he led him to a ragged hole in the ground flanked by bushes. Inside lay a mess of destroyed radio equipment covered in shreds of flesh. James' insides turned to ice when he realized what it was. Vaughan and Sharbaugh were gone. It only dawned on him later that, back on the ridge, for the better part of ten minutes, he'd been shouting at dead men.

Gabe Fieni had a huge smile on his face.

"Fieni, Fieni, Fieni..." The GI with the mail sack was getting irritated as he handed Gabe a stack of Christmas cards one at a time. "Fieni, Fieni..." He checked the name on each envelope before handing it over. Then, flustered, he gave up. "Look, these are all yours."

Gabe laughed and took the pile in his arms. This latest batch pushed the count well over two hundred. Chuckling as he walked, he thought about what his brother had said in a letter just a few weeks ago. *Mom and pop told the church congregation to send you cards.* It was hilarious, but it really meant the world to him. It was a reminder that, even though he was freezing his butt off thousands of miles from home, people still cared about him. Even strangers – people he'd never met – cared enough to send their regards.

"Hey big shot!" One of his buddies saw him carrying the stack of cards. "What are you, the mayor of Pottstown?"

The guys chuckled. It was a big joke by now, though Gabe didn't mind the attention. At least they had something to laugh about. *That's the key,* he always said, *just keep on smiling and you'll make it.*

Martin Dorminy coughed, his lungs aching from the cold. With a disgusted sigh, he shifted about in the stinking pile of manure clumped around his legs. There was no way to get comfortable. The Germans had thrown him into a box car with God knows how many other prisoners. Crammed in like sardines, they tried to kick the animal droppings toward the sides of the car. As more prisoners arrived, however, they were jammed closer and closer to the walls until Martin was sitting in nearly two feet of manure. The biting cold, his wet clothes, and the thick layer of horse feces combined to cause more misery than he'd previously thought possible. Could it get any worse?

The Germans were walking back and forth outside the box car. Martin could hear their voices. But then, in the distance, he heard something else. An engine. It sounded like a plane. He twisted around and looked through a slit in the wall. There was something flying in low over the horizon, beyond the freight yard roofs. The Germans heard it too. They were pointing and shouting, running back and forth and raising rifles to the sky. Martin's heart leaped into his throat. The Allies were coming! An excited murmur passed through the car and the prisoners pressed their eyes against the walls. He saw several fighters racing along toward the train. Flickers of flame spat from their wings and bullets started tearing through the German infantry. Some of them returned fire, shooting wildly into the air. The planes passed directly overhead and swung around hard for another pass. But this time they fired on the train. In a moment of horrifying realization, it occurred to Martin that there was no way for the Allies to know what lie inside the box cars. For all they knew, the prisoners were crates of ammunition or supplies. And they had no way to escape.

Screams erupted from the next car down, mingling with the sickening crunch of splintering wood and the clatter of bullets on metal. Men were dying. The planes kept firing, striking targets in the freight yard. Then they came for another pass at the train. This time they hit Martin's car. Bullets streaked through the sides, puncturing men and kicking up manure. He saw one prisoner take a bullet to the head. His body, pinned against the wall, jerked violently as both eyeballs dangled and swung from the sockets. Martin had never seen anything like it in his life.

Martin shivered as he walked, arms full, towards the box car near the end of the line. Passing a row of corpses, he tried to block out the memory of earlier, when the Germans had made him help pull the casualties from the train. Some were still alive when he drug them from the cars and laid them out on the cement. He couldn't be certain, but it seemed unlikely that any had survived until now. Of course, he had escaped unharmed. Be it through fate or random chance, Martin was one of the lucky ones. Now here he was, playing errand boy for the enemy. He looked down at the thermoses in his arms. The smell of coffee drifted to his nose, and he wrinkled his brow. He hated coffee.

This looked like the place. Martin stopped at a box car with its door open. In the dim light inside, he could make out a number of German soldiers sitting around listlessly. They saw him and motioned for him to enter. So he climbed up and relinquished the coffee. After a moment of awkward silence and stares, they offered him a cup. He hesitated. He didn't really want it, after all, but it was something warm. And besides, they were actually being nice for a change. Maybe it would be best to take advantage of the situation.

Sitting in the dim light of the box car, surrounded by armed Germans, Martin sipped the bitter coffee and stared out into the darkness. Suddenly he remembered something: tonight was Christmas Eve.

Merry Christmas. Well, not quite yet. What a night. Robert Mest sat on the cold ground in a field just outside his engineer supply depot in Belgium. It was impossible to dig a foxhole in the frozen soil, so he'd swept the snow aside and piled it up against the breeze. It was the best he could do. They'd been pulled from the depot and told to watch the skies for paratroopers. Anticipating an attack made him nervous. *Paratroopers are tough in any language,* he thought, *and I'm not really a combat soldier.* He gripped his carbine tightly and tried to ignore the nicotine craving gnawing at his insides. Smoking was forbidden during the blackout, and he was half dead for lack of a cigarette.

Robert thought about the past week. Things had changed since the enemy breakthrough. For one, his German POW laborers were taken away to the west somewhere. *Probably so they don't try to rebel or some nonsense.* He couldn't imagine them giving much trouble, but if the enemy lines drew close anything was possible. Regardless, he'd been doing a lot more heavy lifting lately. With supplies constantly moving east into combat zones – and even to other depots – this meant busier days with fewer workers on hand. But it was nothing compared to what the men on the front lines had to deal with. Robert knew this, and he was proud to be supplying them. *They count on me,* he thought, *They don't know who I am, but I'm the guy who gets their stuff to the front.*

He heard a branch crack in the woods to his right. It was probably just the wind.

Ed Stallman sat in the dark at Bastogne. He was hungry, tired, and sick of fighting off the Germans. They'd been coming at them for days on all sides of the town, probing the Americans' defenses and launching little offensive strikes. *Well, maybe not that little,* he thought. The paratroopers had already pushed back their fair share of infantry and tanks, thanks in part to some sneaky maneuvering. He recalled stringing together makeshift tank traps from AT mines and rope, then pulling them across roads to disable the vehicles so they could plant explosive charges and kill the crews.

This is worse than Market Garden. He sighed and looked up at the sky. It reminded him of parachutes, which reminded him of how badly they needed supplies. *The air drops are supposed to be coming, but when?*

A rumbling in his belly reminded him of the time. Feeling in his pack, his fingers closed around the crackers he'd been saving for three days. Something about them struck him as funny, and he turned to his friend.

"Hey McKinley, guess what?"

"What's that, buddy?"

"It's Christmas dinner!"

McKinley smiled. "Okay, wait 'till I get my two crackers out."

The two men laughed and ate their Christmas cracker feast in the dark. It was all they had for now; hopefully help would come soon.

Paul Fett chewed on a Hershey's Almond Bar and watched the planes moving overhead. It was the last of his Christmas mail, and he savored each chocolaty bite. A friend from home had sent him a whole box of the candy bars, but he'd shared most of them with his buddies. This last one, though... it was a fitting treat for the show before him. Allied planes were out and about, hitting German positions in the woods ahead. It was the first time in a long while, or at least in his memory, that the weather was fair enough for the air support to come out in force. Cold still, at least the skies were clear.

Boom, something shattered in the distance. Some sort of bomb, no doubt. Paul hoped they'd hit something important.

"Who's in charge here?"

Stan cocked his head toward the friendly voice behind him. There was an officer – he looked like a captain – talking to a group of soldiers huddled in the rear. Something was up. It was the captain from the reserve company sent to relieve them. If he was here, did that mean they could leave?

"I can take you out of here."

It was music to his ears. How long had it been? Ten days? Stan could barely keep track of the time. It was all the same: shooting, waiting, shivering. If there was a way out, it was most welcome.

"I can get you out, but we have to go now."

Stan didn't hesitate in the least.

There couldn't have been more than fifty men with them as they left the ridge and began trudging through the snowy night. *Where are the others,* he wondered, *are they dead?* It was impossible to tell, but it put a terrible feeling in his stomach to think that they'd been killed. Some of them were his friends.

It was three in the morning, bitter cold, and pitch black when Stan arrived back in Allied territory. His escape from the ridge had taken at least seven or eight hours, and he was finally reaching his breaking point. *Sleep,* he thought, *I need sleep.* So there were no complaints when his ragged band of soldiers was taken to a schoolhouse and told they could bunk for the night. The captain told them to head inside. Trudging up the stairs, Stan's eyelids grew heavy. Just a few more turns, a few more steps... He flopped down on the third floor and fell asleep almost instantly.

Only three hours later, Stan was jostled awake and rushed downstairs. They were moving out already. Though trying his best, he couldn't eat a thing for breakfast. He felt terrible, and seeing the bacon and eggs sizzling before him was tortuous. *My stomach must be the size of a golf ball by now,* he thought. Ten days without food had taken its toll and he was paying for it now. *Flapjacks!* He noticed the pancakes next to the eggs and cursed his weak body.

"Clean your weapons!" An officer entered the room suddenly and barked an order. "We're taking off!"

Stan gave a sigh and moved away from the food. At least he'd kept the coffee down. *The caffeine should help a little.*

Once outside, the men were loaded on trucks and driven through the snowy woods. Stan's teeth rattled in his head from the vehicle's vibrations on the frozen road. He was used to the halftracks; he wondered if theirs had ever made it to Paris.

Eventually the truck lurched to a stop and the men began piling out into the snow. Stan hopped down, slung his rifle over his shoulder, and rubbed his hands together. The others were moving ahead already, filing along the road towards some murky objective. A place called Bastogne, someone had said. The name meant nothing to him. It was just another dot on a map crawling with Germans. So he got into line and walked. And shivered. And listened. Machine gun fire came drifting in from the haze ahead, and he took a deep breath. Whatever it was, he hoped Bastogne was worth the trouble.

"Go! Move!" Stan's pulse pounded like thunder in his ears as he willed his legs to move faster. Bullets sliced through the air around him from a machine gun emplacement ahead in the trees. He couldn't see it, but it certainly saw him. Left, right, left right... his legs pumped and hammered into the dense snow. *Just a little farther.* The edge of the field was so close. *Can't give up now.* He was beyond exhausted, operating on pure adrenaline and little else. Three hours of sleep after ten freezing days in a foxhole. A bullet whizzed right by his head, hissing like a snake as is passed his ear. *Move!* He focused on the tree line drawing closer with each painful stride. *Almost there!* Something hit the ground in front of him, kicking up plumes of icy snow and nearly tripping him up. But he caught his balance, pushed forward, and made a leap into the trees ahead. Bullets chipped away at the bark for a moment, then retreated back into the field for easier prey. Stan hunched over, his frame heaving as he gulped down air. Men were filtering into the woods, shuffling between the trees and trying to avoid the German gunfire. They were the lucky ones. Some were lying in the field still, cut down by bullets. He could see them where they fell.

From his position, leaning against a tree, hands on knees, Stan's eye caught something startling. He stood upright and grabbed a fistful of his jacket. There were holes in the fabric large enough to poke his fingers through. Bullet holes. *My God,* he thought, glancing back towards the field, *somebody is looking after me.* The machine gun fire had abruptly ceased, and in the eerie silence came the wails of wounded men. He thought of his mother and gave quiet thanks that she didn't know where he was, or what he was doing.

Jerome Merkel stood on a snowy hillside in Belgium, looking down across a frozen creek and into the little town beyond. It was afternoon, and he was enjoying a rare moment of peace with a captain he knew from the artillery division. The forest was quiet for a change; both men savored the calm.

Jerome felt relaxed for the first time in recent memory. No Germans, no artillery, no airplanes – it was a rare treat. So they stood and talked for a while, swapping stories and reminiscing about home. Jerome thought about his family. *I wonder how long it'll be until I see them again.* He sighed and tugged idly at a thin pine branch, snapping it off and pulling the needles out one by one. The town at the base of the hill looked beautiful in the crisp daylight. Stone walls, church steeple, slanting shadows – it was like a painting.

Crack! A gunshot suddenly echoed nearby. Jerome nearly jumped out of his skin. He turned to the captain, pulse racing.

"Hey, we should get out of-"

But he froze. The captain lay in the snow, contorted and bleeding from a hole above his eye. *Oh my God...* Jerome bolted into the trees, weaving back and forth to make himself a difficult target. He could feel eyes digging into his back as he ran. *Don't stop! Keep going!* He was terrified.

Most times, Jerome didn't even consider the fact that he might be killed. He fought, waited, fought some more – it was all just part of being a soldier. But at times like these, during truly dangerous moments, he started to think about life and death. And as he sprinted through the snowy Belgian woods, praying he wouldn't be shot, he began to wonder if he might not make it home.

It wasn't snowing any more, thankfully. But the ground was still frozen solid. Richard Walton gripped his entrenching tool and flinched as a small explosion went off nearby. Someone was blasting little craters to help get the foxholes started. It was startling to hear, but helpful. They'd been dropped off in these God-forsaken woods under cover of darkness and with little direction but to dig. Anything that made it easier was welcome.

Richard dragged the last pine branch into place then stood back and examined his work. The foxhole was covered almost entirely. *Good,* he thought, *now for the finishing touch.* He cleared a small opening and reached down into the hole, retrieving a blanket. They were lucky enough to have two each, so he could afford to put one up top. So he spread it out, covering the branches, then pulled it over the gap as he crouched down inside. It was warmer down there, but not by much. As he huddled on top of the pine needles he'd scooped into the bottom of the hole, he wrapped the second blanket over his shoulders and tried to stop shivering. It would be morning before long, but he couldn't sleep. He was too worked up from the past few days and from imagining what lay ahead. Not long ago he'd been on a truck, racing along through endless fields and forests that all looked alike, poking his head out and never noticing a difference. Luxembourg City was the only notable exception. He recalled the way it looked as they passed through, snow dancing in the streets. It was so different than home. Everything here was. *Wherever this is,* he thought.

Richard's reflection was suddenly interrupted by a rumbling in his gut. More bowel trouble. It came and went, and today was one of the worst ones. Not wanting to soil his carefully constructed foxhole, he jumped up and pushed the makeshift roof away before climbing out and scampering off into the woods. The icy breeze was jarring, and he tried to ignore it as he searched, cursing, for a safe place to relieve himself in the dark.

One of the saddest things Gabe Fieni ever saw was a makeshift hospital in a snowy field in the Belgian woods. He drove a surgical team there and dropped them off, and as he sat in his jeep he was shocked by the suffering on display before him. Hundreds and hundreds of wounded men – maybe even thousands – lay in rows upon the ground with just enough space to walk between them. The white ground was stained with blood where the overworked medics tramped back and forth in endless frustration. There were just too many injuries to take care of.

Gabe recalled the times he'd spent in surgery as a technician. The doctors often joked around and carried on for hours at a time as they stitched up one casualty after another. He never thought this was appropriate behavior, but as he sat gazing at the field of wounded men it suddenly made sense. *This is what they have to look forward to,* he realized, *other people's unending misery.*

With a melancholy glance, he turned the jeep around and started back to headquarters.

Stan Blazejewski's feet felt like they were frozen solid. The only feeling in them was a constant piercing ache from the cold. He winced and hobbled along as his company marched along. They'd been pushed back just a few hours ago, but were moving forward once again. He didn't know how much more he could take.

A jeep came bounding up behind him and he heard a voice.

"Hey buddy, you don't look too good." It was a medic.

Stan turned and responded. "It's my feet. They're frozen."

"Come on, I'll take you over to battalion aid station and we'll see what your problem is."

What a relief. Stan climbed into the jeep and they zoomed off towards the rear.

As he soon found out, his feet were in pretty bad shape. Though there was still some circulation in them, they were purplish and numb. When the doctor stuck a needle into Stan's heel, he didn't even feel it. This, combined with extreme exhaustion and malnutrition, was enough to get him taken off the line. So he was taken to an air evacuation hospital and flown back to England.

Stan couldn't have been gladder.

The horizon was barely visible beneath the cloudy, moonless sky. Richard Walton squinted into the darkness. He could make out a straight line of trees meeting the snow just a few hundred yards across a firebreak cut through the forest ahead. But the night played tricks on his mind. Was there movement on the other side? He thought back to the night before, when they'd bumped into a German patrol out here. They'd only fired five or ten shots, but that was enough. He hoped they wouldn't find anything tonight.

"You see that tree over there? The tall one on the horizon?" The first in command was talking quietly and pointing a finger out across the clearing. "Go over there and see if you can find anybody on our left flank."

Richard swore under his breath as his group of six broke off and stepped away from the tree line. Chances were they'd be out until daybreak, and they'd have to cross the firebreak to get back. But then it would be light, and there might be snipers. *Nothing I can do about it now*, he thought, and he fell into place near the end of the patrol line. Picking their way past fallen trees and frozen stumps, nobody said a word. But he knew they were thinking the same thing he was: *We have a long night ahead of us.*

He was right. The little patrol wandered through the tangled woods for hours in search of enemy activity, jumping at shadows and unexpected sounds along the way. Eventually the eastern sky began to glow and the GIs realized how long they'd been gone. So, quickening their pace, they hurried to complete the patrol.

Snow crunched softly under Richard's boots as he stared straight ahead. With nothing to see but trees and deep shadows, he focused his attention on his ears as he walked. Cracking branches. Footsteps. The occasional burst of a gun far away. These were ordinary noises. He was looking for something unusual. Patrols could be boring or terrifying, depending on what you found. But it was always tense. He hoped, at the very least, the remainder of this outing would be uneventful.

"Did you hear that?"

"Shh! Listen!"

The point man slowed his pace and they all pricked their ears. He could hear it, too: the faint sound of metal tapping metal, probably a mess kit. They crept along the tiny path, following a set of tire tracks into the murky dawn. Richard wondered how deep they'd moved into the enemy lines. Probably not far, though the idea of a static front was almost absurd. They'd moved so much and so often, it didn't seem entirely impossible that they're return later to find the enemy in their foxholes. But still, there was that noise ahead.

"Germans!"

A hushed whisper passed along the line. There were people out in the trees, and they weren't speaking English. He could hear them laughing and eating.

A rustle from behind caught his attention. A German soldier had tripped his way out of the woods onto the path and was standing dumbfound in the snow. The GI behind Richard acted on instinct, raising his rifle and pulling the trigger. A shot rang out but missed. Then his weapon jammed and he swore furiously. The German panicked and began fumbling with his Mauser, tugging at the bolt. But Richard was faster. He stepped into position and squeezed off a shot. The German fell dead. Off in the woods nearby a dog started barking and the enemy laughter had stopped. Shaken, the men turned and began running. They dashed off into the trees, leaving a line of six tracks past the dead man in the snow.

Morning was creeping higher by the minute, blanketing the trees in soft light and brightening the shadows. This was a dangerous thing. Richard's patrol jogged quickly along, darting from tree to tree and trailing a ragged patch of footprints behind them. He breathed quickly, worn out from the long night of searching in the dark. They had left the path behind and were slogging their way toward the fire break. He could see it now, just ahead, a bright spot beyond the trees. Would there be Germans?

At the edge of the woods they all stopped, hesitant. The coast was clear, or so it seemed. And the sun was low on the horizon, so there were shadows still deep enough to hide in. They had to get back and there was no other way. So, taking long breaths, they dashed into the clearing and began zigzagging across the open ground. It was a nerve-wracking move. Richard could feel eyes boring into the back of his head; could feel the enemy's gaze upon his neck. It felt horrible. *It's just in my mind. Keep going!* The edge of the fire break was so close. He gritted his teeth and ran faster. Twenty yards, fifteen, ten... They were almost into the woods. Five yards, then...

A sharp crack and a ringing in his ears. He stumbled forward and fell to the ground. Rough hands grabbed his jacket and he felt himself being dragged into the shadows. His helmet was laying in the snow a few feet away, a jagged coil of metal torn from its surface and protruding like a horn. He raised a hand to his head, felt the gash in his wool knit cap and a tiny trickle of blood upon his scalp. *Oh my God*, he thought, *am I dead?* But he was very much alive. He was sniped in the head, but by some miracle the bullet skirted his skull and went blasting out of the helmet.

On a snowy day in mid-January, James Angert stepped out from behind a clump of trees into a clearing near his base camp on the Elsenborn Ridge. A colonel was waiting ahead with something in his hand. He approached the officer and saluted.

Confirming James' name and rank, he reached out and pinned a Bronze Star on his jacket. "For meritorious achievement in connection with military operations against the enemy from 16 to 21 December 1944, in Belgium," he said.

James swallowed hard, taken back by the commendation. What had he done to earn it? *We were all out there*, he thought, *I can't be the only one to get this.* Of course he wasn't, but at the moment he felt the spotlight upon him. It made him proud but also a little uncomfortable. *Maybe it was that radio duty with the colonel.*

James didn't understand why he'd earned a Bronze Star. He also didn't feel particularly special. None of the men who fought at the Bulge thought of themselves as heroes; they simply did what they were trained to do.

8

FLYING THE HUMP
CHINA BURMA INDIA

"Like toys, the planes were tossed around in a deluge of rain or in a howling snow storm, ice driving hard against the windshield, forming on the wings and props and in the carburetors, unimaginable turbulence... It was challenging and frightening..."

Carl Constein, China Burma India, 1944

The China Burma India, or CBI, Theatre of Operations was a strategically important yet often overlooked area of conflict during world war two. The United States and Great Britain, who were fighting the Japanese, were assisting the Chinese resistance to the Japanese invasion of China, and also protecting India from Japanese attack. Commanding these forces were U.S. General Joseph "Vinegar Joe" Stillwell, British General Sir Archibald Wavell, and Admiral Lord Louis Mountbatten.

The Japanese sought to defeat China and invade India via Burma. Burma provided the back door into China for both sides of the conflict, and the main avenue for Japan's attack into British India. Incidentally, this support of China kept eight hundred thousand Japanese troops busy and unavailable to fight against the Americans in the Pacific Theatre.

Most of the ground and air combat occurred in the isolated jungle and mountainous areas of Burma. With the Japanese in control of the coast of China, the Allies needed to use the port of Rangoon in Burma to bring supplies and equipment to the Chinese. From there supplies were taken overland on the Burma Road to Chinese forces led by General Chiang Kai Shek, in Kunming. This route also brought supplies to the volunteer U.S. air group in China and Burma known as the Flying Tigers led by Claire Chennault.

In March of 1942 when the Japanese captured Rangoon, and soon after the southern half of the Burma Road, the Allies could no longer supply China over land. With little time to waste, unarmed American C46 Commandos and C47 Dakotas began to airlift supplies and equipment into China from bases near Ledo, Assam Province, in northeastern India, over the Himalayan Mountains. This dangerous 500-mile route over the highest mountains in the world, in the worst weather conditions imaginable, became known as the "Hump." Due to severe weather, Japanese air attacks, impossible visibility, and equipment that failed in sub-zero temperatures, the loss of over five hundred planes and thirteen hundred pilots and crew members would be suffered before the Allies regained control of the overland route. This wouldn't occur until January of 1945.

On Sunday, December 7, 1941, Jack Benny was performing the second half of a two-part radio program, *Dr. Jekyll and Mr. Hyde*, and Arthur Youse was settled comfortably into an old upholstered chair in the family's living room. He chuckled along with Benny's antics, hanging onto every word from his favorite entertainer. But the broadcast was abruptly interrupted by an anxious report: Pearl Harbor had been attacked. Annoyed by the disruption, Arthur listened to the grim news but didn't quite realize the significance of the event. So for the rest of the day he put the whole thing out of his mind.

When he arrived at work the next morning, Arthur found everyone discussing the attack on Pearl Harbor. He felt awkward not being able to contribute; all he could do was complain that the Jack Benny Show had been interrupted. Eighteen-year-old Arthur didn't know what the war was all about. At the time it seemed like a small event, barely worth his attention. He just didn't realize the significance of what was happening in the world.

In the space of a year his understanding of current events grew considerably, until in October of 1942 his feelings were quite changed. So he did what seemed right: he enlisted in the army. It wasn't because he thought he'd be drafted, but rather because he'd come to believe so strongly in freedom. Much of this was the doing of his father, a former marine. He knew that freedom had to be earned, and sometimes the only way to do that was to go out and fight for it. His father had taught him well.

The army wasted no time in sending Arthur to Atlantic City for basic training. It couldn't have been better, he thought. He lived in hotels right on the beach. Quickly finishing the training, Arthur's unit left town in one of the worst snow storms Atlantic City had seen in years. Arthur remembers the squall was so heavy that each man had to hold on to the soldier in front so they wouldn't get lost. To Arthur, this was just one big adventure. He'd had a good time so far; basic training was like being in the Boy Scouts. And being away from home wasn't too difficult. But it wasn't so easy for some; one of Arthur's fellow recruits couldn't handle army life and jumped off a third floor balcony to his death.

When asked by the army where he wanted to go, Arthur's reply was firm. "Air Force - ground crew member." He knew he was lucky to be given a choice, and he was pleased to be shipped to radio school at Traux Field in Wisconsin. There he'd be trained as a radio repairman, followed by a few weeks of training for overseas duty in New Mexico to hone his infantry skills. Arthur's brief time in New Mexico was productive; he'd trained for the infantry and had a little fun, too.

Basic training under his belt, Arthur boarded a converted bomber in Miami, Florida in June of 1943 for shipment to Africa. The bomber took off and headed south for a brief refueling stop in Brazil, then headed for a final refueling on Ascension Island before flying to Cairo.

Arthur never showed much interest in ancient history, but he found the sights and sounds of Cairo a fascinating distraction. And visiting the pyramids made him realize that these great wonders were something very special after all. He and a buddy even climbed up on a camel and sat to have their photo taken.

Arthur enjoyed his brief visit to Egypt, but he was most impressed by something he had witnessed from the window of the bomber that brought him to Cairo. He saw a rainbow, but it was a complete circle off in the distance – three hundred and sixty degrees.

One more refueling and the bomber that carried Arthur to war left Egypt behind and flew to Karachi, India. Because of an error in his military occupational specialty report, Arthur flew on to the Chabua Airfield, in the Assam Valley in northeastern India. It was one of the British bases where pilots took off to fly the hump into China.

Chabua needed crew members, particularly radio operators. But Arthur was not trained to be an operator; he was a radio repairman. Fortunately, this distinction would get him through the war alive. Chabua had few radios to repair. Flying the Hump was so dangerous that a lot of radios never came back.

A relieved Arthur was sent back to Karachi just about the time it was turned over to the Americans. But he was the only radio repairman there and he had little work to do. There was very little organization; Arthur remembers officers and enlisted men working side by side on whatever needed to be done. On the first day, Arthur had just arrived and he didn't know who to report to. The Americans were just getting settled and doing the best they could to get organized and Arthur was impressed by the way in which the men worked together.

"Hey, can I help you?" Arthur asked a man who was repairing a plane engine.

The man, who wore civilian clothes, looked up and replied, "Sure, grab that wrench."

Arthur picked up the wrench, thinking how strange it was that nobody was wearing a uniform. He didn't know it then, but the man repairing the plane was an officer.

The camp began to grow as more and more Americans were shipped in. Arthur was pleased to be put in charge of the radio shop, and with three shifts going round the clock, Arthur, a newly assigned shift chief, was a busy man. But it was sometimes tough to get organized. Just twenty years old, he barely knew what it meant to organize subordinates.

Sleeping in tents was okay with Arthur until the monsoons arrived, leaving the base covered in two feet of water for several weeks and forcing them to wade their way to the mess halls.

By June of 1943 Officers began arriving. Arthur's first communications officer was named Solomon Wolfe. Now he had somebody to give him directions. Before that, when the planes came in he'd just go out and ask the crew if there was anything he could do for them. Most of the work done on the planes involved replacing the radios since they took too much time to repair.

Additional runways were under construction to accommodate heavier air traffic and the larger B-29's that were brought in near the end of the war. Arthur was surprised that the labor to build the runways was done mostly by Indians, many of whom were women. They carried large baskets filled with earth on top of their heads and never held onto the baskets.

Arthur didn't have much contact with the locals, and he rarely went into town. His free time was spent playing cards with his many new friends on base. He was one of the few who liked the food in the mess halls. Hamburgers, SOS... he even liked the SPAM. Arthur also enjoyed the occasional K rations that were served when the mess hall ran out of food. And of course, there was always special for the holidays. So Arthur never complained; he ate whatever was served to him and enjoyed every bite. *I wasn't on the front lines where you couldn't get food.* He knew that he was fortunate; but Arthur was grateful too.

The base was often overrun with bothersome little monkeys running wild all over the place. When the British moved out, the Americans left their tents behind and moved into the barracks. They had wash lines outside, and the monkeys would swing from one to the other. They would sometimes have fun with them when they first moved into the barracks. They would give the monkeys beer. They'd beg for it, and after they gave it to them, the monkeys would swing and miss the wash lines. As the base became more and more populated, the pesky little monkeys pretty much disappeared. But the men were never at a loss for antics.

Nighttime coffee at the mess hall became a ritual for Arthur and a few of his buddies. Other than their laughter, the mess hall was relatively quiet in the evening, with the exception of one memorable occasion.

Arthur went over to the mess hall for coffee one night with a bunch of the guys. They were sitting there drinking coffee, when all of a sudden a little crate snake started coming across the floor and everybody jumped up on top of the table. Then one of the guys explained to Arthur that a crate snake was very venomous despite its diminutive size.

On a few occasions when the need arose, Arthur volunteered to serve on a flight crew as a radio operator. For as long as he could remember, Arthur loved flying and joining a flight crew got him off the ground and up into the clouds where he could observe the world from its most beautiful vantage point. Flying also bumped up his pay by fifty percent, and by his thinking, operating the radio shouldn't be too difficult, in spite of the fact that he'd had absolutely no training as a radio operator.

Arthur had a great deal of confidence in himself; after all he'd been a Boy Scout and had earned a merit badge for learning Morse code. Radio messages were all done in code at that time, so a very confident Arthur put his name on the volunteer list. Soon after, he boarded a transport plane for his first trip across the Hump. The C-46 raced down the runway loaded with supplies and lifted off on a dangerous journey over the Himalayas.

When the pilot asked Arthur to get him a weather report out of Calcutta, Arthur replied, "Okay, sir." Arthur knew most of the codes so he was able to get the necessary information. But he was about to learn that Boy Scout code was not quite the same thing as radio code.

Although sending a radio message was easier than receiving one, responses were generally sent back to the operators at the approximate speed in which they were received. But Arthur didn't know that when he quickly transmitted the pilot's request for a weather report. When it came back just as fast, however, he didn't know what it meant. *QRS*, he responded, *please repeat*. The other operator repeated the message, only slower. But it was still too fast. *QRS, please repeat*. It came back again. By now Arthur was mortified, but he had to get the report. So he asked once more and the message returned at about five words per minute – which, of course, he managed to understand.

When the plane finally landed in Calcutta, the radio operator had just come off shift when he came looking for Arthur.

"I wanted to see who I sent that message to," he said, "I was about to give up on you."

Shortly after his humiliating incident, operators began using voice transmission, much to Arthur's relief.

Arthur was not a frequent flyer, but he was needed occasionally so he spent some time in the air. He stayed in radio maintenance in charge of a shift and continued to fly once in a while. Some of the radio operators suffered from air sickness, but Arthur never did - probably because he loved flying so much.

The only time he was ever seriously concerned on a flight was during a run to Agra, India. It was a rough trip in the C-47 with a pilot and co-pilot, a major and a first lieutenant, who were filling in to just to keep up their flying status, getting in some flight hours. The pilot wouldn't use the radio finder equipment to navigate. He didn't trust it. He was the only pilot Arthur ever flew with who got the maps out and followed the river.

On the way back to Chabua the pilot took off but the plane wasn't gaining altitude.   Arthur was becoming concerned. The co-pilot realized the problem immediately. The pilot, who was not familiar with the plane, was taking off on one engine only.   Each engine had a separate control, and the pilot was coaxing just one of them.   The left engine was straining under the pressure to gain altitude and the right was operating just above an idle.

Arthur's time at Chabua was, for the most part, free of enemy interference. The base never really came under fire. Arthur was a lucky man and he knew it.

When Carl Constein was seven years old he wasn't aware that Lindbergh and his *Spirit of St. Louis* had crossed the Atlantic Ocean. It was a historic event to be certain, but not to Carl who was lost in the antics of childhood: riding his bike, playing baseball, going to movies, and once playing pilot on the second floor of a friend's garage in a homemade plane with a wooden cockpit.

At the age of twelve, Carl had his first airplane ride in an old World War I army biplane, a barnstormer, whose pilot gladly took anyone aloft for one dollar.

"Hop in kid," the pilot said with a grin, "and hang on!"

The flight was exhilarating - exactly what he'd expected. But it was the unexpected that captivated Carl and would stay with him for the rest of his life: the breathtaking beauty of a miniature world spread out beneath the wings, stretching as far as the eye could see. Carl was spellbound.

This flight set the stage for what was to come. Carl was a courageous and adventurous young man. Eleven years later, his courage and his exhilaration for flying would be put to the test.

Unlike many young people struggling through adolescence, Carl paid attention to world events. He was especially attuned to the war, even staying after school to discuss the conflict with his favorite teacher. He was an ambitious lad, cutting grass and working at the local grocery store on weekends in Fleetwood, Pennsylvania, for two years before graduating from his small high school.

Times were tough but Carl's loving mother had saved some money for him to attend Kutztown State Teacher's College, and combined with the money he'd saved, he was well on his way.

Carl was a college senior when Japan attacked Pearl Harbor, and he was stunned by the news. By now most of his friends were in the service, and Carl wanted to join too. No boy in Fleetwood could have been more eager to go to war. Carl aspired to become an officer in the army, but he needed to get his degree first. Without it he'd have little chance of getting into Officers Candidate School.

Carl did get his degree but soon learned that all OCS schools were closed. Devastated, he asked to be called up as soon as possible, and on New Year's Day in 1943 he was inducted into the United States Army.

After thirteen weeks of hellish basic training in Philadelphia, Carl was given what he liked to pretend was a top secret military mission: guarding the coal piles for the Philadelphia Electric Company. It wasn't, of course, and Carl was frustrated. *I gave up a boring civilian job for a boring army job,* he fumed, *and it pays ten times less.* In retrospect, it didn't seem like a very smart decision. *I have to get out of this outfit,* he thought, *I just have to.*

Carl was miserable right up to the moment when an idea popped into his head.

He was on guard duty, gun on shoulder, marching back and forth, back and forth, past the coal piles. Back and forth! He wanted to scream. No one to talk to, completely alone. The sky was black and clear as Carl suddenly gazed heavenward. A single plane droning slowly past in a course that followed the stars caught Carl's attention and he smiled. *That's it! The answer to my prayers – aviation cadets!* Carl would ask his Captain in the morning.

"Absolutely not, permission denied," he screamed at Carl.

He was devastated.

"Get the hell out," he added, and Carl made a hasty retreat.

But Carl was determined. One chickenshit Captain wasn't going to stand in his way. *I'll go to the recruiting station,* Carl resolved.

Saturday seemed a lifetime to wait, but Carl's patience paid off.

The recruiting officer said to him, "Aviation Cadet Training is the highest priority. All organizations are under orders to release personnel who wish to apply."

Carl inhaled deeply, his relief an audible sigh. He still had to face his superior officer.

Called in by his Captain a few days later, Carl stood rigid as the man barked in his face. "You sure as hell better not wash out of cadets."

Carl grimaced at the onslaught but stood firm.

"If you wash out, I'll have your ass back here so fast, you won't know what hit you!"

The man boomed a dismissal and Carl spun on his heel and got the hell out.

Carl couldn't stifle a smile. He knew without a doubt that he'd be one of the best cadets to ever come of the program! Or die trying!

Near the end of October, 1944, Carl boarded a Pan Am C-54 for the Crescent run to India. Well trained, he'd been assigned to fly the Hump. Not his first choice by any means, but he was prepared.

Carl's flight was cut short when the plane stopped in Bermuda to correct an engine problem. There would be other stops as well: the Azores, Casablanca, Tripoli, Cairo, and Abadan, primarily for refueling. Ultimately he reached his destination, Karachi.

After three weeks in hot, dusty Karachi, the C-46 that they had picked up in Casablanca headed down the runway for Assam Province, home to Chabua, the largest of the Hump's airbases. It was late October, the monsoons past, and Chabua was dry and hot and seemed quite deserted. But Carl soon learned that it was a hotbed of activity with planes coming and going every few minutes.

Delivered to his quarters by a Sergeant driving a Jeep, Carl was told to find himself an empty bed. He did. The empty bed had belonged to a Hump pilot who had recently been killed, but Carl didn't know it at the time.

Carl felt a strange uneasiness about the C-46. It had two powerful engines and could easily scale the vast Himalayas, the tallest mountains in the world. *The craft, with its 108 foot wingspan and only two engines*, Carl thought, it *seems too big to be powered by just two engines*. He couldn't shake the feeling.

And Carl was right. Just six months into its service flying the Hump, the C-46 was found to have many problems and Carl would experience some of them for himself.

But his greatest challenges would be the result of weather. There were powerful westerly winds, downdrafts, and severe turbulence from flying through cumulonimbus thunderclouds that were far too high to fly over. And deadly ice that would accumulate on wings and clog carburetors.

"Jap planes?" Carl queried a pilot who had served his time and was waiting to be shipped home.

"Not anymore," he was reassured.

Carl was frightened by stories of engine failures. Many planes had already been lost. And he knew that the chance of surviving a bailout was unlikely. That wasn't an option for Carl. He would survive and eventually go home to his lovely young bride who was waiting for him. He would not disappoint his Amy.

Seven *hundred and fifty hours flying over the Hump*, Carl thought, *and a pilot could go home.*

Carl had just finished dinner, his first of many. *SPAM*, he mused, when a voice calling his name disrupted his reverie.

"Here," Carl acknowledged.

The voice in the Jeep instructed Carl to report to flight operations at 2200 hours.

Already? Carl couldn't believe what he was hearing. *I just got here!* Carl was ready to fly; he'd just hoped it wouldn't be today.

Three agonizing hours later, Carl was settled into the co-pilot's seat of a C-46, watching lightning illuminate the night sky. Torrential rain pummeled the plane in steady sheets. Carl was certain they wouldn't take off in this weather.

"Hell, this isn't bad," the pilot chirped.

Carl swallowed hard. *This is it!* He thought about Amy and home. The pilot was on his last flight, going home after this one. Ironically, it was Carl's first. The whole set of circumstances didn't bode well with him.

Their flight wasn't the only one that night as Carl had imagined. In spite of the storm, there was a great deal of activity on the base but that fact did little to ease Carl's apprehension.

Pounded by rain and crosswinds, the big bird lumbered down the runway loaded with 55-gallon gas drums.

Faster, faster! Carl cringed as he saw the end of the tarmac rapidly approaching.

And just like magic, the craft reached its take off speed of 85 miles per hour and lifted off effortlessly. Instead of feeling relieved, Carl's eyes grew wide as the plane flew into snow and ice which was accumulating on the windshield and wings. *We're just a toy,* Carl thought as the plane was tossed about relentlessly by turbulence unlike any Carl had ever experienced in all his days in training.

Flying on instruments, the men continued to battle the elements, climbing higher and higher until they finally reached 12,000 feet. *Stars!* Carl rejoiced silently. He was elated by the vision of the heavens above him, myriad stars unending, the storm well below him. But the tranquility was fleeting; the left engine backfired again and again, shaking the plane uncontrollably before starting to cut out. Carl broke into a sweat.

The pilot made the wise decision to turn back and instructed the radio operator to set the compass on Chabua. "No mayday, yet," he added.

The left engine continued to knock loudly as they turned and flew back into the storm. As the crew struggled to keep the craft level, Carl thought, *we're going to lose that engine.*

Fortunately they didn't. In fact they landed the plane with little effort, having left the storm behind in their final approach at two hundred feet.

After debriefing, log book entries, and a shot of Old Crow, Carl and the Captain said their goodbyes.

This was Carl's first day on the job. No one said it would be easy. He went back to his bunk and slept it off.

Carl was informed he would be flying about every other day. Day flights were preferable for obvious reasons, but Carl took whatever he was given. He dreaded being awakened during the night by the Charge of Quarters when a voice in the dark and a beacon of light awoke him for his flight.

Every day Carl thought about his wife, Amy, and how he longed to be home with her. He thought of his mother too - that kind woman who'd given him the dollar for that first flight - and he wondered about his father, who was wheelchair bound since his terrible stroke three years ago. Then he'd start counting the hours he needed to go home.

Carl was assigned to nine additional flights in November, netting him a total of sixty-seven hours and twenty minutes. A lifetime shy of the seven hundred fifty hours he needed, or so it seemed; and he was determined to be finished by the first of June. That would mean one hundred flight hours per month. He also was looking forward to becoming a "first pilot." All he needed was two hundred hours in the air. Carl was well on his way.

One particular flight unnerved Carl. The pilot was reading a paperback book and smoking a cigarette as he taxied down the runway and queued up for takeoff. He didn't speak one word to Carl. Not a good sign. Carl was already dreading this flight.

The plane in front of them was having trouble. Carl could tell. It hadn't lifted off the runway when it should have. *Something's very wrong, he thought.* And moments after liftoff, it crashed and exploded into a cloud of dark smoke.

The pilot gave it half a glance, then returned to his cigarette and his book.

But Carl was shaken. He dreaded takeoff more than anything; particularly since the C-46 was so prone to engine trouble. He'd experienced this first hand and now it had happened again.

November passed uneventfully for Carl in spite of some very anxious moments in the air, but December brought with it sad news from home.

Carl was having lunch when the base Chaplain sat down next to him. He recognized the man's insignia and knew instinctively that something had happened to his father. Carl finished his lunch in silence, delaying the inevitable, and then followed the Chaplain to his office.

Carl was right; his father was dead. He had succumbed to pneumonia. Carl requested leave; he needed to see his family more now than ever. His request was denied. He wasn't even permitted a phone call to his mother. He sat in the Chaplains office and wept.

A few hours later Carl reported for duty. It was three in the afternoon. He met his pilot at operations and together they filed their flight plan. Carl would be given no time off; he would have no time to mourn.

Carl had flown eleven missions over the hump from the first of December to the time Christmas rolled around. Most of those trips were uneventful, with the exception of one of his pilots who'd lost an engine and panicked. Carl had been forced to pitch in to save the plane and crew when they were denied permission to land due to another mayday. Carl had taken great pride in the fact that he knew the hump routes like a road map. He'd studied every route and had taken to carrying bits of paper with maps and routes drawn on them. And he knew alternate landing sites, which is what saved their lives that day.

Carl wasn't scheduled to fly on Christmas Day, but it didn't really matter to him. He was lonely and thought almost constantly about Amy, his mother who was alone now, and his father who he'd recently lost. Carl attended the base church service and sang a carol or two, but was discouraged that no one had done any decorating for this important holiday. There was no reminder anywhere of the holiday Carl loved so much.

Very much like servicemen and women all over the world, in trenches, on ships, or in the air, Christmas was a sad day for Carl. He would be glad when it was over.

Most hump pilots agreed that flying the C-46 could pretty much be handled by one man, unless of course there was trouble, in which case two heads were better than one. Today was one of those days.

It was January 6, 1945. The flight plan to Chanyi had been filed. The sky was an eerie shade of gray. Carl's pilot, a cheerful, confident man named Henry, looked heavenward and said, "Frankly, I don't like the looks of it."

Those were not comforting words to Carl, but at least he was comfortable with the pilot he was paired with today. They had no way of knowing that they would become participants in one of the most terrifying and devastating days in the history of flying the hump.

Carl felt it in his bones. *Something just wasn't right.*

The continuous merging of three powerful air masses, lows coming in from the west over the Himalayas, lows from Siberia, and highs coming in from the Bay of Bengal, resulted in turbulent weather and dangerous flying conditions on a regular basis.

The night before his flight, Carl had a quick look at the eastern sky before he turned in. The weather was always on his mind. The skies were clear except for cumulus clouds over the Himalayan's first ridge. *The usual,* Carl thought, trying to put the weather out of his mind.

Carl opened his eyes early the next morning to a sense of dread. He knew something was different. Although he tried to shake it off, a feeling of foreboding slowly settled over him.

Captain Henry piloted the craft to a smooth take off, but within minutes they were battered by severe turbulence. Both men grabbed the controls; compass needles spun out of control and both men shouted through a wall of torrential rain and sleet just to be heard. Carl reached for his parachute.

No radio signal came through. Henry said, "We'll take an aural null."

He set the frequency and waited for silence. The static in their headsets disappeared and they knew they were headed toward the station.

Sadly many pilots forgot their training on aural null. He found out later that thirteen planes were lost in the weather today.

The men were battling winds of more than one hundred miles per hour. *My God, we've blown off course,* Carl thought. They were about forty miles to the north. The pilot turned a sharp right and headed northeast of their course. The turbulence got worse, and the plane tossed about like a toy. Carl looked at the wings; they were covered in thick layers of ice. Hail the size of golf balls pummeled the plane mercilessly. But the prop de-icers were functioning, tossing chunks of ice against the fuselage. And the windshield was icing up. Carl felt sick. He'd never been this frightened. Or this busy.

The men continued to rely on aural null readings to guide them to an alternate base for emergency landings.

Carl, grateful to have the calm and capable Henry as a pilot, heard a loud crack behind him. The radio operator had bounced from his seat and cracked his head on the ceiling. Carl got up to check on him. He was okay.

To keep the plane on course, the men agreed to perform a risky procedure called "crabbing" whereupon the plane was pointed 30 degrees south of their course as they flew sideways like a crab for the next hour. Between that and Carl's earnest prayers, they made it back to the base.

The C-46 began its descent and landed hard in a fierce tailwind. The men smiled at each other as they taxied and parked the plane.

Carl sighed deeply as they hurried through the rain to operations. *At least we won't have to fly back in the storm; surely they'll close the hump today.*

Henry spoke first, "Where do we sleep, Captain?"

The operations officer looked squarely at the pilot and said, "I'm not authorized to allow you to remain overnight."

"Who the hell is?" Henry barked. "We can't go back in this stuff!"

The men had no choice. "It's the same story; everyone must go back." Their orders were to return to Chabua that day. Going against orders was not an option, although it crossed Carl's mind.

Carl was devastated. He began to pray.

Carl and the Captain downed some eggs and coffee before climbing back into the cockpit. Four long tense hours later, they touched down in Chabua, but not without fighting for their lives. Their radio operator reported five more maydays, pilots who were hopelessly lost. But they had survived. Carl thanked God, smiled at Henry, and lifted his glass of Old Crow to his lips.

Thirteen planes were lost that day. More than five hundred would be lost over the hump before the war would come to an end. And thirteen hundred pilots, co-pilots and crew members would die.

Carl flew the five hundred mile route from Chabua Airbase in India to China and back ninety-six times, first as co-pilot, and later as pilot. He flew C-46 Commandos, and the much more dependable C-47 Gooney Birds, preferring the latter. He always felt challenged while flying the hump, and often a bit frightened. And he knew that he was lucky to survive.

9

ISLAND HOPPING
LATE PACIFIC

"I took the bombs over and dropped them on the Japanese. I had enough missions to come home, but I volunteered to come back and was assigned to Tinian, which is where I saw the Enola Gay before it dropped the bomb."

John Henninger, Tinian, 1945

Cy Greenburg rushed onto the deck of his LST to investigate the commotion he'd heard from below. *What the heck is this?* He saw sailors crowding around the stern, so he moved closer.

"The captain caught himself a shark," one of the men said, laughing.

Cy pushed his way forward and saw that it was true. The captain, rod bent into a U shape, was struggling to reel a small shark up onto the deck. But it was thrashing and swinging back and forth wildly. The fishing rod looked like it was about to snap.

With a grunt the captain braced himself against the rail and withdrew his pistol before squeezing a round off in the direction of his catch.

Everyone froze. *Did he seriously just shoot that fish?* It was so ridiculous Cy could hardly believe it.

Then the captain swore, and a chuckle passed through the crowd; he'd missed the shark and hit the side of the ship. Cy looked down, saw a tiny hole in the hull, and began laughing himself. What a story this would make someday.

Ralph Mason squinted through his forty five power long glass and furrowed his brow. *Peleliu*, he thought, *what a mess.* He was standing offshore on the Honolulu's signal bridge, and the whole invasion lay before him. He was supposed to be watching for signals from the men on the beach, but there wasn't much to see. There wasn't much of anything else, for that matter – the island was little more than a blasted heap of rock at this point.

Ralph swept his gaze to the landing craft coming in over the coral reefs. Some of the men, overloaded with gear, were drowning in the surf. A lot of others got shot while still in the water. He watched one man advance onto the sand and take a hit before a buddy came up and threw him over his shoulder. They were both cut down as they limped away. *What a waste.*

The island itself was almost completely barren. Hours of naval shelling had ripped the foliage to pieces, scorched the rocky terrain, and laid waste to anything man-made within sight. Ralph couldn't imagine how the Japanese were still putting up a fight. *It's insane.* They must have been burrowed deep underground to withstand such bombardment. He shuddered to think of what the men in the LCIs must have been feeling.

Howard Withers and his marine unit were hammered down in the sand not far from where the Higgins boats had left them off. He was one of the first men to land on the beach at Iwo Jima and he lay pressed into the volcanic surface in a shallow crater, waiting for the rest before going over the top. Bullets flew wildly; and artillery fire boomed relentlessly overhead. Several of the boats took direct hits on the way in. *How many guys were killed just trying to get to the beach.* Howard winced at the thought. "Oh, God," he mumbled through his teeth, there were dead men all over the beach.

Before Howard climbed over the side of his ship and into the Higgins, he glanced at the horizon. Three hundred and sixty degrees. He was completely surrounded by ships. Spread out across the water were carriers and destroyers, LST's, LCI's and minesweepers. And others too numerous to count. The aircraft carriers encircled the fleet. *At least we have back-up,* Howard thought. He was comforted by the enormity of the fleet, but unnerved by the sheer number of Japanese planes. Bombers. Fighters. Kamikazes. Howard swallowed the lump in this throat and climbed over the side.

This was day two and the marines just barely had a foothold on the island. A long way to go before securing the airfields. Howard was here to blow the Japs out of their strongholds. In spite of massive naval bombardment, the island was still operational. The island's natural

terrain provided great fortification and the Japs were dug
in like rats.   If artillery didn't get them, the satchel charges
the men carried would.

At the base of the hill that is Suribachi, marines lay
scattered in silent repose.   For them the war was over.
They had given their lives for the hill.   Others lay
wounded, their cries muffled by the din of mortar fire.
Richard Wheeler was one of them.   He'd been advancing
toward the hill with four buddies when shells started
raining in.   The men dove for cover, but not quickly
enough.   Richard was badly wounded; his jaw shattered
by shrapnel and a gaping hole in his cheek oozed blood
and gore.   Suddenly another shell exploded.   Agonizing
pain!   One of his calves was sliced open.   For a few brief
moments Richard thought he might die, then he saw the
shattered legs of the man next to him.   A medic was
speaking to the man in soothing tones as his breathing
became shallow.   And then the medic took care of Richard.
Richard would live; but the marine next to him was gone.

On day three the battle still raged as the American flag
was raised on Suribachi.   Richard Wheeler's unit had taken
the hill and if not for his wounds he'd have been there
with them.   He was proud of them all.

When the men saw the flag go up they started
cheering.   *You'd think it was a football game!*   Howard
Withers thought.   But the fight was far from over.   Howard
kept low.   Creeping on his belly he inched forward
sticking his eighteen inch bayonet into the grey volcanic
sand hunting for mines.   If he was lucky, he wouldn't find
any.

On John Allison's eighteenth birthday, he was serving aboard the minesweeper USS Success at the invasion of Iwo Jima. It was a momentous day, both for him and for the men landing on the beaches. He watched in awe as bombers swarmed overhead, blackening the sky and bombarding the island with more firepower than he'd ever thought imaginable. They came in great waves, setting the shores alight like a gigantic gas can. Fire, smoke, ash – it was an incredible display.

At one point the Success was ordered into Buckner Bay to draw fire away from the landing craft, and the crew spent some very tense moments as their ship was peppered with gunfire. Their life boat was blown up and numerous parts of the minesweeper absorbed bullets and shrapnel. But the kamikazes were the worst obstacle. They came at the ship dead on, screaming out of the skies like treacherous bats.

Luckily, his ship managed to avoid the air attacks and survive the initial invasion. When the flag was raised on Mount Suribachi, John watched from the deck of the Success. All hands were called up to witness the bittersweet moment, and as he stood there he couldn't help but think of all the men who had died. Their bodies were floating on the tide.

Cy Greenburg walked down the front ramp of his LST and felt his boots sink into the sand. *Solid ground,* he mused, *such a rarity of late.* He was on Luzon, free of duty for a few hours while the crew unloaded cargo, so he thought he might go for a walk.

Moving a short way along the beach, he took a deep breath and stretched. It was nice to be ashore for a change. Suddenly he noticed a small group of people staring at him from the edge of the tree line. They were clearly civilians, and by their attire he could tell they were poor. Something about the look in their faces tugged at his heart, so he turned and approached them.

"Hi," he said with a smile, "do you speak English?"

One of the men nodded. Cy wasn't sure what to say, so he just blurted out the first thing that came to mind.

"Is there anything I can get you? Anything that you want?"

As soon as the words came out, he realized what the answer would be. *They'll ask for food, of course.* But what he heard next surprised him.

"Soap," the man replied with a pleading gaze.

Cy didn't know what to think.

"Alright, wait here. I'll be back."

Walking back towards the ship, he was struck by how humble the man's request was. The civilians were clearly hungry; it was impossible not to see. But they wouldn't take food from the sailors who were fighting to free them from Japanese oppression. Instead, they asked for soap. It was sad and touching all at once.

Cy went to his ship's storekeeper and asked for a handful of soap. Then, returning to the people on the beach, he handed it over. The appreciation in their eyes made his day.

Ross Beeler had just finished loading ammunition into the tail turret of the B-29 that would carry him on a bombing mission to Japan in the early morning hours before dawn. He was tired, but grabbed some chow before hitting the sack early. He'd be awakened for his briefing in just a few hours.

The crew of eleven were told they'd be flying to Japan to destroy the naval aircraft factory at Kure, Renenu, but a last minute change would put them on another plane, not the one Ross and his crew had taken the time to load. The men grumbled about the change as they drove up to the line in the rain. No explanations were given for the last minute switch, and Ross hated last minutes changes.

On board, Ross heard the engines roar to life and felt the Superfortress inching forward. He smiled at his best buddy, Richard Becker, who was seated next to him and prepared himself for takeoff. *Richard seems distracted, lost in thought,* Ross mused.

Clovis Army Air Force Base, in Clovis, New Mexico was where tail gunner Ross met his B-29 crew, including his best friend, radar operator, Richard Becker, seated next to him. The crew trained together and on Feb 18, 1945 flew a B-29 Superfortress from Sacramento to Hawaii, to Kwajaline and on to Saipan. When they arrived at Isley Field in Saipan, their plane was assigned to another crew and they were assigned to the bomber, Mrs. Tittymouse.

Richard Becker glanced at Ross and thought about his younger brother, David, back home. As the engines of the B-29 roared to life, Richard recalled sitting at the kitchen table in his family's modest city row home with David. They were just boys and Richard the elder was teaching David how to build a model airplane. They'd spend hours gluing together the delicate wooden frames and paper wings, then attach the propeller and rubber band before dashing outdoors to send the miniature aircraft aloft. Soon flying them became routine and the boys had to seek new ways to entertain themselves, in particular, the dangerous habit of setting the planes aflame and launching them from the attic roof. Their mother never knew about their daring antics; there was no sense in worrying her.

Richard's thoughts returned to the present, to the sound of powerful airplane engines, to the feeling of the huge craft inching forward beneath him preparing to take him away. *Another bombing run*, he thought. He'd always loved planes and had thought about flying, but now a familiar sense of foreboding enveloped him, haunting him and filling him with apprehension. Richard thought about his mother, and how she would cope if something happened to him.

He thought about his baby sister, Christine, and how she'd been born to take his place. He'd uttered those very words to Fannie Becker, Ross' mother, back in January during a brief stopover to say hello.

Since his last furlough in January, Richard had the feeling that he would not come back from the war. His brother David somehow knew it too, and Richard sensed it that cold day at the Outer Station when David's arms were wrapped tightly around him. He'd mentioned it to Ross, too, when they arrived here in Saipan, but Ross shrugged it off. Ross wasn't going anywhere, except home when the war was over.

Richard thought about the personal items he'd left on his cot this morning. *Regulations*, he thought shaking his head. If an accident occurred, the Chaplain was required to send it all home. Chaplain Cowder was a good man, but Richard wouldn't want that job for all the money in the world.

Richard thought about Sunday service sitting in the old Chapel tent on metal bomb fin crate seats with Cowder's assistant, Alex Miller, playing the folding pump organ. And he thought about the new Chapel, the one he had help to build. The memory made Richard smile.

But something was wrong. Richard's headset crackled, then cleared. The voice on the radio was Lobely's, the flight engineer; he was reporting to the pilot, "Number two engine is not putting out full power!"

"Check it again," the pilot snapped back.

With one B-29 taking off every thirty seconds, on alternate runways, there was very little time to turn back. The flagman had given them the go ahead and they were far too committed to the two-mile runway to abort take-off.

By the time the plane lifted off, the number two engine was in flames and two of the additional three engines were not putting out full power. Ross sat frozen in time and remembered his brother Bill who was killed in Italy last year. *What will my parents do if I die too?* They had both cried when he'd enlisted in Aviation Cadets.

Descending over the cliff at the end of the runway after liftoff usually boosted the plane for the climb, but not today; and the sluggish engines had put the plane too close to the water. The pilot made a quick decision to jettison the payload, five two-thousand pound bombs, then shouted, "Close those damned bomb bay doors, quick!"

Ross was seated in his standard emergency position for take-off "just outside the rear pressurized chamber between the radar operator and the central fire control gunner, with his back to the wall." He was frightened now as he reached to warn the two men.

But it was already too late. Seconds after the pilot jettisoned his load, the plane hit the water hard and snapped in half. Ross was engulfed in seawater as the sinking plane sucked him beneath the surface.

Ross regained consciousness and bobbed on the surface like a cork. He had swallowed sea water and gasoline, and was bleeding profusely from a gaping wound on his head. The waves swelled to twenty feet then fell again, blocking his view of the plane, but he was certain he watched the tail section go under.

The Superfortress went down about five miles north of Marpi Point, Saipan. Ross could see other B-29s taking off and coming towards him. He was hanging onto a thermos he'd found floating in the water. *I can signal for help with the aluminum lid*, he thought desperately. But the planes couldn't see him; they'd turned off their landing lights before reaching him. Ross cursed them. Nobody knew they'd gone down. That's what Ross thought.

Ross never felt so alone in his life. Or so scared.

Jimmy Saunders, the radio operator, was alive. He called out and Ross answered him. "Are you alright?" Ross was overjoyed at the sound of his voice.

Jimmy said, "Yes, are you alright?"

"I'm cut up, Jimmy, but I'm okay."

Then Ross heard another voice in the dark. *It's John, he's alive!* John Bierkortte, the left gunner, came rushing down the side of a swell close to Ross. The two men swam towards each other. "Hold onto my vest! We'll be easier to spot if we're together," Ross ordered as he reached for the man.

Jimmy grabbed Ross's vest and the men held on to each other as they rode up and down the towering swells. "Don't get too excited," John told Ross as they silently prayed for help to come. Ross's face was laid open badly and John was startled when he first saw Ross. He didn't hold much hope for the badly injured man.

Against the darkness Ross saw an outline; a sub-chaser had come to rescue the men. The water was rough, dangerous, and the vessel could not get close enough. A line tossed in Ross's direction fell short. The ship left them, but returned a short time later.

It was 4:40 am when the sub-chaser returned. The men had been in the water for only forty five minutes, but it seemed a lifetime to Ross and John. A man with a rope tied around his waist dove into the violent swells and swam towards the men. Ross was so happy; he hugged the man, and then followed the rope until he reached the ship. His attempt to climb on board failed and he fell back into the water. Finally someone grabbed him by his flight suit and hauled him on board. Exhausted and injured, Ross collapsed on the deck and was taken below deck for treatment.

Ross was given first aid as Jimmy Saunders, the radio operator, was plucked out of the water. Howard Lobely, the flight engineer, and John Bierkortte, the left gunner, had also survived the crash and were picked up as well.

Ross was later told about the other three men who were found alive. Seven of his crew of eleven men were missing, including his best friend, Richard Becker. Ross was devastated. The sub-chaser had heard another man yelling for help but spotted no one. John and Jimmy had seen two men alive in the water right after the crash, but they disappeared into the waves and the darkness.

The ship continued its search but found no one else alive, and no bodies. At daybreak, one of the officers attempted to dive into the water to retrieve what he thought was a body; he was wrong, it was a shark. In daylight the search was halted; the water was full of sharks.

As the men were ferried to a hospital on shore, an extensive search began in daylight for the missing crew members. No one else was ever found. All the men were put on rest leave, given jobs on the ground. None of them would fly again. Ross certainly did not want to.

The crew of the amphibious cargo assault ship USS Palano had just finished unloading her cargo at Saipan. Now she was resting quietly at anchor just offshore. Ken Stoudt stood on deck and watched the sun slip into the horizon. Over on the island, B-29 bombers were starting to take off. Like angry bumblebees, they charged down the runway and lifted into the darkening sky, bristling with bombs for the Japanese.

"Three, four, five," Ken counted as they took off.

They did this every night.

"Eight, nine, ten."

He never got tired of watching.

Cy Greenburg participated in the amphibious invasion of Okinawa, unloading men and vehicles onto the beach while the larger ships screened for enemy aircraft. At first there were no problems, but as time wore on Cy began to hear more and more gunfire outside.

He was sitting in the engine room on ready alert, minding his own business, when he decided to take a look outside. Poking his head through the top ladder, he was startled to see Japanese planes swooping over the invasion fleet, dropping bombs and firing their guns. Antiaircraft rounds streaked into the air from ships all around, slicing through the kamikazes and showering the water with debris.

Suddenly a plane zeroed in on the LST and came straight for them. The pilot didn't fire or drop a bomb – he simply plowed headfirst into the ship. Cy felt the LST lurch as the kamikaze slammed into the bow. *They got us!* Smoke was pouring through a gap in the hull from something burning below. *The ammunition,* he suddenly realized, *it hit the ammo storage!* If the munitions caught fire, none of them were likely to survive. So he jumped up onto the deck, cutting his side on the ladder, and raced to the rail. *We have to get away!* And with that he jumped overboard.

The LST, as fate would have it, did not explode. The ammunition stores remained intact, despite nearly being struck by a Japanese plane. Cy was forced to swim several hundred yards to shore and wait for the ship to come beach itself.

The ship, though damaged, remained seaworthy enough to operate on its own. So, staying at Okinawa for a while longer, Cy had an amusing encounter.

Putt, putt, putt, bang! Cy looked up and smiled. *Here he comes again, regular as clockwork.* A tiny plane was bobbing on the horizon, flying low above the Okinawa shoreline. The guys called him Putt Putt Charlie, and for good reason. His Japanese aircraft was the most rickety thing imaginable; they could hear the engine sputtering from miles away. Every day or two, at precisely the same time, he flew in from somewhere and made a few rounds of the bay. Nobody bothered to shoot him. He was harmless enough and the information he gathered was likely useless at this point. *And besides,* Cy thought, *if we shoot him down it'll put an end to the diversion.* Cy liked the guy, personally. Zooming along fifty feet above the water, he would grin from ear to ear before flying off into the sunset. This always gave Cy a chuckle. *Let him have his fun, he's no threat to us.*

Ken Stoudt had been spending his recent days traveling from island to island, ferrying cargo and supplies wherever they were needed. Because the Palano had assault capabilities, he knew he'd likely be involved in the invasion of Japan. This was something he dreaded, as he'd seen enough of war already. But as time wore on he started to accept this likelihood; *why worry about it,* he figured, *if my time is up, so be it.*

At the start of August the Palano steamed to Samur in the Philippines to take on stores. Then she was off to Leyte to collect troops for the invasion. Everyone was busy with preparations; the sea was a whirlwind of activity.

Then suddenly it was over. The atomic bombs fell and two cities were reduced to ashes. Japanese men, women, and children perished in vast numbers. It was horrific, yet necessary. For as many deaths that occurred, countless more were prevented.

The Palano sailed into Yokohama and dropped off marines who would become part of the occupation force in Japan. Dead enemies, mines, and countless other debris littered the water. Ken would flinch with every explosion. *Another mine...* Sharpshooters picked them off as the ship lumbered along. There were so many.

But not all was grim. Off the shores of Japan, Ken laid eyes on something remarkable – something far away, pristine and untouched by war: Mount Fuji. It was beautiful.

Ahead of him the great Pacific stretched out to the endless reaches of the globe. Breathtakingly blue, it was a stark contrast to the remnants of war he was leaving behind. Charred islands, shattered ships, bodies adrift in the waves – he would tuck these away in his mind for now. He was no longer the boy who'd left home at seventeen, who'd never ventured beyond his hometown of Reading. War had touched him; it had forever changed him. And he had gazed at the beauty of Mount Fuji. That was something he would never forget.

10

INTO THE RHINELAND
GERMANY

"I had seven or eight German prisoners in the jeep by myself... I was a kid of nineteen... but I had kids in that jeep that were thirteen and fourteen years old. I had grandfathers in that jeep. They used everybody in the war... This was the Wehrmacht, the people's army. It was what was left of Germany."

George Moore, Germany, 1945

John Gallagher took a deep breath and steadied his nerves. Whistling birds, creaking pines – the sounds of the German forest filled his ears. He embraced the calm, let it cover him like a blanket and block out the terror of what he was about to do. Eight inches of snow lay before him – a tranquil sea of white that masked the danger hiding beneath. It was smooth and unbroken but for a trail of footprints and the ragged crimson hole where Captain Wells lay writhing. *How many yards between us*, he wondered, *and how many mines?* Odds were, there were a lot.

John's engineering company was supposed to be clearing trees for a roadway near the Siegfried Line. They'd been taking odd jobs like this since their decimation at the Bulge, so they were used to operating in the dense woods. But something today had caught them off guard. An army jeep, left alone in a snowy clearing, had snagged the attention of Captain Wells. Leaving the road to investigate the mysterious vehicle, he had stepped unwittingly into a minefield. And at the worst possible moment, dead center in the field, he had set one off. Now he was bleeding and unable to move. To make things worse, another man had tried to help him – a private named Cook. He suffered the same fate.

John dropped onto his stomach and tried to concentrate. It was up to him to rescue these men. Brushing snow away with his left hand, bayonet gripped in his right, he inched slowly forward into the minefield. His heart pounded in his ears. *Focus, John, focus.* It was terrifying. Each sweep of his hand risked triggering a mine, and even if he found one before it got him, there was no guarantee he could disarm it. So he crawled along, foot by foot, in nervous silence. His legs ached from pressing into the freezing ground. His fingers were numb from the snow. But he had to keep moving. The captain was just ahead; he could hear the groans. *And Cook... I have to help them both.* He pictured himself reaching them, clearing an area and getting things under control. But he wasn't sure how he'd get them out. *Is anyone else coming? Can they help?* He turned his head gently and glanced back toward the others. A few of the men were following along behind him, sticking to the path he'd cleared. *Good*, he thought, *I'm not alone.* Then he looked forward again and heard a click, and for the briefest instant time froze. The bright snow, piled nearly a foot high in front of his head, was the last thing he saw before a tremendous blast cut off his senses.

Blackness. Blind and cold, grasping in the dark. Paralysis. *I can't feel my body.* Voices drifting in from the void. Shouting. Terror. *Are those my screams?* His heart rattled madly, his breath came in gasps. *Am I dead?* John floated in a lifeless void, rolling lightly upon an unseen current. He was senseless, motionless. He was blind but he could see. Suddenly his wife, Stella, appeared before him. She was beautiful and soothing. Then he heard voices as before, but clearer. The twenty third Psalm entered his head. *The Lord is my shepherd; I shall not want.* It comforted him. *He maketh me to lie down in green pastures.* But he wasn't active in the church. He didn't know this verse. *Where is it coming from?* He couldn't answer the question, nor could he explain the sensations in his being. *I must be dead*, he thought, *or close to it.* And though he didn't know it, he was very much right. *He leadeth me beside the still waters. He restoreth my soul...*

The flak was hitting close. Very close. Between the B-24 bomber's roaring engines and his thick flight helmet, Frank Lashinsky could barely hear the bursts on most missions. But something was different today. The distant puffs were drawing nearer by the minute. And they were loud. Frank was crammed into his tail turret as usual, scanning the horizon for signs of the Luftwaffe. From the amount of flak being thrown their way, though, he doubted he'd see enemy fighters any time soon.

An unusually fierce boom rocked the plane, followed by the clattering metallic rain of shrapnel bouncing off the bomber's fuselage. It unnerved Frank, made him feel like a target. The Germans were unloading a firestorm down there, and he couldn't help but wonder if they were actually aiming at him personally. It certainly seemed that way.

Another blast, this time just beside the plane. It buffeted the aircraft violently. Then another, on the other side. Then a sharp crack pierced the din and Frank was thrown upwards. He smacked the top of the turret, tossed about by the bucking plane.

"What happened? What the hell was that?" A startled voice squawked in Frank's ear over crackling static.

The rattle of flak returned as razor shards of metal peppered the fuselage, tearing a starfield of holes in the plane. Frank's heart raced. *That was the closest hit yet.* But it was closer than he realized. Looking down, he spied a sliver of metal, two inches long and razor sharp, resting on the floor. It must have missed him by inches. *My God*, he thought, *I've used up my luck for today.*

John Rowe hopped down from the back of the truck and pointed his rifle at the German motorcyclist sitting in the middle of the road. His Tiger Patrol buddies hopped down behind him.

"Looks like we got another one," John said with a grin.

The other guys laughed and approached the enemy soldier. He didn't look like he'd put up much of a fight; on the contrary, he seemed a bit confused.

"So what should we do with it?" One of the GIs was talking as he liberated a pistol and dagger from the prisoner's possession.

John knew exactly what he was going to do. "I guess we'll have to take it with us." He pointed to the German. "And him too."

He was talking about the vehicle, of course. It was no secret that John loved motorcycles. Whenever he found one unoccupied or abandoned, he made a point to *requisition* it for the Tiger Patrol. *We have to get transportation somehow*, he always said. The bikes were mostly German, and they were usually lying along a road or parked outside a house. He would ride them until the gas ran out, then put some American fuel in the tank and hope for the best. That never really worked, though, so he'd never been able to keep one for long. *Not a problem,* he mused, *I have a new ride now.*

Five minutes later John was cruising down the center of the road, smiling widely and loving every moment. And behind him sat the German whose motorcycle he'd just claimed – his very own prisoner. Headquarters was still a ways off; John planned on taking his time.

Bumping, droning, mechanical sounds. Exhaust fumes. *Where am I?* John Gallagher woke, groggy and disoriented, to find himself in an airplane. He was lying on a litter suspended from the ceiling in what appeared to be a cargo aircraft. It was dark, hazy – but at least he could see. How long had he been blind? *Two weeks, at least.* It was horrible. He could only recall pieces of his life since the minefield – tiny scraps of memory scattered about at random. He remembered riding in some kind of truck or ambulance, unable to see but in horrible pain. Each bump in the road was agony, and he could still hear Captain Wells crying out in his mind. But it wasn't really him crying out. *They were my own screams.* There was just so much pain – the agony of bone rubbing bone still haunted him. *The bones!* He raised his arms feebly and winced at the bandages wrapped tightly around the stumps that were once hands. *Agony.*

For the first time, John began to feel sad for his loss. *What's beneath these bandages? How will I function?* He felt helpless and lost – an anonymous GI wounded and discarded by war. But then again... *Maybe this was the Lord's work,* he thought. *Perhaps this is my calling.* It was some comfort to know that maybe, in some small way, his misfortune was meant to be.

"Hey, I've got an idea." George Moore's buddy had a sneaky expression on his face. "Let's get a jeep and go down to the Rhine."

George furrowed his brow. *We probably shouldn't do that,* he thought, *but on the other hand, it's dark and pretty quiet out there. We probably won't be missed.*

"Okay," he said with a nod, "let's go."

Within the hour he and two friends were bouncing along a road through the German countryside, wondering what kind of adventure they could get into. It was safe enough where they were, but the area was still under blackout conditions. This meant extremely limited visibility, which in turn meant that they didn't notice their destination until they were practically embedded in it.

A wine cellar, a big door in the side of a hill with an endless supply of alcohol locked away – this was their target. George screeched to a halt, jumped out of the jeep, and gathered his wits. Then the three GIs walked right in and tried their best to look official.

The American guards inside must have been tired, because they barely raised an eyebrow when George requested eighty quarts of wine and champagne and signed the paperwork *General Eisenhower.* Or maybe they just didn't care. Regardless, the three tricksters were barely out of earshot when they started laughing about the heist.

"I can't believe that worked," his buddy chuckled.

It's going to be a good night, George thought. But he was wrong.

A flashlight flickered at the side of the road ahead. George slowed the jeep and approached to find an engineer poking around behind a vehicle.

"Hey, watch out," he turned and shouted, "We have a lowboy parked up there on the right hand side." He pointed forward with the light.

George put it into second gear and swerved wide to the left. There was the lowboy, parked right where the engineer said with a halftrack sitting on top. But there was another one that he hadn't mentioned, and it was dead ahead.

The jeep's headlights didn't warn them of the obstacle until it was too late. Before George could react, his little vehicle rear-ended the lowboy and threw them all through the windshield. But even worse, the eighty liters of alcohol in the back followed along, bottles smashing to pieces as they flew.

George and his buddies never got to enjoy their plunder. After picking themselves out of the mess of broken glass and jeep pieces, they took inventory and discovered that only a handful of bottles had survived the wreck. And considering that they were drenched in wine and reeked like a vineyard, none of them felt like drinking. So they cleaned themselves up and walked back to camp, all the way discussing how they would explain the missing jeep.

Richard Wenrich tightened his grip on the rifle stock and pricked his ears toward the sound on the road ahead. The German night was murkier than usual. He couldn't see a thing beyond the feeble lamplight, but the sound of footsteps reached out to him from somewhere beyond the shadows. Whoever it was, they were getting closer. He crept forward, feet softly tapping the dusty road, eyes straining into the darkness. There was a shape ahead, low to the ground. A battered German motorcycle, lying helpless in a ditch, betrayed its owner's fate. Dark stains peppered the ground beyond, and Richard could just make out the form of a dead soldier in the grass. He remembered the shots from earlier that day, and wondered what the man's story was. Had he been trying to escape to the rear? Maybe he was just lost. In either case, it seemed a senseless way to die.

The footsteps ahead grew louder, forcing Richard's attention once more. They sounded tremendously close now, and he swallowed a lump in his throat as wild speculation raced through his head. But he was on guard duty; he couldn't flee or go hide in the bushes. It was his job to stand in the way of whatever was coming and issue a challenge. However, that didn't mean he had to do it alone.

Richard turned to his buddy waiting back at the guard post. "Here comes a whole group of them!"

The other man drew his rifle close and tried to muster his courage for an intimidating pose. But as Richard faced those footsteps in the dark, he didn't feel very brave. *They're here!* The footsteps were just beyond the light now.

"Halt! Identify yourself!"

His challenge was met by silence, and for a frightening instant Richard thought he might be in over his head. Then a man stepped from the shadows and his heart leaped. *It's Paul,* he realized, *Paul Rupp.* His friend gave a sly grin as a small group of GIs appeared behind him, followed by the uniformed figures of at least fifty Germans.

"We have a group of prisoners here," Paul announced proudly before continuing on.

They passed in silence, heads low, marching with heavy strides. Richard couldn't believe it. *Talk about making assumptions,* he thought. The Germans weren't so fearsome without their weapons. They just walked along looking sad. Even after they'd faded into the night, he could still hear them moving away.

Richard checked his watch. Barely an hour left on guard duty. He looked forward to getting some sleep.

"Four hundred feet, there's a big ditch out there, Les. I'll tell you when we get there."

The tank commander's voice chirped over Lester Groff's radio headset. Squinting through his driver's periscope, he gunned the engine and burst out into a muddy field. A handful of other Shermans were visible ahead, and beyond them a ruinous city skyline poked out of the smoky haze that clung to the horizon. Cologne was burning. Dark acrid plumes shot skyward and mingled with the low-hanging clouds. It was apocalyptic.

"Take it easy, Les. Slow down a little."

Lester refocused his attention as the tank bucked over an earthen hump and rattled the crew. His periscope flashed a glimpse of sky for a moment, then faced down again as the vehicle rounded the peak of the crest. Gunfire thundered ahead. Was someone shooting at them? He saw a large ditch approaching quickly ahead.

"Twenty feet... ten... five... you're ready to drop."

He eased the Sherman up to the edge, then *bam!* The tank dropped with a tremendous thud, thirty tons of metal sinking into the soft earth, treads grinding. Lester was blind. Rocks and mud obscured the periscope.

"Go about fifty feet. There's a big tree stump. You'll feel it."

Crunch. There it was.

"Okay, you're ready to come up. Be on guard."

Lester floored the gas and rocked the Sherman up out of the ditch. For an instant, the front half of the vehicle hung in the air at a sharp angle, exposing its soft underside. *Come on, come on,* he thought, *get on with it!* This was one of their most vulnerable moments, as he'd learned firsthand near the start of his career. *There!* The vehicle lurched forward just enough to tip the balance, and with a great slam the front end came crashing down onto the top of the embankment.

"Ow!" The loader let out a small yelp as he knocked his head into a piece of metal. "Anybody got any bandages?"

A slight chuckle crackled over Lester's headset. Bumps and bruises were something of a joke by now. They all had them and there was little to do about it. *A few scrapes are nothing compared to having to eat, sleep, and go to the bathroom in here,* he mused. They did what they had to do.

The gunfire outside was growing louder. *And closer,* Lester realized. They were still in the field and he felt exposed. There was plenty of concealment just ahead but they'd have to advance across open ground to reach it. *Just a bit farther.* Something very nearby fired loudly and he swallowed a lump in his throat. It had to be the Germans.

A horrific jolt suddenly rocked the Sherman and a tremendous bang deafened Lester. *No!* Time seemed to slow as a German tank round pierced the hull and burst inside the gunner's compartment. He could hear it strike; could hear each piece of shrapnel clatter and slice its way through flesh and metal. The gunner and commander screamed together as it tore them to pieces. *I have to get out!* Something struck the unspent munitions and they started popping. One by one, then all at once – live shells exploding and firing wildly inside the tiny space. It knocked the wind from Lester's lungs as the chain reaction slammed him forward in his seat. And the gunner's severed legs, spurting jets of warm blood, came tumbling down into his lap. *Move! Get out!* He was stunned, covered in gore and pinned inside the tank. Everything hurt. And it was hot. The choking stench of smoke and oil threatened to overwhelm him – something was on fire. A high pitched squealing pierced his thumping ears, punctuated by the tapping bursts of machine gun rounds cooking off. *Oh God, he's trapped!* The machine gunner was burning alive barely two feet away, shrieking like an animal. Running on adrenaline, Lester summoned his last ounce of strength and threw open the overhead hatch. It was almost impossible to move; he was beginning to black out. *Keep going!* But if he stopped now he was dead. He caught a glimpse of the gun barrel jammed above the next hatch over, trapping his buddy in the inferno beneath. *There's nothing I can do. Nothing...* He gasped, crying out as a sharp pain shot through his left side. Rolling out of the driver's compartment and over the side of the Sherman, Lester dropped into a deep rut in the mud. He hit with a violent jolt, and as his body settled into the soft earth he saw shards of silver light pulsing in his eyes. *Is this it? Am I dying?* Blackness closed in on the edges of his vision, choking the light and drawing him into himself. With a trembling hand he clutched at the Bible in his breast pocket – his father's parting gift. It was cool to the touch. *Dear Lord,* he prayed, *if you bring me through this... if*

you take me home I'll do your work for the rest of my life. He
meant it. His chest heaved in great shuddering breaths.
The pain was unbearable. *I swear to this!* And suddenly,
time froze once more as the darkness gave way to clarity.
In answer to his prayer, or perhaps because of the
extraordinary stress, something remarkable happened. He
no longer knew if he was awake or asleep, alive or dead,
but he saw a vision. There, robed in blue and appearing
before him, stood Christ at Gethsemane. Lester repeated
his prayer. *I will do your work for as long as I live.* It was the
last thing he remembered.

*Lester's prayers were answered and he was saved, though it
was by the hand of Allied medics. Lying unconscious in the
mud, covered in blood and soot and pale as a corpse, Lester was
very nearly left for dead. But the fellow who found him took a
second look. Something caught his eye – something he couldn't
quite put his finger on. And when he felt for Lester's pulse, he
was astounded to find him alive – though barely. Thus he
escaped the loss of his sixth tank and was taken off the front, the
only surviving member of his crew.*

Gabe Fieni's truck rattled noisily along a pitted road in
the anonymous German hinterlands. None of his
passengers – not the major in the passenger seat, the
captain in the back, or the half dozen nurses and privates –
knew exactly where they were. Gabe, of course, had
memorized the mission map with a critical eye, so he had a
fairly accurate idea of their present position. This was a
crucial part of his job, as he was forbidden to carry maps
lest they fall into enemy hands. The downside, however,

was that his passengers sometimes questioned where he
was taking them. And as they bumped their way along in
silence, the major next to him seemed to be growing
anxious.

There was an intersection ahead. Gabe rolled to a stop
and eyed the signposts. One pointed left, a bold arrow
indicating the direction of Bonn. *That's not correct,* he
thought, *it should be the other way.* He wracked his brain,
trying to recall the map directions from earlier. *It should be
to the right.* He was certain of it.

"It's that way," Gabe said to the major, pointing in the
direction opposite the sign, "they must have turned that
sign around."

"Nonsense," he replied, "keep going."

Gabe tried to argue but there was no reasoning with
the man. And of course, he was outranked. There was
little he could do but turn left and follow the altered
signpost. Thinking about what might lie ahead was
worrying enough, but it bothered him doubly to realize
that, by taking the wrong route, he had effectively left his
mental map and gone into strange territory. He was
driving blind now.

Before long the terrain around them changed. They
left the fields and hills that had accompanied them for so
long and entered a thickly wooded area. After several
minutes the road bent sharply, forcing Gabe to slow down
and make a hard uphill turn. He felt the tires dig in and
spin a bit, and he flashed a glance in the mirror. The
trailer, loaded with medical supplies and hitched to the
back of the truck, swerved wildly. But it was still there.
This definitely isn't right, he thought. Suddenly he heard

small arms fire in the woods nearby. Was it coming from the top of the hill? It was hard to tell.

"Sir," Gabe said in a calm but firm voice, "we are going the wrong way. This is leading us into an ambush and we need to turn back."

But the major was adamant. "Keep going," he ordered, with more than a hint of apprehension in his tone.

Gabe looked over and noticed the bizarre look on his face. It was almost as if he was wearing a calm mask, a cool expression that said he was in control. But beneath it, emerging from the facade, utter terror was poking through. He seemed to know exactly what was about to happen, but couldn't bring himself to accept it. And when Gabe realized this, he could barely contain himself. Rage welled up in his chest. *Idiot,* he fumed, *he's going to get us all killed!* He wanted to do something rash – to mutiny and take command. His mind was a hyperactive well of violent thoughts. But he refused to do anything stupid, so he took a deep breath and steadied himself. *Stay calm. Keep your head.* He gripped the wheel tightly. *They're going to need you.*

An instant after this thought crossed his mind, Gabe's vehicle crested the hill and his adrenaline shot up abruptly. In the right lane, just ahead, three American trucks sat at wild angles, crumpled and burning, thick plumes of smoke pouring from their ruined chassis. He slammed on the brakes.

"You see," he shouted at the major, "do you see what's going on now? He was furious.

But the officer didn't get a chance to reply. German mortar shells started pouring in, striking the road and trees very near the truck. The first one sent shrapnel flying in their direction, shredding the truck's canvas top and pummeling the trailer.

"Get out!" Gabe turned toward the back and screamed at his passengers. "Get out and hit that ditch over there!"

Half a dozen figures leaped from the back of the truck and raced to the depression at the side of the road. The major, shell shocked, stumbled along after them. Then, turning back, he looked at Gabe with a puzzled expression as Gabe gunned the engine.

"I'm coming back for you," Gabe shouted, "Don't move."

Then, throwing the truck into gear and flooring the pedal, he sped off down the road and pulled a sharp U-turn. Pieces of shrapnel were flying everywhere, clattering off the truck and tearing canvas. *Come on, come on! You can do this!* It was a horrifying ordeal, but he clenched his knuckles and focused on the road ahead. *You're going to make it out alive!*

"Get in! Hurry!" Gabe was back at the ditch, rolling along slowly enough for his passengers to join him. And this time he was facing the right way. "Get in the truck!"

The captain and his enlisted men piled into the back with the nurses, but the major simply ran alongside the truck.

"I've lost my camera," he moaned, "my Leica."

"Sir, if you don't get the hell in the truck I'm leaving you here!"

The captain swore. "That thing is worth a lot of money!"

But his bravado melted away as a mortar shell pounded the earth very close beside him, and he jumped into the passenger seat with a curse. Gabe floored the pedal once more and the truck sped away from the ambush, trailing explosions and splintered trees behind it.

A short way down the road, Gabe started to feel pain in his back. The adrenaline still surged in his veins, but now that the danger had passed he was becoming more and more aware of his body. He took a hand off the wheel and pressed a finger to his back with a wince. *Blood,* he thought, *but not much.*

"Sir, I think I was hit. My back is burning."

Suddenly another mortar shell burst ahead of the truck. Then another. The Germans must have been firing blindly, just guessing at the truck's position as it sped away. *Lucky shots.* He tensed up again and hoped they'd make it out of range soon. Then he heard a woman shout from the back.

"I'm hit!" It was one of the nurses.

Gabe kept driving. He couldn't stop now. He had to make it out of these woods, to get them all to safety.

A quarter of an hour later, Gabe sighed and leaned his head on the steering wheel. "Please," he muttered as the major leaned toward him, "take care of the nurse first." He gestured toward the rear with his thumb and the major nodded.

The nurse's wounds were minor, like Gabe's. The major, working from the back of the truck, removed shrapnel from each of their backs. Miraculously, they were the only injuries sustained during the ambush.

Judging from the destroyed trucks they'd seen on the road, things could have been much, much worse.

Once everyone had been tended to medically and tempers were cooled, the major called everyone out into a circle behind the truck. He stood there, looking a bit sheepish, and cleared his throat.

"Look, we made a big mistake back there," he began. "But if any of you report this, I'll see to it that you're court martialed." He suddenly regained the cocky fire in his eyes as he looked down at them over his nose. "I have a lot of clout with a lot of important people. Don't you ever forget that."

An awkward silence followed as the enlisted men flicked nervous glances back and forth. It was one thing to refuse to accept blame, but threatening them was another matter entirely. Gabe seethed once more. *What a coward.* As before, though, he knew he had to keep his head. *At least we survived*, he thought, *that's what matters right now. When all this is over, then we'll see about blame.* But he felt that the incident would soon be forgotten. After all, there were bigger things to be dealt with. And perhaps the major had learned his lesson.

Gabe took a deep breath and took a step toward the truck. He had to get them back on track and safely to their objective. They were miles out of their way and in unfamiliar territory. It was going to be a long drive.

"Goddamn Germans are lousy shots!" A flustered GI was shouting threats at no one in particular from the back of the truck that Charles Gryniewich was driving. He was part of a tiny convoy – no more than four or five vehicles –

tasked with crossing the Ludendorff Bridge at Remagen without being blown apart by the enemy units stationed on the other side. This was easier said than done, as the Germans were sitting up in the hills overlooking the Rhine, taking potshots at will and generally causing havoc.

Charles knew it was late at night, but he couldn't take time to look at his watch. Small arms fire and mortar rounds were pouring in, often striking dangerously close to the truck and spitting shrapnel everywhere. He had to jerk the wheel sometimes to avoid shell bursts – not that it helped very much. The truck looked nearly as bad as the bridge with its countless holes and shredded canvas top. He just hoped the Germans' aim wouldn't improve until they were safely on the other side. *But who am I kidding*, he thought, *I'm not going to make it.* Squinting ahead into the dark, looking down the length of the bridge illuminated by sporadic flashes of gunfire, he felt a cold lump forming in his gut. There was too much debris, too many wrecked *things* sitting like corpses along the way. *They've been hitting this bridge for God-knows-how-long. It's just a matter of time.*

Another round exploded within feet of the truck, just behind the passenger side door. Someone in the back screamed.

"Keep going! It's okay!"

Charles didn't know who was yelling, and he didn't need to be told to keep moving. But whoever was hit wouldn't stop wailing back there. He imagined some terrible shrapnel wound, guts tumbling out and blood everywhere. It made him shudder. *Why isn't anyone firing back?* He wished someone would put artillery up into those German positions, but he knew that was out of the question. It was too dark to see anything but tracer rounds and explosions.

He heard an engine whine. Was that a plane? *Well that's it,* he thought, *they've got us now.* A strange feeling washed over him. He wasn't actually scared – just *accepting* of his fate. He felt that, barring some kind of miracle, he was going to end his days on this bridge. Tonight would be the last night of his army career. He entered a sort of trance, eyes focused softly ahead as the gunfire flickered and reflected off the truck's windshield. And it was in this daze that he lost track of time and drove until he was jarred back to attention by a bright glare off to the right. It was another convoy – one significantly less fortunate than his own. Truck after truck sat engulfed in flames just beyond the end of the bridge. As he drove back onto solid ground and made a sharp right turn, he passed them by and slammed into a wall of stench. Burning flesh. It wrenched his gut and made him gag. But it only lasted a moment. Charles realized he was safe and gave a sigh of relief. The bridge was behind them, and from what he knew it was relatively safe ahead. *How much luckier could I be?*

Though they were out of immediate danger, Charles had to keep driving. There was a town ahead, something that started with an E. He couldn't remember the full name, though he knew roughly where to find it. But it was late and they were behind schedule – not to mention exhausted. So when the convoy rolled up to an abandoned farmhouse after a mile or two, they decided to stop for some rest.

Stepping from the truck, Charles and the other GIs fanned out, keeping an eye out for enemy activity.

"Let's see if anyone's home."

They approached the darkened house, rifles ready, and stepped through the doorway. Silence. Splitting up, they searched the building room by room. In the end, the only surprising thing they found was a large cask of wine in the cellar – which they quickly decided to requisition for Uncle Sam. *Well, if I'm going to die,* Charles thought as he downed a gulp of the wine, *I'm going to die happy.* It was with this attitude that he and his buddies drank their worries away and spent the night in the abandoned farmhouse, happy to be alive. They would regret it the next morning when they woke with hangovers, but for now it was enough just to be safe and happy.

The very next day, Felix Uhrinek had his turn at crossing the Ludendorff Bridge. Jammed in bumper to bumper traffic, he sat in his halftrack and watched the excitement around him.

Billowing smoke drifted in from the shoreline, obscuring parts of the bridge and making it difficult to see down the whole length. It might have been a smoke screen, but he couldn't be sure. *Is something burning over there?* In and out they drove, passing through thick puffs, catching glimpses of the action at intervals. At one point a plane passed overhead – a Luftwaffe dive bomber. *They're still trying to take out the bridge,* he realized. A crackling burst of antiaircraft fire flew skyward and bit into the plane. The pilot banked hard, fighting for his life, and went screaming away with smoking engines.

Felix could hear small arms fire coming from the opposite bank – rifles and machine guns popping randomly less than a hundred yards ahead. He flinched as a stray round pinged against the bridge trellis. *What the hell is going on up there,* he wondered, *this is supposed to be cleared.* A least this wasn't as bad as the Bulge, or even the bloody Hoertgen Forest. Still, he didn't like being shot at, regardless where he was.

The halftrack swerved to avoid a rift in the bridge, jarring its passengers. The train tracks in the surface had been covered with metal plates to avoid snags, but some of them had shifted or been blown off by artillery fire. Every time the vehicle rolled over a gap it bumped abruptly. *What a mess,* Felix thought, *this thing looks like it's going to collapse.*

Somewhere in the distance artillery started booming. He hoped it wasn't pointing at them.

"Art!" Frank Lashinsky's heart skipped a beat as he shouted into his helmet mic. Scrambling forward, he watched in horror as the B-24's side hatch abruptly slammed shut, pinning his buddy's foot to the fuselage. Now he was hanging outside the plane helplessly as the crippled bomber sank smoking towards the battlefield below. For the first time, Frank froze. He just didn't know what to do. Should he wait? Try and force the hatch open? Grab his foot and try to pull him back in? If Art really was wedged, he might be hurt or unconscious. Setting him loose could be a death sentence. But if he didn't get that hatch open, Frank and the others would go down with the plane.

Steeling his nerves, Frank moved into position and weighed the odds. With a deep breath, he removed his helmet and reached for his friend's foot. But then, with a sudden pop, the boot before him fell away and the hatch was freed. Art had literally slipped out of his shoes. All Frank could do was hope his friend would reach the ground safely. Then he, too, pushed free of the plane and went sailing out into the open sky.

Frank's head was spinning. The sudden blast of icy air was jarring, though he had long gotten used to the cold. He strained his neck and looked back as he fell, trying to catch a final glimpse of his plane before it plummeted, and saw two flak rounds explode violently on either side of the fuselage. *I got out just in time*, he realized, then he pulled the D ring on his chute.

The jerk of his parachute opening tugged uncomfortably on his harness straps. But he'd experienced that before. What caught him in awe was the noise. On his first jump, he'd been wearing his helmet, and in muffled silence had drifted down from the skies over Yugoslavia. But now, four thousand feet above Hungarian soil, the horrific sounds of war threatened to overwhelm his senses. He could hear, with startling clarity, bombs thundering in the distance. He could hear flak bursting above and gunfire from below. But clearest of all, and most disturbing, was the whizzing of bullets as they passed near his body. Looking down, he saw puffs of smoke. The Germans were shooting at him.

Tugging on his shroud lines, Frank tried desperately to dodge the enemy fire. Left, right, left, right... he swung back and forth precariously. The maneuver made him harder to hit but dangerously increased his speed. He strained to stay oriented, keeping a sharp eye on the rapidly approaching earth. By now he could make out a maze of trenches and barbed wire directly below. It was impossible to guess exactly where he'd land, but it almost didn't matter. It all looked the same down there. And in any case, there was no time to adjust his fall. Before he knew it, the ground slammed into his heels and he was rolling about in a tangle of silk and wires.

Frank freed himself from his chute and looked around wildly. Where the hell was he? Barbed wire and mud stretched out in all directions. He craned his neck, scanning the sky, suddenly awed. The air raid, he realized, looked entirely different from this new perspective. After twenty five missions he was seeing things from the ground. Fingering the boot laces tied to his harness, he thought about changing his shoes. But then something caught his attention. A man's bare head was poking up from a trench just a short distance away. For a moment, Frank didn't know what to do. But then the man beckoned him with a gesture. *Well, he didn't take a shot at me*, Frank thought, *that must be the way to go.* So, keeping his head down, he scrambled through the barbed wire maze and hopped into the trench. A moment later, his heart sank.

"Pistol." The hatless man held out his hand, palm up. His voice was calm but firm. Frank's eye moved along the grey sleeve to the swastika above his breast pocket. And then he noticed the eight or ten other Germans in the back of the trench. They stared at him with cold eyes. *Well shit*, he thought, *they got me.*

In that instant something remarkable happened. During his entire career in the air force, Frank had imagined this moment time and time again. He wondered if, as an airman used to sailing above the clouds, he'd be able to keep his wits if he ever faced the enemy dead on. He'd heard stories of men freezing or panicking, freaking out or refusing to act, and the question had always remained in his mind: *what would I do?* Now he knew. He was calm. It was with this thought that he unfastened the pistol in his shoulder holster and handed it to the German soldier. He was afraid, but in control. He would not freeze.

Within minutes Frank was being led through the trenches at gunpoint. After a confusing number of turns, he arrived at a tiny shelter cut into the earth. It had a roof overhead and a dirt floor, upon which a German officer sat working through a stack of maps and paperwork. He motioned for Frank to sit, so he did. And he stayed there for several hours in complete silence, just wondering what they were going to do to him.

As dusk approached another guard arrived and took Frank away. They left the trenches and walked up to ground level, and he could see they were heading for the rear. The guard spoke some English, and at one point he turned to Frank.

"If you manage to live for three months," he said, "you'll be a free man."

Frank could see the hollow sadness in the man's eyes. He clearly understood what was happening to his country; he knew the war would be over soon. Frank almost felt sorry for him.

Eventually they came to a river and entered a flat-bottomed boat. Shoving off, the German crew began rowing towards the far bank. Frank idly put a hand in his pocket, reserved to his fate, and felt something that worried him. *Bullets!* He suddenly realized that, though his captors had taken his pistol, they'd forgotten to search him for ammunition. *I should get rid of these somehow,* he thought, *they probably won't like me having them.* So he watched the Germans, and when they weren't looking he started dropping bullets into the water. *Splash, splash.* They heard the sound and froze. *Uh oh!* He wasn't sure what to do. But they were looking out at the water, not at him. *They don't know it was me!* It was a relief, but there were still bullets left in his pocket. He waited until the boat started moving again and dropped a few more. Then some more. It continued like this until he was out of ammo.

"Strip off all of your clothing!"

Frank was really worried now. The Germans had marched him into a town on the far side of the river. He was on the second floor of a drab building that appeared to be some kind of command center, and an angry-looking German officer stood before him. *Don't panic,* he thought, *just do what he says.*

A few moments later Frank's clothes were on the floor and the German still looked angry. *Okay, now I'm naked and they're probably going to torture me.* He eyed the potbellied stove sitting in the middle of the room. *They'll probably use that for something.*

"Where did you come from?"

It was an easy enough question, but Frank had been trained to resist interrogation. *Just your name, rank, and serial number,* they taught him. So that's what he gave.

The officer's mood didn't improve. "Where did you come from?"

Frank gave the same answer.

"What unit are you with? What was your target?"

The questions kept coming, and Frank continued his usual reply despite his interrogator's anger. *Name, rank, serial number! Name, rank, serial number! Nothing else!*

"You're lying!" This one caught him off guard. "We know you're lying because there was a captain on board your plane."

Frank swallowed hard. *How do they know that?* His pilot was a captain. *Maybe it was a lucky guess?*

"We haven't picked up any captains yet, and you're the last man we have." The German leaned in close, eyes flickering in the lamplight. "So it must be *you...*"

Name, rank, serial number, Frank answered.

The man abruptly stood up, stretching up to his full height. He was quaking furiously. "And what will you say when we say we're going to execute you?"

Frank thought about this, but he figured it didn't make a difference anymore. So he held his chin up.

Name, rank, serial number.

"Bah!" The officer swore and kicked the chair before storming from the room. Frank let out a nervous breath and watched a guard approach. *Well now they're going to kill me for sure,* he thought. But the guard threw him his clothing and told him to get dressed, which was reassuring.

Dressed once more, Frank was roughly ushered down several flights of stairs into a hallway with an open door at the end. Just outside he could see a brick wall, unadorned and filthy. For a moment, his heart leaped into his throat. *An execution area!* He'd seen this before, time after time in the movies. The bad guys always put the hero up against a wall before shooting him. *Before I know it they'll be offering me a cigarette and a blindfold.* Then a bullet would end his life unceremoniously. *No!* He could escape! He just had to disarm the guard. But he was too far ahead now. He'd never close the distance in time. What could he do?

The guard moved in closer and gave Frank a shove past the wall. *We're not stopping?* It was a relief, but he felt a little bit foolish.

Frank was eventually taken through the town to a house that the Germans were guarding. He was physically and mentally exhausted by now, so the thought that he might get to rest was encouraging. And as he stepped through the door, he saw a very welcome sight: Five members of his flight crew were inside. If he was going to be a prisoner, at least he would be with friends.

George Moore bumped along down a German country road all alone in his jeep. Well, he wasn't entirely alone. Half a dozen German prisoners sat crammed along with him, staring idly into space and looking rather morose. He'd been trying to stay positive throughout the war, but seeing these Germans was depressing. None of them were fit to fight, yet here they were, prisoners of a foreign power. *That kid can't be older than fourteen,* he thought, glancing in the mirror. *And that guy is old enough to be my grandfather.*

The GIs had been seeing a lot of this lately – enemy soldiers who were surprisingly young or old. *It's like they're running out of people.* Most of them seemed glad to surrender; they didn't want to be fighting any more. He thought he might be able to cheer them up, so he reached in his pocket and pulled out a box of cigarettes. They gladly accepted.

George sighed. *This is what's left of the Wehrmacht, the people's army. It's all Germany has left.*

"Keep rowing! Keep rowing!"

Lungs aching in the damp Rhine river mist, Richard Walton braced himself and tugged hard on the oar gripped tightly in his fingers. Just over the whistle of bullets and between artillery bursts, he could hear the engineers shouting frantically.

"Keep your heads down! Don't stop rowing!"

Tracers were hitting the water on all sides of the boat, skipping off the river surface and hissing like snakes.

"It's a goddamned crap shoot," someone yelled.

From above and to the left came the rush of artillery, then a sickening rip as the shell tore apart. Shrapnel splintered the wood at his feet and he froze for an instant, gazed fixed between his legs. In the flickering flare light he could see water lapping at his boots. And there was blood in the boat.

Richard had to keep rowing. *I'm not going to die here!* He was the only surviving member of his company, and he sure as hell wasn't going to let the Germans knock him off now. So he pulled with all his strength, determined to make it to dry ground. *So close*, he thought, *just a little bit further.* It only took minutes but it seemed like ages.

The boat bumped to a halt and the men came tumbling out. Boots slipping on the slick pebble shore, Richard slogged his way out of the water, up onto a grassy slope, and into the ragged vineyard beyond. The tangle of grape vines and sagging trellises offered little protection from the bullets whizzing above his head, so he moved quickly. *With my luck*, he thought, *I've survived the river crossing only to be hit now.* But somehow he didn't believe that. Up ahead the Germans were firing down at the GIs, though it was becoming more and more sporadic. Were they retreating?

"There a twenty millimeter hitting us from that promontory." Someone nearby was barking commands between gasps. "If we get to that line it can't see us."
The man was right. Richard scrambled through the mud and slapped his body into the hillside, hugging the ground for cover. He breathed deeply, gulping great lungfulls of cool night air and fighting to steady his pulse. Steam rose from the pile of soldiers huddling against the earth around him.

Back near the boats, staccato gunfire erupted every few seconds, but up on the slope it grew quiet. Men piled in from behind, and Richard craned his neck to watch them climb the hill. He'd come farther than he'd realized. The muddy slope ran up from the riverbank, through the ratty vineyard, and continued up to where he lay. And it seemed, or at least he hoped, that the Germans above could no longer target them.

"Up the hill! Let's go!" the sergeant was egging them on.

Richard scrambled over the crest of the embankment and shouldered his rifle. Nothing. A smoky haze lingered atop the enemy positions, but the enemy themselves were nowhere to be found. The Germans had fled.

Richard's company gave chase, moving quickly across an open field and setting up a defensive line in a wooded area beyond. They waited there in silence. Would the Germans return?

A familiar, throaty roar abruptly passed overhead and the men gave a shout as a pair of Mustang propellers flickered above the trees. Looking up, Richard cracked a tiny smile. Air support had arrived. *They must be after the gun just upstream*, he thought, *though they could have gotten here sooner*. Better late than never. A loud burst of machine gun fire confirmed his guess, and for a moment he felt good knowing that the river crossing would be safe for the others. But something was wrong. It sounded too close.

"Get down!" A cry went up from the men in the woods. "They're shooting at us!"

Richard jumped sideways as bullets tore through the grove, kicking up dirt and splinters and slicing through branches as they went streaking by almost horizontally. The P-51s roared again and he suddenly realized what was happening.

"We're behind the damn gun!"

Whoever said it was right. He bolted behind a tree and held his breath. The planes were overshooting their target. More gunfire. More splinters. Teeth clenched, he muttered a silent prayer over and over. *Please God, get me through this. Don't let it end this way.* Time seemed to crawl as the fighters made another pass. Tracers seared the air, illuminating the grove, flashing one after another. It was violent and beautiful all at once. Then it was over.

"Anyone hurt?"

No answers. The men around him stirred slowly. Some were lying down. Others were behind trees. It didn't seem to have made a difference. Richard's pulse was pounding and he suddenly remembered to breathe. *Exhale, inhale, repeat.* He wiped a bead of sweat from his face with one soggy sleeve and rose to his feet. His knees ached. His feet were wet. As the Mustangs rolled off into the distance, he stepped out from behind his tree and glanced up. *Thanks*, he thought, then fell into stride with the others.

The forty and eight rattled along on the tracks, shaking the thirty-some odd men who shared Frank Lashinsky's half of the boxcar. Wedged among the mass of prisoners, he peered across to the German guards. They looked alert. A web of barbed wire, strung diagonally from door to door, separated them from the POWs. Frank and the others had been sitting listlessly for a few hours now, just waiting for whatever came next. The dejected men around him seemed to share his attitude.

With a sudden jolt and a metallic screech, the train car began to decelerate. *We're stopping,* he thought, *maybe they're finally going to shoot us.* The Germans had been threatening to kill them all for some time now. Maybe it was a ploy to demoralize them; he couldn't really tell. They certainly didn't need help being depressed, though – riding on a filthy train, crammed in like sardines with no food or water was more than enough to ensure that. Still, Frank tried hard to stay positive. There seemed little to look forward to, but he felt that, somehow, he would make it home. He'd survived long enough to think that maybe someone wanted him alive. Many of the Germans seemed almost as apathetic as the prisoners, as if they knew the war was being lost. He felt that they might even gladly surrender if they encountered the Allied front. But the enemy was still in charge of him for now, and as the train ground to a halt he wondered what was in store for them this time.

The guards were saying something he couldn't understand. They always sounded a little angry. Or maybe they were just frustrated. But for all their bark, the regular army guys weren't so bad, really. It was the SS who really rattled his nerves. They were embedded here and there, always watching with cold eyes. If anybody was going to kill the prisoners, it would be them. Frank figured they knew their days were numbered. Ever since Malmedy the Americans were gunning for them, and they knew it. The only question was whether or not the rest of the Germans could keep them under control.

There was a noise outside, then a blinding glare as the doors were thrown open. Frank squinted out into the daylight. It looked like they were still in the woods. The guards were shouting and ushering their captives off the train with nervous looks. He hopped down and got his bearings. They were in the middle of nowhere, that much was certain. The tracks ran off in both directions, bordered by thick trees for as far as he could see. But there was an open area near where he stood, down a slight slope past the tracks. The Germans were prodding them along in that direction. He suddenly felt a pit in his stomach, though he had no choice but to follow. Just ahead the men were stopping. Was this it? Were they going to be killed in the woods like animals? He wondered if he could make a break for it when the shooting started. No, they were too far from the tree line. *They've got us*, he thought with a hint of despair, *no way out*. For the first time in his memory, he felt utterly powerless. *I've dropped off the face of the earth. No one knows where I am.* It was a horrible feeling. *My family will never know what happened.* But fate, it appeared, had other plans.

Frank's foot splashed lightly and he glanced down. A stream. They were supposed to drink. In the span of two seconds his fear melted away as he realized they would survive this stop. Around him the prisoners were bending down to quench their thirst in the cool water flowing past his ankles. Relieved, he joined them. The stream was far from pristine, but he could barely remember the last time he'd been given water. He drank for what felt like ages, savoring the moment. They were safe enough for now, and that was all that mattered. One day at a time. One stop at a time. That's how they survived. He hoped the next would bring similar fortune.

Charles Gryniewich watched the scenery roll by as he drove his truck down a muddy road. The German countryside reminded him of home sometimes; it had the same trees and hills. The people, though – that was another story entirely. He and his buddies had tossed some candy to the German kids back in town earlier. They were probably orphans; he felt terrible for them. *You don't see people like that back home*, he thought. The hollow eyes, the sallow complexions, the yearning stares – it pained him to think about it. *Their country is destroyed. No wonder they mourn.*

The commanders were always reminding the soldiers not to harm the civilians. Charles figured this went without saying. *Don't treat them like we're the conquerors*, he always maintained, *that just wouldn't be right.* He wondered if the German people were as tired of war as he was. *Probably more so*, he thought, *as bad as I've had it, it's almost been worse for them.*

Martin Dorminy trembled as he watched the Russian soldiers drag a struggling German sergeant into the central yard at Stalag IV-B. The Red Army had come through the gates only hours earlier, and already they were exacting revenge.

Martin recognized the sergeant's face even through the mask of fear. There was no forgetting him. One of the meanest bastards he'd ever met, the German had made Martin's life miserable time and time again. And now it seemed the tide was about to turn.

The Russians threw a rope around his ankles and strung him up on a pole. He thrashed wildly, spitting insults that none of them understood. *Arrogant to the end,* Martin thought. One of the soldiers produced a bayonet, and without hesitating began sawing at the sergeant's groin. He screamed horribly as the man sliced down toward his stomach, spilling blood and innards onto the dirt. *Oh my God...* Martin grimaced. Of all the things he'd seen, this was one of the worst. But he couldn't look away. Something compelled him to watch.

The German sergeant was gutted like a pig and died in front of the men he'd so often tormented. Was this justice? Many of the inmates thought so. Whatever it was, it was only a small gesture of the anger and frustration that lay bottled up inside millions of people in every corner of Europe.

Richard Wenrich was resting inside a barn next to the German mansion his company was occupying when a sudden explosion pierced the air. The timbers above him rattled, showering dust and bits of straw down onto the floor. *What the hell was that,* he wondered, jumping to his feet and rushing outside.

It was midday and the sun was high overhead. He shielded his eyes with a hand and squinted towards the commotion. Soldiers were scurrying out of the barnyard, up a little dirt lane to where a wrecked jeep sat smoking. The driver was dead; Richard could tell even from this range. *Poor bastard,* he thought, *must have hit a mine or something.* He stopped in his tracks. *A mine?* It suddenly dawned on him how many times he'd walked along that road. Then somebody shouted "booby trap" and the truth hit him like a thunderbolt.

For two weeks German deserters had been swimming across the Elbe River, not far from the mansion where Richard now stood. They came across in little groups usually, no more than ten or fifteen at a time. The Russians were coming and the Germans figured they stood a better chance surrendering to the western Allies, so they risked the swim and turned themselves in. And at least a dozen times, Richard had marched them past the spot where the ruined jeep sat. *It was rigged to blow all this time and I never set it off.* What an eerie feeling. He wondered, though, how many times this might have happened in other places – how many times he'd randomly avoided death and not known it. The way things were going, it didn't seem entirely unlikely.

The man was Austrian. He had short stubbly hair and sunken eyes, and his tattered uniform clung loosely around an emaciated frame. The look in his face spoke of fear and hopelessness. And of hunger. Frank Stevenson could barely stand to look at him; the pity was just too great.

"They trusted me," he said, his voice a wavering whisper, "The Germans permitted me to go where others could not."

Frank saw pleading in his eyes. *Let me show you,* it said, *somebody needs to know.*

So he followed in silence as the man hobbled from building to building. He saw the ovens, the graves, the rooms stacked with clothing. The man showed him everything, and when he finished there was nothing more for either of them to say. The scene was beyond words.

This is why we're here, Frank suddenly realized, *This is what we've suffered for: to save them.* His heart swelled with anguish and purpose all at once, and he found himself weeping. Dachau was free.

It was April when John Gallagher found himself aboard a hospital ship bound for the United States. After such a long time overseas, he was finally going home. His wounds were finally stabilized and it would be a long road to recovery, but at least he was alive. Sadly, his hands would no longer be the same. Yet *I'm still here,* he thought, *I have a purpose to serve.*

Days passed as the ship crossed the Atlantic on the warship line. During the night it was lit up like a beacon to announce itself as a hospital vessel. It was late in the war, though, and John wasn't worried about the Germans any more. He just enjoyed sitting on deck, feeling the breeze on his face and knowing he'd see his loved ones soon. This was the best feeling in the world.

John sometimes felt sad, however. He often thought of the Bulge, and of the retreating he'd done. Somehow it still didn't feel right, especially now that he knew how many men had been killed or captured. *We failed them,* he sometimes told himself, *we didn't fulfill our duty.*

Two days from home the ship received sad news: President Roosevelt had died. For a while everyone was very somber, but John knew it wasn't the end of the world. America had stuck together through adversity, and now things were getting better. Even without Roosevelt, life would go on. *We'll be okay,* he thought, *we're going to make it through this in the end.*

11

LOOKING BACK
REFLECTIONS

"I was in a meadow when I heard that Roosevelt had passed away. It was April, before the war was over. I think we were concerned... He was our commander in chief; certainly we were fond of him. That was a different war. Everybody knuckled down for everybody. It was a joint venture; everybody knew the country was behind them."

George Moore, France, 1945

When Paul Wolfinger was drafted in February of 1943, unlike most men, he was given a choice. Since his heart was already set on the navy, the decision was an easy one.

Paul took his boot camp in Sampson, New York, then attended electrician's school in Kentucky. By October 6, 1943, he was on a shakedown cruise in the Chesapeake Bay on the newly commissioned auxiliary repair and salvage ship ARS 36 Swivel. Paul, who would ultimately travel from Virginia to England, Scotland and Wales, and from France to Belgium and Holland, performed critical salvaging operations necessary for the war effort, particularly clean up and salvage work on Omaha and Utah Beaches.

On August 22, 1945, Paul was on leave in the beautiful city of Paris. With the capitulation of Japan just one week earlier, the war was over and Paul was feeling pretty good; however, he missed his sweetheart, Fern, who waited patiently for him back home in Reading, Pennsylvania. So he sent her the following telegram:

> *WESTERN UNION*
> *To: Miss Fern Hetrich*
> *PARIS LOVELY ... LOVLIER IF YOU WERE*
> *HERE ... GREATEST VICE GLASS OF BEER*
> *...WILL WRITE ... ALWAYS REMEMBER*
> *THAT I LOVE YOU ... PAUL WOLFINGER*

No wonder she waited for him!

Sometime after WWII ended, Joseph W. Yourkavitch found a letter in his mail box. The name on the return address was Gustav Schmiedel. The address was not familiar to Joe, as it was written in German. But Joe understood the word Deutschland.

During the Battle of the Bulge, Joe was captured on the 16th of December at St. Vith along with much of his unit. They'd been outnumbered, surrounded, and were ordered to strip their weapons and bury them. Their fight over, the men were marched through ice and snow for days to boxcars that took them to prison. Cold and frightened, yet still hopeful, the men sang Christmas carols during their week-long march.

The fifteen prisoners in Stalag IV-F were treated better than most. Joe was lucky and he knew it. The few guards in charge of the camp were older men, nearly seventy years old, and Joe said "they were pretty nice." He remembered one guard in particular. His name was Gustav Schmiedel. The letter read as follows:

Gustav Schmiedel
Bucholz – Sa.
Deutschland
Sowjet – Zone

Lieber freund Joseph!

I am referring to our acquaintance in prison camp in Hammerunterweisenthal and I always hoped that I would receive a letter from you. Since I did not get one, I would like to know how and if you got home and how you and yours are. Hopefully you and your loved ones are as healthy as I am. Also we don't have to go hungry. Our way of life is very simple and things are still not plentiful. I would like you to remember me and that you give me a sign that you are alive. I often talked about your humanitarianism that you prisoners had to put aside and I think about the time I was allowed to spend with you. I wish you good luck in the future.

Yours very truly.
Your friend from long ago
Posten – Schmiedel

"The greatest sight in my life," said Ralph Lerch "was seeing the Statue of Liberty from the deck of our ship." Ralph had just arrived home from the war and was standing on the flight deck with a few thousand men. On shore was a large sign that read "JOB WELL DONE."

"Let's not all go over to one side, you'll tip 'er over," Ralph's Captain joked, smiling at the men.

Ralph was thankful to be home in the great old USA. He had had a feeling from the time he was trained as a medic that he wasn't going to come home. But here he was, in New York Harbor! He never had the opportunity to serve as a combat medic; he'd been assigned to a medical supply depot instead. "Sometimes I feel guilty that I wasn't a combat soldier to experience what those boys went through," Ralph said. "But I had a job I was proud to do, and I liked the army."

Ralph was sent to Indiantown Gap for discharge, but was detained for a case of pyorrhea which required treatment. His parents surprised him with a much welcomed visit to Indiantown Gap. "I didn't recognize my father;" Ralph remembered, "he got awful gray."

Ralph was finally discharged from the army a few weeks later in January of 1946. He hopped on a bus which took him to the Franklin Street Station in downtown Reading, Pennsylvania. Because Ralph hadn't told anyone he was coming home, he arrived home to an empty house. Or so he thought.

When Ralph opened the front door, he was stopped in his tracks. Pepper, his much beloved bulldog was glaring at him, teeth bared. "I was standing in the front door in my army overcoat," recalls Ralph, "and my bulldog, Pepper, challenged me." After three long years, Pepper had forgotten his best buddy until Ralph inquired, "Pepper?" The dog leapt into Ralph's arms and licked his face. Boy was it good to be home!

When the war in Europe ended a frail Paul Fett remembers "taking that steel helmet off and throwing it as far as I could throw it. It weighed a ton!"

Paul was going home now, by ambulance, and taking with him the hepatitis he'd picked up somewhere in Europe; hepatitis he would carry with him for the rest of his life. Be he didn't care; he had survived the war, and he was going home!

Russel Rightmyer was in Paris the day that victory was declared in Europe. He was in his quarters at the hospital when he heard the news.

Assigned to the 108th General Hospital in Paris, Russel was a trained medical tech assigned to a surgical team. He had just finished a long shift. "It was tough duty," particularly during "gruesome times," Russel recalled, but "doing it every day you soon got accustomed to it and went on with your life."

Russel considered himself one lucky guy, and thought, *it was better than being on the front lines, getting shot at or even killed.* He calls his service a "wonderful experience."

At one point Russel felt "somewhat ashamed that he did not serve in a combat unit." He has finally put those feelings to rest.

Russel changed his clothes and went out to celebrate. Everybody was in the streets, partying, celebrating one of the greatest days in history.

"I went out and celebrated," Russel smiled at the memory, "A grand long celebration."

Kenneth "George" Reitnouer learned a lot about leadership during his time in the army. He'd been drafted in March of 1943 and took basic training at Camp McQuaide, California. "Basic training put our muscles in the right place," he smiled as he spoke.

"I wanted to go to the navy, but the navy wouldn't take me; I was color blind, terribly color blind, so they put me in the army which was all right. I had no qualms about that."

George remembers the impenetrable fog at balmy Camp McQuaide. "In the afternoon the fog rolled in, then at 7:00 in the morning it rolled out again. We knew our way from the main PX to our quarters in the fog." George was trained on artillery which "was an experience in itself because I never saw anything that big," and then he was shipped to Key West, Florida, assigned to a Coastal Defense Unit.

In Key West George's unit trained on 3-inch coast artillery guns, world war one types. And George loved it! The unit was on 24-hour alert, but the men had free time to play baseball and swim at the beach. George's only complaint was "there were too many sailors. There were ten sailors to every G.I. At the USO dances sailors were always cutting in!"

George's unit practiced a lot of night firing during their training in Key West. Large drums for use as targets were placed strategically on the water. During the night the local pelican population took up residence on the targets. "The drums were loaded with pelicans!" George said. "They'd land on these drums and the search lights would come on... we were required to shoot if the searchlights went on. We never knew who was out there!" With the lights on, the men could see the pelicans; there'd be ten or twelve in a row, and the men had 50 caliber water-cooled machine guns. The birds were decimated in seconds, bit and pieces afloat in the water, feathers adrift in the breeze.

Needless to say, the residents of Key West were up in arms about it. The army was killing their beloved native birds. "Somebody took the blame for it," George said, "but it wasn't me!"

In March of 1944, George's unit was de-activated and the men were loaded into trucks and taken to Miami to become part of the 4th Coastal Defense Command.

"I had a lot of seasickness. The navy pulled targets for us and it seems like my name came up quite often to help. We went out on little tugboats to pull the targets; it was a bumpy, rolling ride. The targets were out about three miles; the guns were good for about 5 miles." The targets were no larger than four feet square and George and the men easily blew them out of the water.

As a child, George grew up in Oley, Pennsylvania in a close-knit family. "Oh, boy, were we ever..." George smiled at the memory. We played baseball, went swimming in the creek, went hunting, and learned to work hard on a farm. "My father was a 'one-liner;' he kept us in stitches, and my mother kept us in line.

After world war two, George went on to serve in the Korean War. When asked what he did in the service, George said, "I didn't do much." But George was proud to serve his country and will always remember it as "a great experience overall."

When Carl Mengel of the 821st Signal Wire Maintenance Corps looks back on his experience during world war two in Newfoundland, he says, "I had a wonderful military experience... I was just one of the lucky ones. When I think of those guys who were in the war zone... oh, my God... how they trudged, what they went through, the Battle of the Bulge. My God, we were at repeater stations. We had plenty to eat; we didn't have to worry about whether we would get something to eat, or if we were going to be fired at... No, I just wasn't in the war, thank goodness. I was lucky. Somebody had to do it."

Tommaso Gentile was a baker in the Italian Army. His unit, forced to retreat from their fight in Tobruk, eventually surrendered to the British in Tunis. They had run out of ammunition and were stranded in a deserted air field just outside of town waiting for a flight to take them home to Italy. Tommaso was relieved to be free of the war, but he was apprehensive at the prospect of becoming a prisoner of war.

The British were overrun with prisoners, and to Tommaso's relief, he was turned over to the United States. For seven days he and several hundred other prisoners sat cramped in boxcars headed for a camp in Casablanca. "We cut air holes in the side of the boxcar," he recalled, "and I put my mouth in the hole to breathe." The men were given breaks only twice a day for food and toilets.

A few days into their trip, the prisoners heard a loud thump and the train came screeching to a halt. Two cars were damaged and removed, and the prisoners were transferred to the three remaining already crowded boxcars. Tommaso does not know what the train hit, but the rest of the journey to Casablanca was more uncomfortable than before.

Tommaso remembered, "In Casablanca I was in a field outside of town. We were fed a lot of corned beef…the Americans treated us well." He remembers a swarm of locusts that came through the camp. They were so thick he could see only a few feet in front of his face.

One month later, Tommaso was transported to the United States in a liberty ship. "I wore my life vest for the entire journey," he said. "You never know, the Germans might shoot the ship!"

"It took twenty-two days to get to the U.S. When I got to New York, I kissed the floor," Tommaso recalled, tears welling up in his eyes. It was 1943, and even though Tommaso was a prisoner of war, in his heart he was a free man. He was showered and processed, then shipped by rail to a camp in Missouri to wait out the war.

One day the prisoners were asked, "Who wants to go to work?" Tommaso immediately volunteered even though he was not required to work. He was paid eighty cents a day to pick potatoes, and was given one pack of cigarettes a week even though he didn't smoke. And Tommaso was grateful. So much so that he decided to join the U.S. Army.

On March 14, 1944, Tommaso, in his lovely broken English, proudly announced that he had "signed up to join the United States of America to the best of my ability."

Slightly premature, Lewis "James" Matthews, III was born at home on the kitchen table, put in a shoe box, and placed in the oven to keep him warm. His diminutive size at birth had no effect on his childhood, however; he grew to be a strapping lad, spending much of his time on the beautiful Chesapeake Bay near his childhood home in Takoma Park, Maryland.

James like many young men feared the draft and enlisted. Having had some college at the University of Maryland, James enrolled at King's Point Academy for the Merchant Marine. Right from the start James knew he'd made the right decision and he graduated in October of 1943 with a B.S. in Marine Transportation. His younger brother, Stephen, followed in his footsteps and graduated the following year.

James' first assignment was deck officer on the USS Herald of the Morning, a cargo ship with five holds. He was responsible for navigating, steering the ship, tracking depth, handling mooring lines and anchors, and keeping all equipment in good working order. In October of 1943 the Herald of the Morning left San Francisco with a load of petroleum destined for Pearl Harbor. She traveled alone, unescorted; there was no convoy to protect her.

In January of 1944 James was transferred to the SS W.B. Rodgers, a Liberty ship, and given the assignment of transporting cargo to support the war effort in the Italian Campaign. James' brother Steve remembered, "They got shot at plenty of times."

James served his country from October of 1943 to the end of the war in August of 1945, primarily in the North Atlantic and the Italian Campaign, and for one additional year serving on vessels traveling primarily to England and France.

Just like the army, navy, air force and marines, the United States Merchant Marine played a very important role in bringing the war to an end. They provided logistical support for the United States during world war two manning cargo ships that transported critical supplies to the battlefronts across the Atlantic, Pacific and Mediterranean. They operated primarily Liberty and Victory cargo ships that transported ammunition, food, weapons, tanks, airplanes, fuel, clothing, medical supplies, and many other items.

Their job was a dangerous one, as many of their ships were sunk by German submarines. By war's end, the United States Merchant Marine suffered the loss of seven hundred thirty marine vessels, with a loss of eight thousand, five hundred men.

Fortunately James was not one of them; he had survived the war. And he was proud of his service in the Merchant Marine.

Lew Carter was homesick already, especially for his sweetheart, Verna. He was sitting in a "cattle boat" gazing up at the beautiful Golden Gate Bridge. A few hours earlier his unit had gotten off the train in San Francisco and was marched directly onto a ship like cattle to the slaughter.

He'd just finished recruit training at Fort Belvar in Virginia and was headed for Honolulu. They weren't told where they were headed, but "everything was marked Honolulu...so we knew where we were going...nobody told us nothing, except...we'll be back in a year."

Recruit training wasn't too bad, but the first couple of weeks Lew was homesick, and heading out to sea now made him feel worse than ever, particularly the churning in his gut. Lew was seasick and he hadn't even left the harbor.

Lew had no idea what lay ahead for him. He could never have imagined that in less than two months he'd be involved in the attack on Pearl Harbor. Or that more than three years would pass before he would go home again.

Lew's family waited anxiously for more than two weeks before a letter arrived telling them he was all right. "Am safe," wrote Lew, to their great relief. Then Lew "wrote and asked Verna's mom for permission...I was giving my money to my mom and dad to put in the bank...I told them to go get so much money and take Verna to Reading and buy her a diamond ring." And they did. Verna was overjoyed and sick with worry at the same time.

Lew remained in Pearl Harbor for nearly two years before moving with his unit to Ellis Island to build an airstrip for the Air Corps. Eager to let his family in on his whereabouts, he figured out a way to let them know without breaking any rules. "You couldn't tell anybody where you were," he recalled, "so I wrote home and said, 'do you remember farmer Miller? I can't tell you where I am, but think of what farmer Miller's name is.' His name was Ellis. His mother wrote back and said, 'I know where you are.'"

Finally, in May of 1945, Lew was given the word that he was going home.

"I went down to the supply sergeant to get new clothes to go home in." Lew said, "He gave me an old coat and I said I don't want it."

"You have to take it," he replied curtly. "You'll only throw it away when you get home."

"It's none of your business what I do with it. I'm not going home in an old coat!" Lew was adamant, and the sergeant handed him a new coat.

Lew was impatient. Comfortably settled into his seat on the train, he looked in the direction of the conductor.

"When we get to Birdsboro, tell me," Lew instructed the man.

"Yes, sir," the conductor nodded his head and smiled at the soldier.

When Lew stepped off the train in his hometown of Birdsboro, Pennsylvania, his family was waiting for him. It was Memorial Day, 1945.

"My mom wouldn't let me take my uniform off," Lew said, suddenly glad for the new coat.

"We're going to go see the parade first," she announced proudly. The war was over, and Lew was home. He never felt happier in his life.

At the age of seventeen, David Voigt enlisted in the Army Air Corps Cadet Program. Called up in January of 1945, he reported to New Cumberland, Pennsylvania with high hopes. From the time David was a boy he remembers thinking, "I want to be a part of this...maybe a bombardier." But David was given disappointing news, "all schools are closed." No pilot, navigator or bombardier schools were accepting applicants. Even gunnery school was closed!

"So they gave us options for tech school," David said, and he easily qualified for radio operator school at Scott Air Force Base in Illinois. David was told after the test that he had a good aptitude for code. "The funny thing about that was when I was in the Scouts, the one test I really couldn't pass was code, so I took Indian sign language." David laughed.

At Scott Air Force base, David attended what he called "code college" where he quickly became proficient in Morse code and typing. After nine weeks of training, he received a certificate for achieving 30 words per minute. David was very proud of that. "I felt good about becoming a radio operator... something like that I figured I could never do."

Shortly after, David was assigned to the 133rd Airways Communication System Squadron at Keesler Field in Mississippi. It was there he heard that FDR had died. "FDR was my hero," he said. "They made us march...it was getting pretty warm at that time, it was April," David remembered. "Then the war ended a month later and we had to march again. It was quite a parade, quite a victory parade."

David was eventually sent to Germany, to a Luftwaffe base in Bavaria as part of the occupation forces. Everything was peaceful; he was free to use public transportation, and the German people gave him no trouble.

"I was surprised when I got to go to Germany and the occupation. The funny thing about the occupation was we never were scared. What kind of occupation situation could you imagine where everything is just about as docile as it gets? During an occupation, you have to be afraid of what people will do. But it never crossed my mind to be afraid. I was an 18-year-old kid. We all felt that way. We knew the war was over, the Germans had surrendered, and we had jobs to do. I don't think we expected any problems." But David knew he'd have to be on his toes.

David enjoyed the job he was trained for. He was happy to be doing his part to help the war effort, but he felt that his job was not anything comparable to what it must have been like on the line. "In that sense, I wasn't tested," he said. But he was grateful. "I felt like every day in the service was a day in college, and I carried that thought all the way through to my master's."

DeLight Breidegam was a skilled cryptographer. In December of 1944, at the age of seventeen, he enlisted in the Army Air Force because his father objected to DeLight's first choice, the navy. In March, "I got a letter...to try out for the aviation cadet program. They'd send me to Gettysburg College for awhile until I could get into the rotation."

DeLight was excited, so his dad said, "okay."

"We weren't going to get paid, but we got tuition and...books and room and board." DeLight was told he'd be attending school for ninety days, but would put in nine months of college before he was called back. DeLight studied "really intensive stuff. I was very fortunate," he recalls, "because it was basically engineering and aeronautics and a lot of military stuff." His double session of studies netted him the equivalent of two years of college. He knew that he was a lucky guy.

Next was basic training at Shepherd Field, Texas, and "getting into shape which I was happy for." And then in May, the war in Europe ended. "I was pretty happy. Some of the guys were told they could leave if they wanted to, but not me; I was going to be involved in the invasion of Japan."

DeLight was sent to Scott Air Force Base in Illinois. The only school accepting candidates was gunnery school, "because the Japanese would kill the tail gunners, making the plane more vulnerable."

DeLight's immediate response was, "What else do you have?"

"Cryptography school," was the reply.

DeLight was interested and asked, "What's that?" And he took the test. Only seventeen out of four thousands men qualified, and he was one of them.

Months passed by and most of the men DeLight had taken basic with were gone, shipped out to their assignments. "I sat there 'till the early part of September and took advanced basic just to give me something to do. Then I was put on a permanent detail working in the laundry."

VJ Day came and went and DeLight was relieved. VE Day was good news; but VJ Day was big news."

But he was still waiting. "I was becoming a cryptographer, and to be a cryptographer you had to get top secret clearance. I had to wait because a letter was sent home to a constable named Frank Reed. He was the only law enforcement in my hometown to check my background, and he responded that I came from a responsible family. So until I got that letter, I had to wait to go off to cryptography school."

DeLight was given leave to go home that Christmas of 1945. The newly trained cryptographer was eager to see his family. Christmas at home revived him, and knowing the war was over, he returned to the Army Air Force with renewed enthusiasm. Gone was the fear of war. DeLight was grateful for his peace of mind.

He returned from leave in January of 1946 to finish out his service as a cryptographer: first in Grenier Field in Manchester New Hampshire, then Washington National Airport, and finally a short stint at the Pentagon.

DeLight remembers the day the President of the United States sent a message to his troops, congratulating them on a job well done. "The message was so long, and the system was so slow, they worked on it for over two days!"

Richard Wenrich wasn't drafted until the summer of 1944, and when the war ended in Europe he did not have enough points to go home. Richard had joined the 84th Infantry Division sometime after the Battle of the Bulge, and went to Berlin with the occupation forces to finish up his time.

"They announced the war was over a day ahead," Richard remembers. "We were in a small town in Germany and everybody had lots to drink, wine mostly, some cognac." They weren't afraid to drink it because they knew the Germans drank it. Richard remembers being in a high school gymnasium when they got the news.

He said, "We were all in there when the captain announced that the war was over. Everybody went wild and had a couple more drinks. But it wasn't right…that was the wrong date. It happened the following day. So everybody celebrated again. We had two celebrations!"

Richard was given a job in the officers' mess hall answering the phone while the officers were eating. "That was the sweetest job I ever had."

Lester Groff was in Marseilles, France when he heard that the Japanese had surrendered. Having fought his way across Europe in a Sherman tank, getting wounded several times, Lester was greatly relieved that he wouldn't be going to Japan. So he and his buddies got drunk.

"We were happy," he reminisced, "we were not going to war. I was with five GIs drinking champagne. We each had a bottle," Lester smiled at the memory, "and we drank our bottles." A mischievous grin spread across Lester's face, "and when we stood up, we fell over. Bump, bump, bump."

And there they lay, for quite some time, sprawled across the floor. And Lester thanked God. He was done with war.

"We were over there in the area when the news came over the PA system that President Truman gave the order to drop the bombs on Hiroshima and Nagasaki the prior day...I felt a sigh of relief. It was over when we got to Tokyo Bay," Edwin Gegenheimer recalled.

The light cruiser, USS Oklahoma City entered Tokyo Bay on September 10, 1945, less than one month after VJ Day. Assigned to occupation duties, it would afford Ed the opportunity to visit Tokyo.

Ed, a sailor at heart, had enlisted in the navy in August of 1944. He'd been assigned to the newly-commissioned Oklahoma City and was very proud of the fact that he was one of its original 1,200 crew members.

Ed remembers being permitted shore leave and visiting Tokyo. "There wasn't much left standing," he remembers, "everything was gone." It was depressing to Ed, and he eventually stopped going ashore.

The Oklahoma City continued its occupation duties steaming around the Japanese islands until January of 1946. After picking up 650 American GIs, the big ship headed for San Francisco.

In the meantime, Ed had passed a test and became a ship's cook. He was happy in the galley, particularly now that the war was over, and enjoyed every minute of time he spent there.

"I remember putting 2,500 pork chops in the ovens; every man got two pork chops. We ate good!" Ed particularly remembers the extra large cans of corned beef, and the corned beef sandwiches that nearly cost him his life.

Knowing there weren't enough rations for an additional 650 GIs, Ed asked his superior officer, "What do we feed 'em, Chief?"

"Give them corned beef sandwiches!"

Ed wasn't too happy about serving fighting men corned beef sandwiches for breakfast, lunch and dinner, but he was one to follow orders.

Two days of corned beef sandwiches set the GIs to grumbling, and by the fifth day, they began making threats.

Ed overheard a very angry voice just outside his window. "The next son of a bitch that hands me a corned beef sandwich is going over the side!"

Ed swallowed hard. He knew the man wasn't joking. "It wasn't fair to those men," he thought, "they deserved better." And that was not the way Ed wanted to die.

The very next meal Ed ran six hundred and fifty additional men through the chow line; the Chief had given the okay. "Run them through the chow line; we're halfway home," he told Ed. Ed wouldn't have had it any other way.

Charles "Charlie" Brubaker and Robert "Red" Wells seemed to have a lot in common. Both were born in Reading, Pennsylvania, to families who lived just two blocks apart. The men even shared the same birthday,

August 3, 1923.   As boys, they ran the streets, played baseball and fished. But their paths had never crossed.

Although Red enlisted in the army and Charlie was drafted into the navy, both men came under assault: Red in the battlefields of Belgium and France, and Charlie in an attack on the English Channel on an LST prior to D-Day.

Charlie was assigned to an LST ferrying men to Omaha Beach at the same time Red was shipped to Omaha Beach by LST to join the fight. While Red fought his way across Europe, Charlie continued to carry troops to Omaha Beach from D-Day on, then turned around and transported allied wounded and German prisoners of war back to England.

By war's end in early May, Charlie was assigned to transport Special Forces, the 474th Infantry Regiment (Separate) by LST to Norway.

At precisely the same time, Red's unit, the 474th Infantry Regiment (Separate) was sent to Norway on those same LSTs.

Both men participated in post war activities: Red in Norway rounding up Germans and POW's, and Charlie collecting and dumping excess ammunition into the Atlantic Ocean.

Finally, near the end of 1946, both men were discharged and went back to the same hometown.

Many years later when Red and Charlie were 84 years old, Red's daughter planned to bring the two men together. With so much in common, the two could finally get to know each other. But sadly Red never made it; he passed away before the meeting took place. At least they knew about each other; someone had taken the time to tell them.

12

THE TRAGEDY OF WAR
AFTERMATH

"At a very young age I got a deep appreciation for life and death. You're never the same. It did make me appreciate life very, very much... what life was about, what death was about. Was I proud to serve my country? Oh my, yes!"

John Allison, Pacific, 1945

Richard Becker's mother, Elsie, sat on the sofa in her living room with the lights turned off, weeping quietly, her bowed head resting in her hands. Her daughter, Geraldine turned on a lamp and asked her mother what was wrong. Elsie had gotten letters before from her son, Richard, and his best friend, Ross Beeler, but none like the one she'd received this afternoon.

"Leave the light off," Elsie whispered, handing the letter to her daughter.

Geraldine reached for the letter and began to cry.

Ross' letter was filled with grief as he gently recounted the events leading up to the accident. He spoke of an engine in flames, a B-29 hitting the water and splitting in half, seven of a crew of eleven perishing in the water at four o'clock in the morning.

Ross went on to say that he and Richard were sitting side by side in the plane before the crash. It all had happened so fast; Richard had simply disappeared in the night. Ross spoke of hitting the water and being sucked under, of being injured and unable to help. He explained the circumstances in the only way he knew how, by speaking truthfully so Elsie would know how her son had died.

But she didn't know. She didn't know about the crash, or that Richard was gone. The war department had neglected to tell her.

Ross had gone to the Chaplain right after the accident and told him what happened. Assuming the family had already been informed, the Chaplain suggested that Ross write them a letter explaining the circumstances. The Chaplain censored the letter and it quickly went through.

Ten days later, the doorbell at the Becker house rang. No one ever rang the doorbell, not in their comfortable close-knit neighborhood. Not neighbors, nor relatives, nor friends. Folks just walked in. Elsie knew who was at her door.

The telegram from the war department was brief. It stated simply that Richard B. Becker had gone missing in action on May 5, 1945.

The family was devastated. Richard's father, LeRoy, who'd been ill with asthma and emphysema, took a turn for the worse and was never able to return to work. Elsie, in spite of her grief, trudged on, working full time and taking care of her family and home.

The night before Richard went into the service, he was working on an airplane that he had carved from a piece of wood. The P40 had a ten-inch wingspan and Richard worked feverishly to finish it before he left home. He managed to finish the plane and he even put a coat of paint on it. And the next morning he was gone.

One month after Richard's death, Geraldine woke up in the night and saw him standing at the foot of her bed. He said to her, "I'm okay," and then he disappeared. The vision gave her a great deal of peace, but she didn't speak of it until six months later. When Geraldine finally told her mother, Elsie responded, "He came to me, too; and to David. He appeared at the foot of the bed as a bright light."

The little P40 that Richard so lovingly crafted sits on a shelf in David's home. And very much like that little plane that David cherishes, Richard is cherished, too. And this beautiful man and the thousands of others who were lost to war will always be remembered in the hearts of family and friends.

George R. Hess, one of thirteen children born to Raymond and Mabel Hess, lived on a farm in the beautiful Oley Valley in Berks County, Pennsylvania. Though his life seemed idyllic, and it was for the most part, George and his siblings worked hard in the fields helping their father to support the large family. George was a handsome young man with blue eyes and light brown hair. He was quiet, easy going, and his lean frame stood over six feet tall.

Like millions of other young men across the country, George was drafted, and in February of 1942, he was inducted into the United States Army in New Cumberland, Pennsylvania. Whisked off to Camp Croft in South Carolina for basic training, twelve weeks later George was a full-fledged infantry soldier.

There are missing pieces to George's army life, but we know that he was ultimately attached to the 157th Infantry Regiment of the 45th Division. Sometime after finishing basic, he boarded the USS Charles Carroll, an attack transport, at Newport News, Virginia for transport to Oran in Algiers. There he would prepare to fight in the Italian Campaign. George left for Sicily and on the 10th of July participated in the invasion. His next major engagement was the invasion of Italy on September 9, 1943 and just three days later, George was captured by the Germans at Salerno.

On the day of his capture, George was injured when he was struck in the neck with the butt of a German rifle. This injury earned him the Purple Heart. He earned the Bronze Star as well for his participation in the Italian Campaign.

Thus began the nightmare that would alter George for the rest of his life.

Immediately after he was captured, he was placed in Stalag II-B in Mooseberg, which was situated one and a half miles west of Hammerstein in West Prussia (now Germany). On the train where they made their final journey to the camp, the thirsty prisoners held their upturned helmets out the doors in an attempt to catch some rain water. The helmets were shot out of their hands by the Germans. Stalag II-B, with about 5,000 other POWs is where George would spend the next twenty-two months of his life struggling to survive as a prisoner of war.

Stalag II-B was a work camp. Most of the prisoners were taken to surrounding farms and put to work. George was initially treated a little better than the others because he spoke Pennsylvania Dutch, but soon after was put to work on a farm with everybody else. He did farm chores and took care of cattle. Others worked in the camp shoe shop or at the post office if you spoke German, and others were taken to Munich to repair craters left by Allied bombs. Munich was still under siege by the allies and POWs died regularly doing their dangerous job filling holes.

Early 1945, the Germans feared the inevitable Russian invasion and quickly began to march their POWs deeper into Germany rather than turn them over to the Russians who would free them. This five hundred mile mass exodus of prisoners from Stalag II-B and many other POW camps became known as a death march.

When one thinks of a death march, one thinks of Bataan. But few know that a death march did in fact occur in Germany between December 1944 and April 1945. Near the end of the war, Hitler gave the order to kill all prisoners. Some were marched into concentration camps and murdered; others were lined up and shot. Fortunately many survived at the hands of allies who intercepted their march.

Tens of thousands were rushed out of camps all over Germany on foot with little or no warning. Sick prisoners were loaded up and taken "away," sadly never to be seen again. The march lasted for nearly three months, and POWs suffered daily from illness, cold, tuberculosis, trench foot, dysentery, polluted water, starvation, and exhaustion. Many died each day. If one faltered, he was shot. POWs were marched in groups of several hundred, long distances each day, with little to eat. They slept on the ground in the bitter cold weather, some of them freezing to death in their sleep.

They lived in filth in the tattered clothing they'd worn for many months, sometimes for two or more years. Some managed to escape by hiding in coal bins or chicken coops, while others were shot for their efforts. Those who fell ill were shot as well.

How George endured this, we will never know, but we do know that he increasingly withdrew into himself. He became quiet and remote, a solitary human in a camp of thousands, a man who wanted to be alone, alone to block out that which he suffered. George survived, but he wasn't himself anymore. George was gone.

Finally, on the third of May, George was liberated by the Yankees. Moments before American troops arrived, he was lined up with dozens of others to be summarily executed. Suddenly the voice of a POW rang out joyfully, "The Yanks are coming! The Yanks are coming!" The Germans took their weapons and fled.

Five days later the war in Europe ended and George went home to his family. He stayed in his room, avoided family and friends, barely able to function. Eventually he was admitted to the Veterans' Hospital in Lebanon, Pennsylvania, where he stayed for the next 20 years. The handsome blue-eyed man who grew up on a farm in the Oley Valley was just a shell of his former self. A beautiful mind, lost to war.

After the war, George rarely spoke again. He would occasionally mutter something unsolicited about his war experiences to a family member, such as, "He complained about the food, and they shot him dead," or, "They shot the helmets from our hands; we only wanted a drink of water." And then George was silent again. Tidbits of information, that's what George gave his family, and they wrote it down so it would not be forgotten, so that George's memory will forever live on.

Five months into George's imprisonment, he wrote the following message on a Stalag-issued postcard to his mother:

> *Kriegsgefangenenpost, Camp des prisonniers*
> *Correspondance des prisonniers de guerre*
> *Stalag II B Postkarte*
>
> *Feb. 6, 1944*
> *Dear Mother: It's been so long since I've heard from you. I'm letting you know that I am feeling fine. I hope you and everybody are having a good time. Well I guess this is all for now. Hope seeing you soon. -George*

John Gallagher had his first airplane ride while lying on a litter hanging from the roof of the plane. It reminded him of the troop ship that took him to Europe; a big ship that could easily have outrun the Germans. John's job was to throw the trash overboard every night, and *boy did I get seasick!* The ship had bunks stacked four high, one on top of the other, and John was on the top. He could hear the water splashing around at night. *What an ordeal.*

John was relieved when the plane finally touched down in England and he could get out of that hammock. It had been a relatively comfortable flight in spite of his injuries. His sight had finally returned, *thank God,* and he was beginning to walk normally again.

John was taken to a hospital in England. There he walked outside on his own for the first time since being wounded. "I was able to walk outside without a helmet, and that was the first I ever could go to the boys' room. I felt so free, I almost cried."

Finally, in April of 1945 John was transferred to a hospital ship that set sail for home. They steamed south of the warship line to keep out of the way of seagoing traffic, brightly lit up at night so all would know they were a hospital ship. John sat up on deck and enjoyed the voyage. *Oh, what a beautiful trip.* Two days outside the United States, John was given the sad news that President Roosevelt had died.

They docked in Charleston, South Carolina and John was carried from the ship on a litter. The only belongings he carried with him were his dog tags, and attached to that was his wedding ring and his school ring. Both rings had been removed from his badly wounded hands by capable surgeons in a field hospital.

John was flown to Walter Reed Army Hospital for additional surgery. He completely regained normal eyesight and no longer had any difficulty walking. "I just had one finger off and they had to decide what to do, as the fingers do not work, only the thumb works on the right hand." John lost his left hand completely.

John came home from the war to the arms of his loving wife, Stella, physically different than before, but grateful to be alive. He never lost his zest for life nor his love of God. And he wasn't angry. But he regretted that he couldn't do more for his country; felt as though he never really completed the job the army trained him to do. Yet without giving any thought to his own safety, John acted to save the life of another human being. John had given generously.

Richard Becker, George Hess and John Gallagher were just three of millions of ordinary men and women who gave their all for their country. Why did they do it? Was it a sense of duty? Love for their country? A hatred of the enemy? Or because they had too? What difference does it make? They did it. And magnificently.

Most survived, but many tens of thousands died. And thousands of others came home less perfect than when they arrived.

They served on the ground, in vehicles, and in the trenches. In the air, on the sea, and along our coasts to protect our nation. The restored peace to a world at war.

And each in his own remarkable way.   They went to war.
Each one ordinary. All of them heroes.

PHOTOGRAPHS

John Allison
Born 1927 in Tamaqua, Pennsylvania
U.S. Navy 1944 Pacific
USS Success Auxiliary Minesweeper AM-310 Pacific
Resides in Wernersville, Pennsylvania

James A. Angert
Born 1920 in Butler, Pennsylvania
U.S. Army 1942
99th Infantry Division – Europe
Wounded in Belgium January 31, 1945
Resides in Wernersville, Pennsylvania

Richard B. Becker
Born 1925 in Reading, Pennsylvania
U.S. Army Air Force 1944
875th Bombardment Squadron, 498th Bombardment Group
Killed May 5, 1945 when his B-29 crashed off Saipan

W. Ross Beeler
Born 1924 in Seneca County, Ohio
U.S. Army Air Force 1943
875th Bombardment Squadron, 498th Bombardment Group
Wounded in B-29 Crash off Saipan on May 5, 1945
Resides in Tippen, Ohio

Willard M. Bickel
Born 1924 in Pottstown, Pennsylvania
U.S. Army 1943
104th Infantry Regiment
Resides in Pottstown, Pennsylvania

Richard L. Biehl
Born 1923 in Temple, Pennsylvania
U.S. Army 1942
1st Division
D-Day Omaha Beach
Resides in Wyomissing, Pennsylvania

Stanley W. Blazejewski, Jr.
Born 1924 in Wilkes-Barre, Pennsylvania
U.S. Army 1943
9th Armored Division
Resides in Downingtown, Pennsylvania

DeLight E. Breidegam, Jr.
Born 1926 in Fleetwood, Pennsylvania
U.S. Army Air Force 1945
Cryptographer
Resides in Lyon Station, Pennsylvania

Charles J. Brubaker
Born 1923 in Reading, Pennsylvania
U.S. Navy 1943 Atlantic
Exercise Tiger, D-Day Omaha Beach
USS LST-511 Amphibious Forces
Resides in Mohnton, Pennsylvania

George Lewis "Lew" Carter
Born 1918 in Birdsboro, Pennsylvania
U.S. Army 1941
34th Combat Engineers
Pearl Harbor Survivor
Resides in Reading, Pennsylvania

Carl Frey Constein
Born 1920 in Fleetwood, Pennsylvania
Army Air Force 1943
China-Burma-India Theatre
96 Missions over the Hump
Resides in Wernersville, Pennsylvania

Martin E. Dorminy
Born 1924 in Fitzgerald, Georgia
U.S. Army 1943
106th Infantry Division
Prisoner of War
Resides in Leesport, Pennsylvania

Paul H. Fett
Born 1925 in Reading, Pennsylvania
U.S. Army 1943
108th Machine Gun Battalion – 28th Division
Resides in Reading, Pennsylvania

Gabriel "Gabe" J. Fieni
Born 1922 in Pottstown, Pennsylvania
U.S. Army 1943
1st Division Medic
D-Day Omaha Beach
Resides in Reading, Pennsylvania

John I. Gallagher
Born 1920 in Lebanon, Pennsylvania
U.S. Army 1943
106th Infantry Division
Wounded in Belgium
Resides in Reading, Pennsylvania

Edwin R. Gegenheimer
Born 1926 in Reading, Pennsylvania
U.S. Navy 1944 Pacific
USS Oklahoma City
Resides in Reading, Pennsylvania

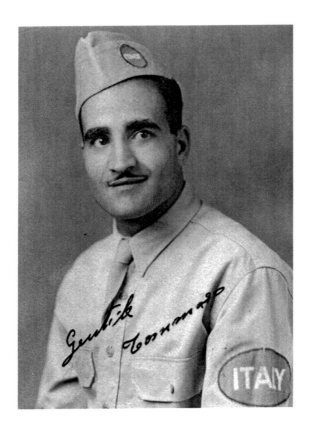

Tommaso Felice Gentile
Born 1919 in Andali, Catanzaro, Italy
Italian Army 1940
Captured in Tunis - May 1943 by the British
1943 Brought to US as a Prisoner of War
Joined U.S. Army March 1944
Resides in Reading, Pennsylvania

Paul Revere Gordon
Born 1920 in Cressona, Pennsylvania
U.S. Army Air Force 1941
B-17 Turret Gunner shot down over France
Wounded in France
Prisoner of War
Resides in Birdsboro, Pennsylvania

Cyrus M. Greenburg
Born 1925 in Philadelphia, Pennsylvania
U.S. Navy 1943 Pacific
USS LST 622
Resides in Reading, Pennsylvania

Lester Groff
Born 1924 in Pottstown, Pennsylvania
U.S. Army 1943
3rd Armored Division Tank Driver
D-Day Omaha Beach
Wounded in Germany
Resides in Reading, Pennsylvania

Charles T. Gryniewich
Born 1924 in Hellertown, Pennsylvania
U.S. Army 1943
78th Infantry Division
Resides in West Lawn, Pennsylvania

Kenneth C. Hart
Born 1923 in Seyfert, Pennsylvania
U.S. Army Air Force 1943
B-17 Ball Turret Gunner
Crash landed in Naples
Wounded in Naples
Resides in Wyomissing, Pennsylvania

George L. Hatza, Sr.
Born 1918 in Reading, Pennsylvania
U.S. Navy 1938 Pacific
USS Tucker
Pearl Harbor Survivor
Resides in Mt. Penn, Pennsylvania

John H. Henninger
Born 1925 in Reading, Pennsylvania
U.S. Army Air Force 1942 Pacific
B-29 Pilot 20th Air Force
Resides in Wyomissing, Pennsylvania

George R. Hess
Born 1919 in Oley, Pennsylvania
U.S. Army 1942
45th Infantry Division
Prisoner of War – Captured in Italy
Deceased

Richard A. Hiller
Born 1924 in Reading, Pennsylvania
U.S. Army 1943
80th Division
Wounded in Europe
Resides in West Reading, Pennsylvania

Geraldine A. Houp
Born 1918 in Oley, Pennsylvania
U.S. Navy Nurse
Panama and United States
Resides in Reading, Pennsylvania

Lyle M. Koenig
Born 1920 in Armstrong, Iowa
U.S. Navy 1939 Pacific
USS Aylwin
Pearl Harbor Survivor
Resides in Bernville, Pennsylvania

Francis J. "Frank" Lashinsky
Born 1924 in Mahanoy City
U.S. Army Air Force1942
Crash landed in Yugoslavia
Crash landed in Hungary
Prisoner of War – Captured in Hungary
Resides in Cornwall, Pennsylvania

Ralph Lerch
Born 1922 in Reading, Pennsylvania
U.S. Army 1943
65th Medical Depot Company
Resides in Reading, Pennsylvania

Ralph S. Mason
Born 1923 in Portland, Oregon
U.S. Navy Pacific
USS Honolulu
Pearl Harbor Survivor
Resides in Reading, Pennsylvania

Lewis James Matthews
Born 1920 in Takoma Park, Maryland
U.S. Merchant Marine 1944
Atlantic, Pacific, Mediterranean
Passed away March 2, 1976

Carl D. Mengel
Born 1918 in Cross Keys, Pennsylvania
U.S. Army 1942
821st Signal Wire Maintenance Corps
Newfoundland
Resides in Reading, Pennsylvania

Jerome N. Merkel
U.S. Army 1942
75th Infantry Division
Resides in Boyertown, Pennsylvania

Robert R. Mest
Born 1923 in Reading, Pennsylvania
U.S. Army 1943
Engineer Supply Depot Company
Resides in Reading, Pennsylvania

Vincent Nester Miller
Born 1921 in Reading
U.S. Army Air Force 1943
B-17 Turret Gunner
Resides in Reading, Pennsylvania

George R. Moore
Born 1926 in Sanatoga, Pennsylvania
U.S. Army 1944
1252nd Engineer Combat Battalion
Resides in Birdsboro, Pennsylvania

Nick Phillips
Born 1925 in Birdsboro, Pennsylvania
U.S. Army 1943
28th Infantry Division
Prisoner of War – Captured in Belgium
Resides in Birdsboro, Pennsylvania

Robert H. Reeser
Born 1925 in Pennsylvania
U.S. Army 1942
80th Infantry Division Medic
Resides in Reading, Pennsylvania

Kenneth "George" Reitnouer
Born 1923 in Oley, Pennsylvania
U.S. Army 1943
4th Coastal Defense Command
Resides in Reading, Pennsylvania

Leroy Renninger
Born 1921 in Bernville, Pennsylvania
U.S. Army 1942
83rd Infantry Division Field Artillery
Resides in Robesonia, Pennsylvania

Russel W. Rightmyer
Born 1925 in Reading, Pennsylvania
U.S. Army Medic
108th Army General Hospital Paris
Resides in Amityville, Pennsylvania

John Rowe
Born 1924 in Philadelphia
U.S. Army
87th Infantry Division
Resides in Schafferstown, Pennsylvania

Sam B. Scales
Born 1919 Roselle Park, New Jersey
U.S. Army 1941
78th Armored Field Artillery
Resides in Reading, Pennsylvania

Jerry E. Schoener
Born in 1924 in Host, Pennsylvania
U.S. Navy 1942 Atlantic
USS Mayrant
Resides in Temple, Pennsylvania

Ed Stallman
Born 1921 in Birdsboro, Pennsylvania
U.S. Army
101st Airborne
D-Day Carentan
Resides in Birdsboro, Pennsylvania

George E. Stauffer
Born 1920 in Pittsburgh, Pennsylvania
U.S. Army Air Force 1944
B-24 Bombardier Europe
Shot down over Romania
Prisoner of War
Resides in Shillington, Pennsylvania

Frank Stevenson, Jr.
Born 1923 in Philadelphia, Pennsylvania
U.S. Army 1943
45th Infantry Division
Resides in Wernersville, Pennsylvania

Kenneth E. Stoudt
Born 1927 in Reading, Pennsylvania
U.S. Navy 1944
USS Palana Pacific
Resides in Reading, Pennsylvania

Ed A. Taggert
Born 1923 in Philadelphia, Pennsylvania
U.S. Army 1942
Americal Division Field Artillery
Resides in West Lawn, Pennsylvania

Felix J. Uhrinek
Born 1919 in Catasauqua, Pennsylvania
U.S. Army 1942
774th Tank Battalion, 3rd Army
Resides in Reading, Pennsylvania

George Vath
Born 1925 in Trevose, Pennsylvania
U.S. Army 1943
1st Division - Infantry
Killed on D-Day on Omaha Beach

David Q. Voigt
Born 1926 in Reading, Pennsylvania
U.S. Army Air Force 1945
133rd Airways Communication System Squadron
Resides in Shillington, Pennsylvania

Richard L. Walton
Born 1926 in
U.S. Army Air Force 1944
87th Infantry Division
Resides in Wernersville, Pennsylvania

Robert "Red" Wells
Born 1923 in Fritztown, Pennsylvania
U.S. Army 1941 Special Forces
99th Infantry Battalion (Separate)
Passed Away April 24, 2008

Richard C. Wenrich
Born 1926 in Reading, Pennsylvania
U.S. Army 1944
84th Infantry Division
Resides in Wernersville, Pennsylvania

Richard Wheeler
U.S. Marines
5th Marine Division Pacific
Resides in Pine Grove, Pennsylvania

Howard Withers
Born 1923
U.S. Marines 1943
4th Marine Division Pacific
Resides in Reading, Pennsylvania

Margaret Schatz Wolf
Born 1921 in Mohnton, Pennsylvania
U.S. Army Nurse
United States and England
Resides in Laureldale, Pennsylvania

Paul M. Wolfinger
Born 1923 in Hamburg, Pennsylvania
U.S. Navy 1943
USS Swivel ARS 36
Resides in Reading, Pennsylvania

Joseph F. Yaklowich
Born 1921 in Reading, Pennsylvania
U.S. Navy 1940
USS Pennsylvania
Pearl Harbor Survivor
Resides in Laureldale, Pennsylvania

Joseph W. Yourkavitch
Born 1925 in Fleetwood, Pennsylvania
U.S. Army 1944
106th Infantry Division
Prisoner of War Europe
Resides in Temple, Pennsylvania

Arthur R. Youse
Born 1923 in Reading, Pennsylvania
U.S. Army Air Force 1942
China-Burma-India Theatre
Resides in Elizabethtown, Pennsylvania

Edward J. Zabinski
Born 1924 in Reading, Pennsylvania
U.S. Navy 1943 Armed Guard
USS Dillworth and USS Marcus H. Tracy
Resides in Reading, Pennsylvania

BIBLIOGRAPHY

Constein, Dr. Carl Frey. *Born To Fly The Hump*, The First Airlift. U.S. 1st Books Library. 2001

Keegan, John. *The Second World War*. New York. Penguin Books. 2005

Kennedy, David M. *Freedom From Fear*, The American People in Depression and War, 1929 – 1945. New York. Oxford University Press. 1999

Personal papers and documents

Reader's Digest. *Illustrated Story of WWII*. Pleasantville. The Reader's Digest Assn., Inc. 1969

Sledge, E.B. *With the Old Breed at Peleliu and Okinawa*. New York and Oxford. Oxford University Press. 1990

Wells Wagner, Sharon. *Red Wells*, An American Soldier in WWII. Charleston. Booksurge. 2006

Wheeler, Richard. *Iwo*. Edison. Castle Books. 2007

Wheeler, Richard. *The Bloody Battle For Suribachi*. New York. Skyhorse Publishing. 2007

CONTACT INFORMATION

If you would like to contact the authors, please feel free to do so by emailing us at the following address:

OrdinaryHeroes2008@gmail.com

www.StephenAndrewWagner.com
www.SharonWellsWagner.com

1898995